Accounti Workbook for Peachtree® 8.0

CHAPTERS 2-16

Prepared by

Warren Allen and **Mary Allen**

Problem Material Prepared by

James A. Heintz
University of Kansas

and

Robert W. Parry
Indiana University

SOUTH-WESTERN
THOMSON LEARNING

Australia · Canada · Mexico · Singapore · Spain · United Kingdom · United States

Accounting Workbook for Peachtree®, 8.0

Acquisitions Editor: Scott Person
Developmental Editors: Sara Wilson and Mardell Toomey
Marketing Manager: Larry Qualls
Production Editor: Marci Dechter
Editorial Assistant: Sara Froelicher
Manufacturing Coordinator: Doug Wilke
Production House: Navta Associates
Cover Design: Patti Hudepohl/Ft. Thomas, KY
Printer: Globus

COPYRIGHT ©2002 by South-Western, a division of Thomson Learning. Thomson Learning™ is a trademark used herein under license.

All Rights Reserved. No part of this work covered by the copyright hereon may be reproduced or used in any form or by any means—graphic, electronic, or mechanical, including photocopying, recording, taping, or information storage and retrieval systems—without the written permission of the publisher.

Printed in the United States of America
1 2 3 4 5 04 03 02 01

For more information contact South-Western, 5101 Madison Road, Cincinnati, Ohio, 45227 or find us on the Internet at http://www.swcollege.com
For permission to use material from this text or product, contact us by
- telephone: 1-800-730-2214
- fax: 1-800-730-2215
- web: http://www.thomsonrights.com

0-324-12452-X

CONTENTS

SECTION 1 INSTALLING AND OPERATING THE PEACHTREE ACCOUNTING SOFTWARE

Installing the Peachtree Accounting Software   1
Installing the Data Files   2
Peachtree Accounting Operating Instructions   4
    Enter or Tab Keys, 4   Case Sensitivity, 4   Peachtree Today Startup Screen, 4
Peachtree Accounting Main Menu Options   5
The Navigation Aid   6
Opening a Peachtree Company Data File   6
Peachtree Accounting Windows   7
Chart of Accounts and Entering Beginning Balances Windows   9
General Journal Entry Window   11
Account Reconciliation Window   12
Displaying and Printing Reports   14
Using the Report Filter   15
Viewing Report Detail   15
Changing Accounting Periods   17
Payroll Entry   17
Sales/Invoicing Window   19
    Sale on Account, 20   Credit Memo, 21
Purchase Transactions   22
    Purchase on Account, 23   Credit Memo (Purchases Returns and Allowances), 23
Payment Transactions   24
    Payment on Account, 25   Cash Purchases (Direct Payment), 26   Real-Time vs. Batch, 27
Backing up and Restoring Data Files   28
    Backup, 28   Restore, 28

SECTION 2 INSTRUCTIONS FOR SOLVING SELECTED PROBLEMS USING PEACHTREE ACCOUNTING SOFTWARE

Chapter 2 Demonstration Problem (02-DEMO)   31
Chapter 3 Demonstration Problem (03-DEMO)   37
Chapter 4 Demonstration Problem (04-DEMO)   38
Problem 4-2A   41
Problem 4-2B   42
Chapter 4 Mastery Problem   44
Chapter 5 Demonstration Problem (05-DEMO)   46
Problem 5-3A   47
Problem 5-3B   48
Chapter 5 Mastery Problem   49

Chapter 6 Demonstration Problem (06-DEMO)   51
Problem 6-3A   53
Problem 6-3B   55
Chapter 6 Mastery Problem   57
Comprehensive Problem 1   59
Chapter 7 Demonstration Problem (07-DEMO)   61
Problem 7-2A   63
Problem 7-2B   64
Chapter 8 Demonstration Problem (08-DEMO)   66
Problem 8-2A   67
Problem 8-2B   69
Chapter 8 Mastery Problem   70
Chapter 9 Demonstration Problem (09-DEMO)   71
Problem 9-2A   73
Problem 9-2B   75
Chapter 9 Mastery Problem   76
Chapter 10 Demonstration Problem (10-DEMO)   78
Problem 10-2A   79
Problem 10-2B   81
Chapter 10 Mastery Problem   83
Chapter 11 Demonstration Problem (11-DEMO)   84
    Sales on Account Transactions, 85   Credit Memo Transactions, 86   Cash Received on Account Transactions, 87   Credit Card Sales Transactions, 89   Cash Sales, 90
Problem 11-3A   91
Problem 11-3B   93
Chapter 11 Mastery Problem   94
Chapter 12 Demonstration Problem (12-DEMO)   97
    Payment on Account (Apply to Invoices Tab), 100   Direct Payment (Apply to Expenses Tab), 100
Problem 12-3A   101
Problem 12-3B   102
Chapter 12 Mastery Problem   103
Chapter 13 Demonstration Problem (13-DEMO)   105
Problem 13-2A   106
Problem 13-2B   107
Chapter 13 Mastery Problem   108
Chapter 14 Demonstration Problem (14-DEMO)   110
    Voucher Payment (Apply to Invoices Tab), 112
Problem 14-3A   113
Problem 14-3B   115
Chapter 14 Mastery Problem   116
Problem 15-1A   117
    Cost of Goods Sold, 117
Problem 15-2A   119
Problem 15-1B   121
Problem 15-2B   123
Chapter 15 Mastery Problem   125

Chapter 16 Demonstration Problem (16-DEMO)   125
Problem 16-1A   128
Problem 16-1B   130
Chapter 16 Mastery Problem   132

SECTION 3 SETTING UP A NEW COMPANY

Completing New Company Setup   135
Setup Checklist   137
General Ledger Checklist   137
Accounts Payable Checklist   137
Accounts Receivable Checklist   137
Payroll Checklist   138
Inventory Checklist   138
Jobs Checklist   138

SECTION 4 DEMONSTRATION PROBLEM SOLUTIONS

Chapter 2 Demonstration Problem Solution   139
Chapter 3 Demonstration Problem Solution   142
Chapter 4 Demonstration Problem Solution   144
Chapter 5 Demonstration Problem Solution   148
Chapter 6 Demonstration Problem Solution   150
Chapter 7 Demonstration Problem Solution   153
Chapter 8 Demonstration Problem Solution   154
Chapter 9 Demonstration Problem Solution   158
Chapter 10 Demonstration Problem Solution   160
Chapter 11 Demonstration Problem Solution   162
Chapter 12 Demonstration Problem Solution   165
Chapter 13 Demonstration Problem Solution   168
Chapter 14 Demonstration Problem Solution   172
Chapter 16 Demonstration Problem Solution   175

SECTION 1

Installing and Operating the Peachtree Accounting Software

INSTALLING THE PEACHTREE ACCOUNTING SOFTWARE

You must install Peachtree Accounting from within Windows™. If you plan to run Peachtree Accounting on a network, you must install Peachtree Accounting on each workstation. The procedure for installing the Peachtree Accounting software is detailed below:

▶ **Place the Peachtree Accounting CD into the CD-ROM drive.**

The opening screen shown in Figure 1.1 will appear with options to Install Peachtree Accounting, Install Online Documentation, or Exit Installation.

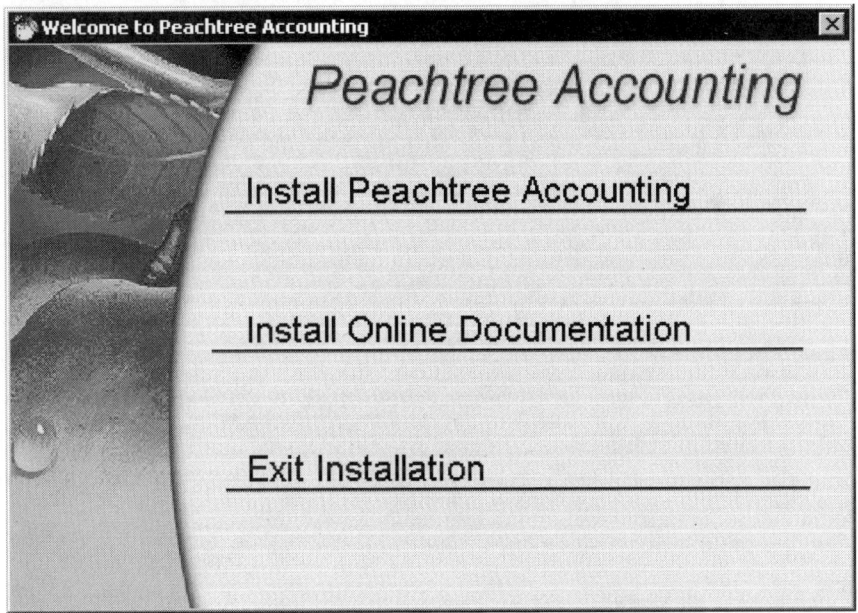

FIGURE 1.1 Peachtree Accounting Opening Screen

▶ **Choose the Install Peachtree Accounting option.**
A Welcome screen will appear.

▶ **Click Next to proceed.**
A License Agreement will appear.

▶ **Click Yes to accept the agreement.**
The window shown in Figure 1.2 on the following page displays offering up to four choices depending on if you are a new or previous user.

Standard Installs everything you need to begin running Peachtree Accounting. You cannot change the location where the program will be installed if you select this option.

Upgrade This option upgrades you from a previous version of Peachtree Accounting, maintaining your current program and data path settings. This option only appears if you have previously installed an earlier version of Peachtree Accounting.

Custom You can set a different path for the program or data files using this option, or choose which components of Peachtree Accounting you want to install.

Network This option allows you to install program and data files in a network environment.

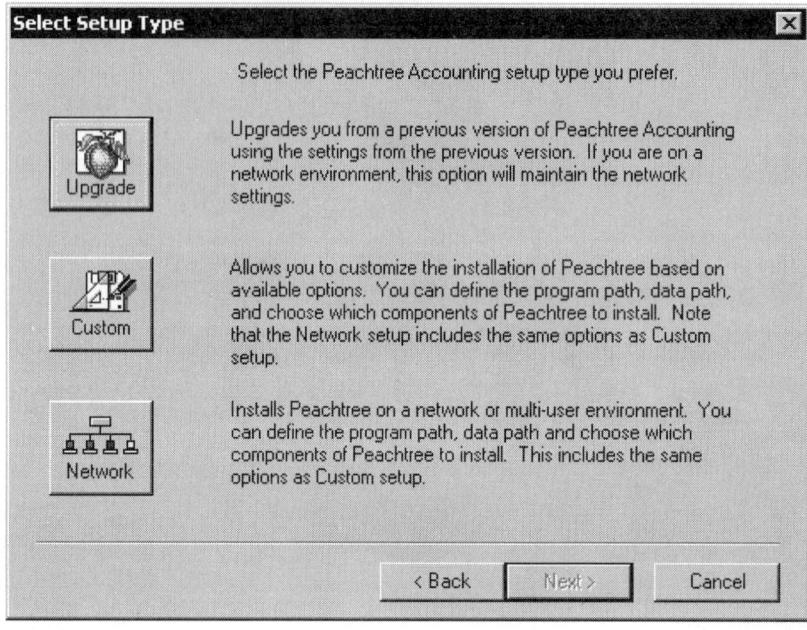

FIGURE 1.2 Select Setup Type Window

▶ **Select either Standard (new users) or Upgrade (previous users) for quick installation.**
   A Select a Program Folder will appear.

▶ **Enter or choose the program folder in which you would like the Peachtree Accounting icons to be contained.**
   Once the program and data files have been installed, a window displays, asking if you wish to restart your computer.

▶ **Choose Yes.**

INSTALLING THE DATA FILES

The opening balance files for selected problems are included on the Peachtree Accounting CD. The setup program and files are contained on the Peachtree CD in a folder named ACCNTNG. Each problem requires a unique data file containing the opening balance data for that problem. To solve a particular problem, you will open the data file that contains the opening balances. As you solve the problem, the computer will be updating information in this file; therefore, each user must have his or her own unique copy of the respective file. If available disk storage is limited or you do not always have access to the computer that contains your data files, there are several options described within the instructions that will accommodate these circumstances. The step-by-step instructions for installing the Peachtree Data Files are detailed below:

▶ **Place the Peachtree Accounting CD into the CD-ROM drive.**

- Select Start, then Run. Type the command to run the setup program, casetup.exe from the CD-ROM drive (e.g., D:\CASETUP, assuming the CD-ROM is drive D).
- When the Welcome screen appears, click the Next button.
- The Select Components Window shown in Figure 1.3 allows you to select which of the available problems you wish to install. The options are described on page 3.

With this option, you can choose which files are to be installed. You can install the files for several chapters, just one chapter, or all the chapters. This option is especially useful if either available storage space is limited or it isn't always possible to access the same folder from one session to the next because the folder you need is on a different computer from one session to the next. Notice that each Chapter has a check mark next to it. The check mark indicates that the problems for that chapter will be installed. If you do *not* want the files for that chapter installed, click on the check mark to toggle it off.

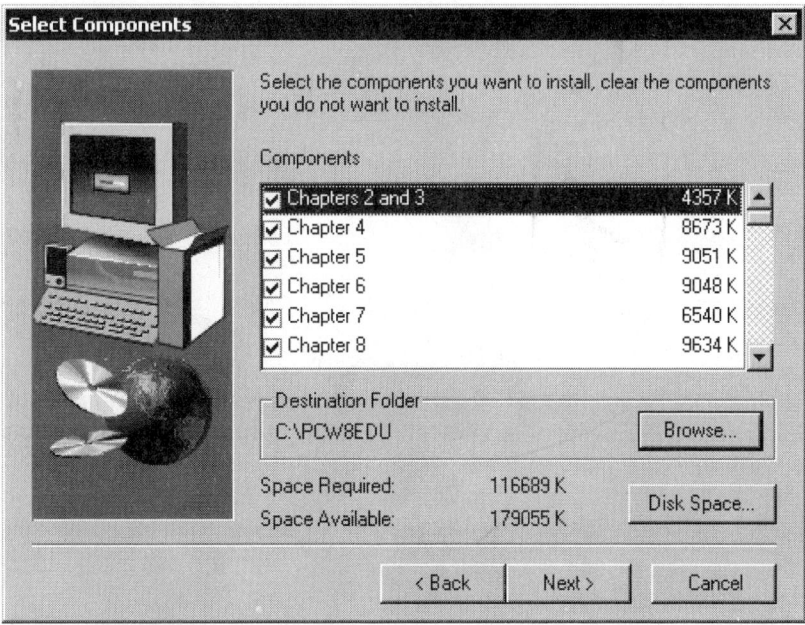

FIGURE 1.3 Select Components Window

- The default folder into which the data files will be installed is PCW8EDU. To install into a different folder, click on the Browse button. When the Choose Folder window illustrated in Figure 1.3 (shown on the next page) appears, enter or select the drive and folder where you would like your file(s) to reside.
- Click on the Next button to proceed with the installation.
- When the Setup Complete dialog appears, click the Finish button.

PEACHTREE ACCOUNTING OPERATING INSTRUCTIONS

Peachtree accounting follows Windows standards for program navigation. Therefore, if you have used other Windows programs, you will have few problems navigating the Peachtree menus and entering data into the Peachtree data entry windows. If you are unfamiliar with the Windows environment, it is recommended that you view the Windows online tutorial lesson in the Peachtree Accounting Help menu.

Enter or Tab Keys

In most Windows programs, you use the Tab key to move from field to field. However, most people find the Enter key more natural. Peachtree Accounting gives you the choice; both Enter and Tab move the cursor to the next field. Shift+Tab or Shift+Enter will move you backward to the previous field.

Case Sensitivity

Some software programs are case sensitive and others are not. If a program is not case sensitive, then "apple," "Apple," and "APPLE" would all be interpreted the same by the software. However, Peachtree Accounting is case sensitive, so each of the above examples would be interpreted differently. This will have implications for you as you work with the software. For example, one of the companies you will be working with has a sales tax code named "Indiana." While you most likely would select the code from a drop-down list, if you chose to key it instead, you would have to key it exactly as shown. If you key "indiana" rather than "Indiana," Peachtree would not calculate sales tax correctly.

Peachtree Today Startup Screen

When you first start Peachtree Accounting, the Peachtree Today screen shown in Figure 1.4 will appear. Peachtree Today is the information center. The welcome page lets you browse product tips, open key areas of Peachtree Accounting, check for the latest updates, and get help on common tasks. All the program options available on the startup screen are also available via the Peachtree menus.

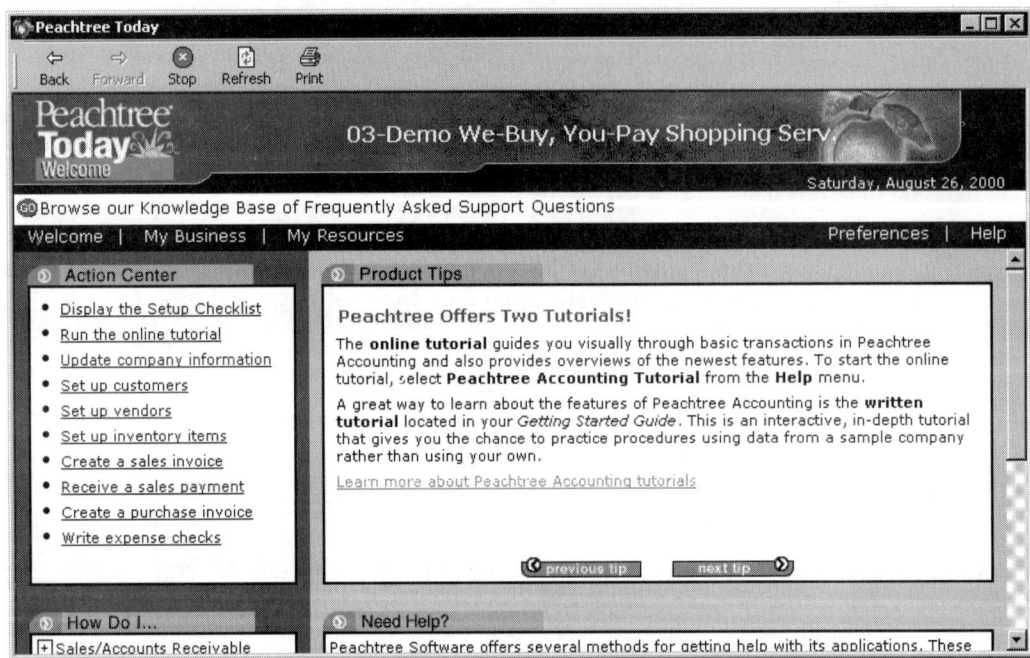

FIGURE 1.4 Peachtree Today Screen

PEACHTREE ACCOUNTING MAIN MENU OPTIONS

The Peachtree Accounting Main Menu allows you to access the various features of the software. There are nine pull-down menus available. The Peachtree menus with the File menu pulled down are shown in Figure 1.5.

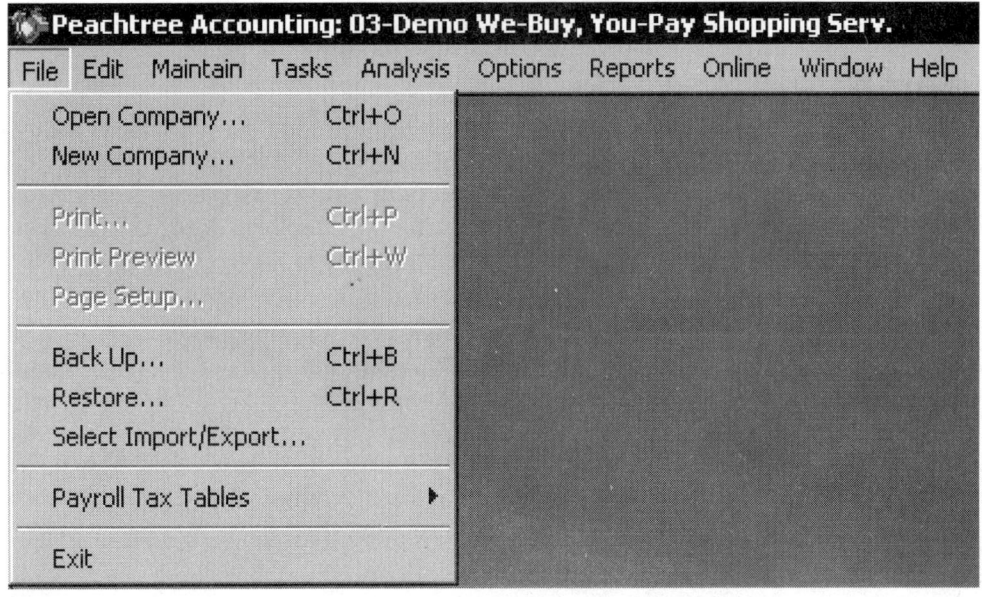

FIGURE 1.5 Peachtree Accounting Menus

▶ Click on the desired menu to pull it down.

▶ Click on the menu option you would like to choose.

Each of the main menu options is described below:

File. This menu option allows you to open an existing company, create a new company, print, do printer setup, back up a company, restore a previously backed up company, import and export data, set up taxes for payroll, and exit.

Edit. This menu provides the standard Windows cut, copy, and paste options.

Maintain. This menu allows you to access the various data entry windows to maintain the accounting data base by entering or editing the chart of accounts, customers, vendors, and employees.

Tasks. This menu allows you to enter the various accounting transactions such as general journal entries, sales invoices, purchase invoices, payments, and payroll transactions.

Analysis. This provides access to graphical overviews of cash flow, collections from customers, and payments due.

Options. These menu options allow you to change the system date, toggle the Smart Guide, Status Bar, Navigation Aid, and Startup Screen.

Reports. This menu allows you to access the various accounting reports by accounting system (accounts receivable, accounts payable, payroll, and general ledger).

Online. This menu allows you to view the Peachtree Today screen, check for an updated version of Peachtree Accounting, or define your internet connection.

Window. This menu allows you to arrange the displayed windows on your desktop, arrange the icons on your desktop, and close all open Peachtree windows.

Help. This menu allows you to open the Peachtree Help system.

The various menu options can also be accessed from the keyboard. To open one of the Main Menu options, press the Alt key and the underlined character. For example, press Alt+F to open the File menu. You can use the up and down arrow keys to move through the menu options, then press Enter to select the option. As an alternative, once the menu is displayed you can key the underlined letter to select the menu option.

THE NAVIGATION AID

In addition to the menu options, you can also utilize the Navigation Aid feature to access these same options. The Navigation Aid allows you to click on icons instead of choosing menu options. The Navigation Aid simplifies the selection of options because it is organized by accounting system (general ledger, accounts payable, accounts receivable, or payroll), so you only need be concerned with options within the system in which you are working. The Navigation Aid is shown in Figure 1.6. If you don't see the Navigation Aid at the bottom of your screen, it has been turned off. To turn it back on, select the View Navigation Aid from the Options menu.

FIGURE 1.6 Navigation Aid

As an example, the general ledger navigational aid is illustrated in Figure 1.7. Notice that the various options are illustrated as icons. To access the desired option, simply click on the appropriate icon.

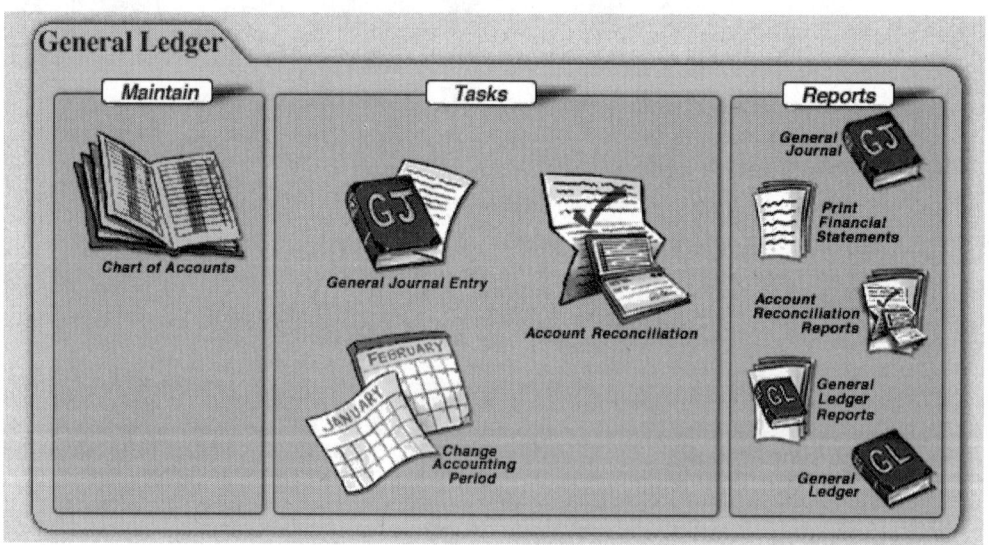

FIGURE 1.7 General Ledger Navigational Aid

OPENING A PEACHTREE COMPANY DATA FILE

The Open Company option allows you to access previously created company files. Each of the selected problems has been set up as a company. Follow the steps below to open a company file.

▶ From the File menu, select Open Company. The Open Company window shown in Figure 1.8 on the following page will appear.

▶ Select the data file you wish to open from the Company Name field and click Ok.

▶ If the company name you wish to work with does not appear, go to the Directories field and double-click the folder containing your data files. The list of data files will appear in the Company Name field. Select the data file you wish to open and click Ok.

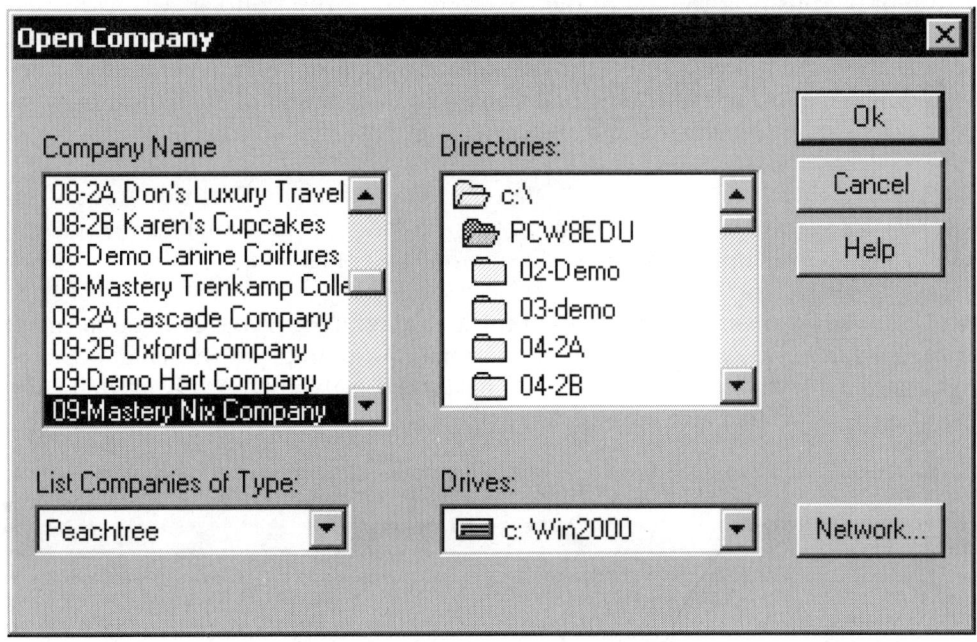

FIGURE 1.8 Open Company Window

PEACHTREE ACCOUNTING WINDOWS

When you select a menu option, a data entry window will often appear. The Maintain Chart of Accounts window, a typical data entry window, is illustrated in Figure 1.9.

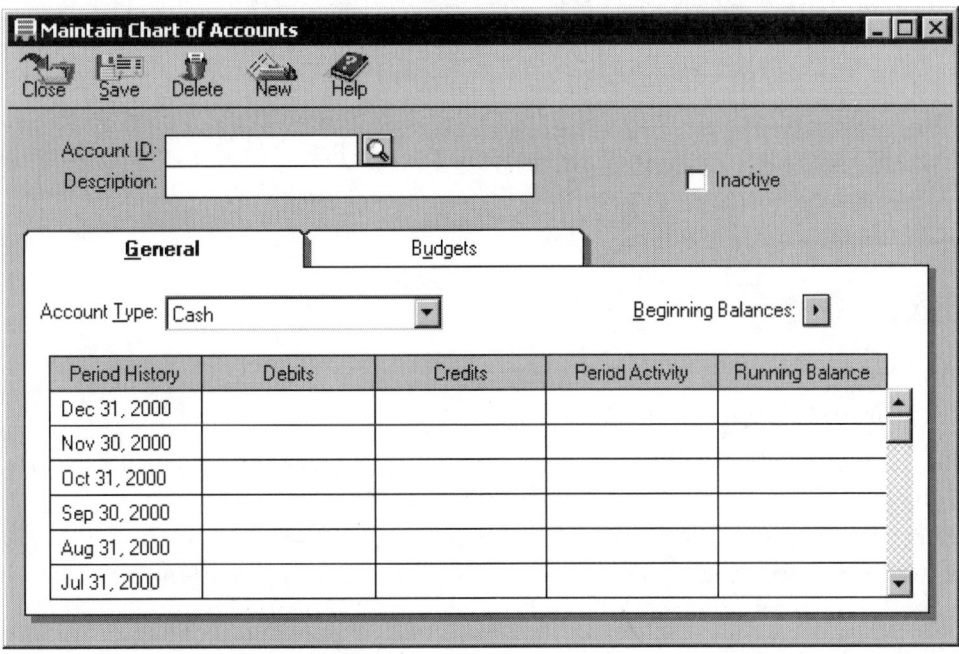

FIGURE 1.9 Peachtree Data Entry Window

Icon Bar. The strip of buttons near the top of the window is called the Icon Bar. The Close button will exit the window without saving any work entered since the last Save. The Save button saves the Chart of Accounts entry just entered. The Erase button causes the entry you are working with to be deleted. The New button will clear the window and allow you to enter a new entry. The Help button calls up the context-sensitive help system and provides useful information about the current activity.

Folder Tabs. Notice the General and Budget Folder Tabs. Many windows in Peachtree Accounting have Folder Tabs that allow easy navigation between sections of the window. You can visualize them as file-folder tabs that you can flip through by simply clicking on the appropriate Folder Tab.

Lookup Boxes. Lookup Boxes are indicated by a button with a magnifying glass. Click on the magnifying glass button to display a list from which you may select an option. An example of the Chart of Accounts Lookup Box is shown in Figure 1.10. You can also display the Lookup Box by typing a ? or by clicking the right mouse button from within the associated text box.

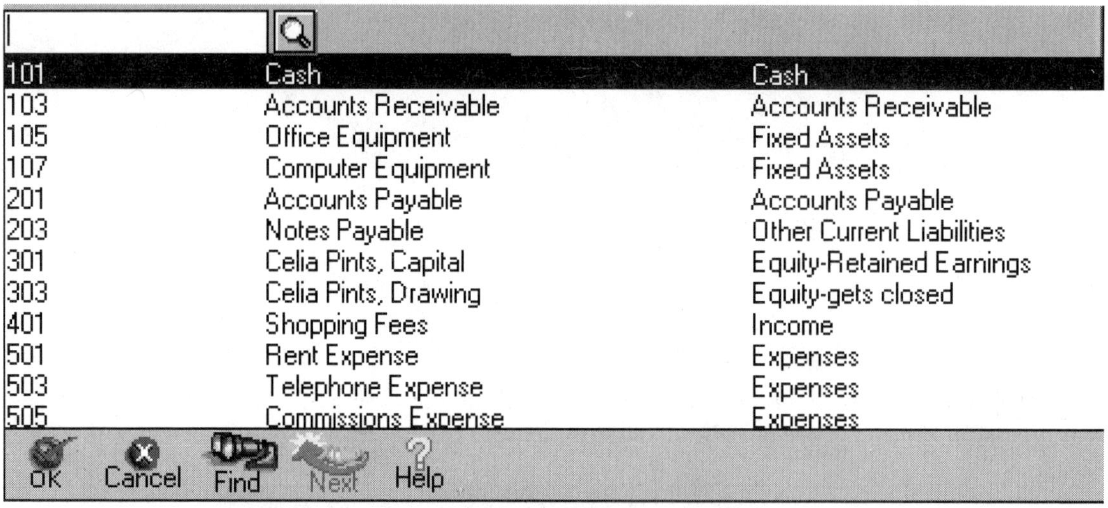

FIGURE 1.10 Chart of Accounts Lookup Box

Drop-Down List. A down-arrow button to the right of the field indicates that a drop-down list is available. Only the options in the list are allowable for the associated data field. The Account Type drop-down list is shown in Figure 1.11.

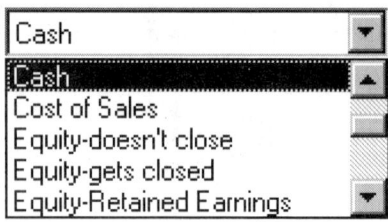

FIGURE 1.11 Account Type Drop-Down List

Status Bar. The status bar at the bottom of the screen provides a brief explanation of the current field. It also shows the current system date and the current accounting period. An illustration appears in Figure 1.12.

FIGURE 1.12 Status Bar

Pop-Up Calendar. All data entry windows that have a date field have available the pop-up calendar shown in Figure 1.13. To bring up the calendar, simply click on the calendar icon next to the date field. There are arrow buttons next to the year and month which can be clicked on to increase or decrease the year or month. Once you have set the calendar to the correct month and year, click on the day of the month. The calendar will close, and the selected date will appear in the date field. A shortcut method of entering the date is available if the month and year of the date are correct and you only wish to change the day of the month: you can simply enter the two-digit day of the month into the date field.

FIGURE 1.13 Pop-Up Calendar

CHART OF ACCOUNTS AND ENTERING BEGINNING BALANCES WINDOWS

The Maintain Chart of Accounts window shown in Figure 1.14 is used to add new accounts, to modify existing accounts, and to delete an existing account.

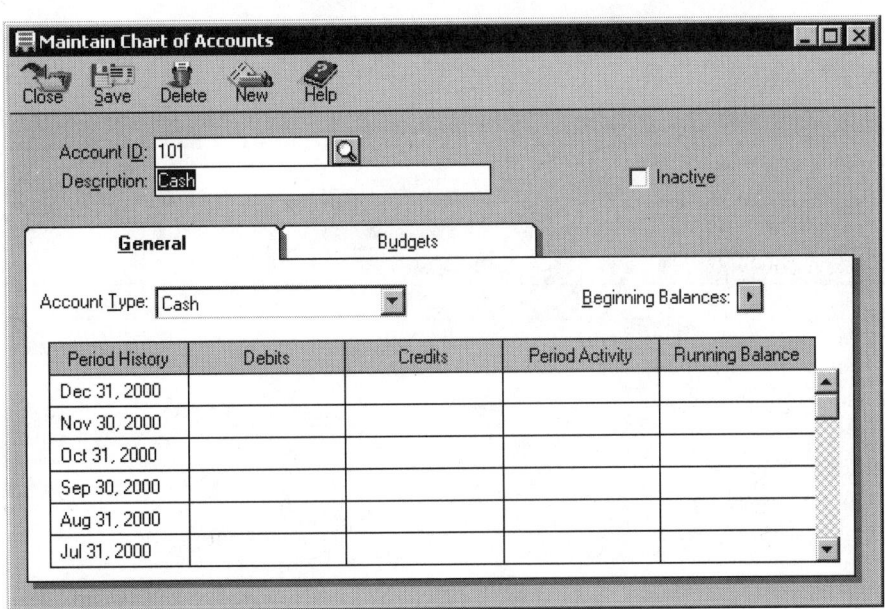

FIGURE 1.14 Maintain Chart of Accounts Window

To add a new account to the chart of accounts, complete the following:

- ▶ Enter the Account Number in the Account ID field.
- ▶ Enter the Account Title in the Description field.
- ▶ Select the Account Type from the drop-down list.
- ▶ Click on the Save button to record the account.

To make a change to an existing account, complete these steps:

- ▶ Click on the magnifying glass button next to the account number, then select the account you wish to modify.
- ▶ Enter the changes to the account.
- ▶ Click on the Save button to record the changes.

Complete the following steps to delete an account:

- ▶ Click on the magnifying glass button next to the account number, and choose the account you wish to delete.
- ▶ Click on the Erase button.

To record beginning account balances, complete the following:

- ▶ Click on the arrow button labeled "Beginning Balances:" near the center of the window to the right of the Account Type field.
- ▶ When the Select Period dialog box appears, choose the accounting period for which you wish to enter opening balance data and click on Ok.
- ▶ When the Chart of Accounts Beginning Balances window shown in Figure 1.15 appears, enter the account balances. Make sure that you enter the decimal point. After entering each account balance, press Tab to move to the next account.
- ▶ After all balances are entered, click on the Ok button.

Chart of Accounts Beginning Balances

Beginning Balances as of December 31, 2000

Account ID	Account Description	Account Type	Assets, Expenses	Liabilities, Equity, Income
101	Cash	Cash	7,665.00	
102	Accounts Receivable	Accounts Receivable	1,300.00	
103	Supplies	Accounts Receivable	300.00	
104	Prepaid Insurance	Other Current Assets	600.00	
105	Tools	Other Assets	3,000.00	
106	Truck	Other Assets	8,000.00	
201	Accounts Payable	Accounts Payable		2,200.00

The Trial Balance is made up of the balances of all accounts. In order for the Trial Balance to be in balance, the sum of Assets and Expenses should equal the sum of Liabilities, Equity, and Income.

Total: 20,865.00   20,865.00
Trial Balance: 0.00
(Difference posts to Beg Bal Equity)

Net Income is the difference of Income and Expense account values. The Income and Expense values making up Net Income are already included in the total.

Income - Expenses: 0.00   0.00
Net Income: 0.00

FIGURE 1.15 Chart of Accounts Beginning Balances

You will notice that as you enter the account balances two totals are updated near the bottom of the window. The first is the total of Assets and Expenses; the second is the total of liabilities, equity, and income. After all balances have been entered, the two totals must be equal. If they are not, you must find and fix any errors or the software will not allow you to proceed.

GENERAL JOURNAL ENTRY WINDOW

The General Journal Entry window is illustrated in Figure 1.16. Follow the steps below to enter general journal transactions.

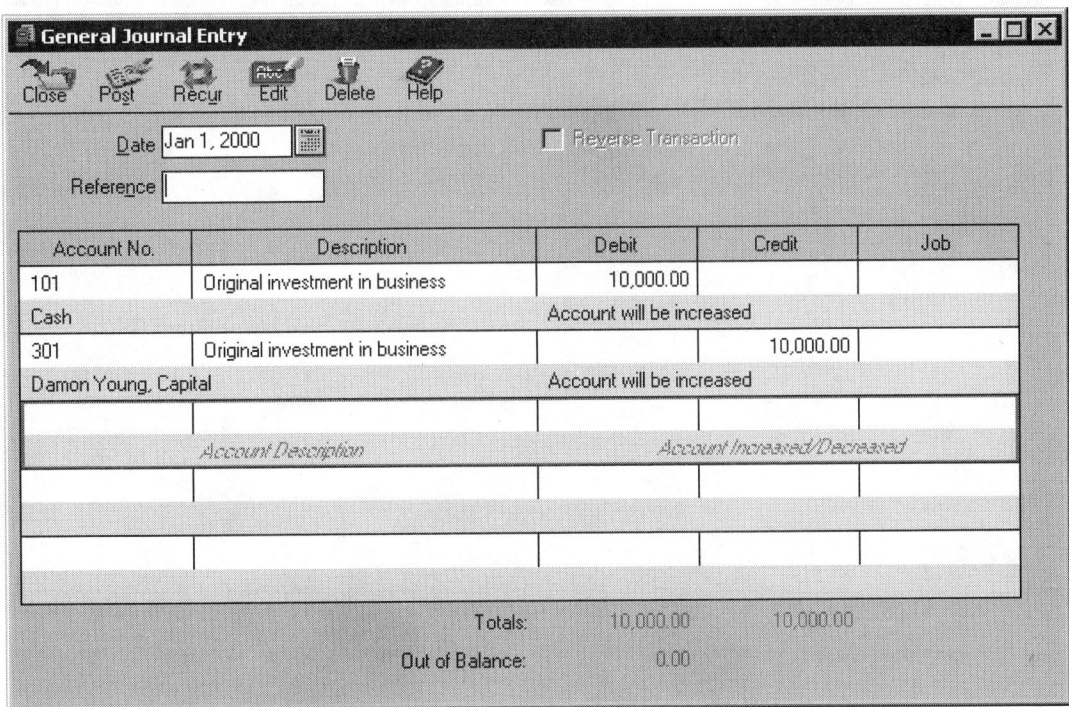

FIGURE 1.16 General Journal Entry Window

From the Tasks menu, select the General Journal Entry option.

▶ Enter the date of the transaction. Click on the Calendar icon next to the Date field to select the date from the pop-up calendar. If the month and year are correct, you can use the shortcut method of just keying the two-digit day of the month.

▶ Enter the reference, if one is provided, up to twenty characters in length. If none is provided, leave the reference blank. Examples would be check number, invoice number, or other meaningful transaction reference that will provide an audit trail to the original transaction source document.

▶ Enter the account number or select it from the drop-down list.

You can add a new account to the chart of accounts by keying a +, by double-clicking in the Account Number text box, or by clicking on the magnifying glass icon, then selecting Records New.

▶ Enter a description of the transaction.
▶ Enter the debit or credit amount (key the decimal point).
▶ After all the parts of the entry have been entered, click on the Post button to save and post the transaction.

- If you wish to insert a leg to the transaction between two existing legs, simply position the cursor to the point where you would like to insert the entry and click on the Add Icon Bar button. The software will open up a space to insert the entry.
- If you wish to remove a leg of a transaction, position the cursor to the line you wish to remove and click on the Remove Icon Bar button.

To make changes, corrections, or deletions to existing journal entries, click on the Edit Icon Bar button. The Select Journal Entry window shown in Figure 1.17 will appear.

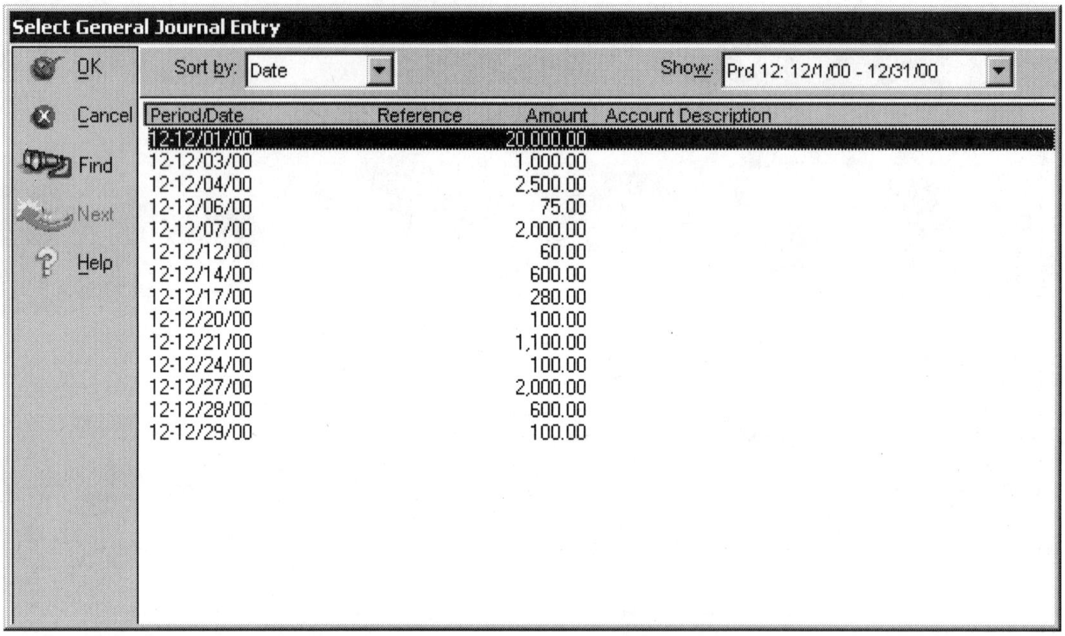

FIGURE 1.17 Select General Journal Entry Window

- Highlight the journal entry you wish to change or delete and click on the Ok button.
- To locate a journal entry, you can use the Find button. A text box will appear. Enter the search argument you wish to search for such as an amount, description, or reference. The journal entry will be located and highlighted. Click Next to find the next occurrence of that search argument.
- Click on Cancel to return to the General Journal Entry window without selecting a journal entry.

Notice that the upper right corner of the window contains a drop-down list labeled "Show" that displays the current accounting period. If you wish to access transactions from a different (not previously closed) accounting period, select that period from the drop-down list. The general ledger transactions for that period will be displayed so that you can make changes and corrections to them.

ACCOUNT RECONCILIATION WINDOW

The Account Reconciliation window illustrated in Figure 1.18 on the following page allows you to reconcile your bank account.

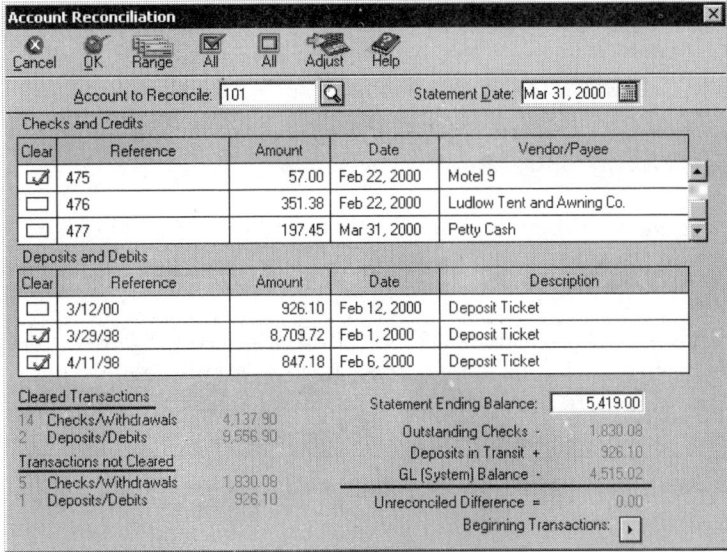

FIGURE 1.18 Account Reconciliation Window

The procedure for reconciling a bank account is detailed below:

▶ From the Tasks menu, select Account Reconciliation.
▶ Select the account you want to reconcile.
▶ Enter the closing date from the bank's statement as the Statement Date.
▶ Enter the Statement Ending Balance from the bank statement in the lower right section of the window.
▶ Mark the Checks and Credits that have cleared (those not marked represent the outstanding checks). Checks and Credits can be marked as cleared by clicking in the Clear box to place a check mark there indicating the item has cleared.
▶ Mark the Deposits and Debits that have cleared by clicking in the Clear box associated with that item.
▶ If there are additional withdrawals or additional deposits, click on the Adjust Icon Bar button.

The Additional Transactions window appears in Figure 1.19. Follow the steps below to enter any additional withdrawals or deposits.

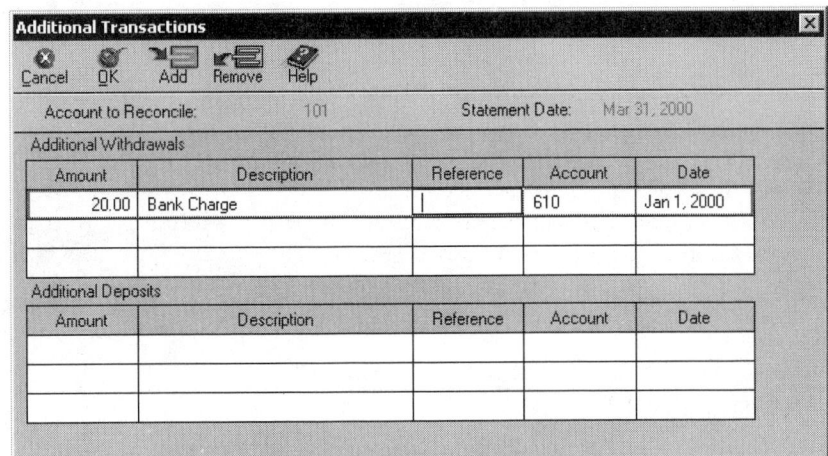

FIGURE 1.19 Additional Transactions Window

- ▶ Enter the adjustments.
- ▶ Click on Ok when finished.
- ▶ These transactions will now appear in the Account Reconciliation window.
- ▶ Mark the new adjustments as cleared.
- ▶ When you are finished reconciling, click on Ok.

DISPLAYING AND PRINTING REPORTS

Reports can be directed either to the screen display or to an attached printer. While many standard reports are available, reports can be customized to meet specific needs. Often, the data files will contain reports customized to meet the needs of a particular accounting problem. Follow the steps provided to display and/or print reports.

- ▶ Select the menu option you want from the Reports menu shown in Figure 1.20.
- ▶ Select the area of Peachtree you want from the Report Area. The reports available for that area will display in the Report List section.
- ▶ Select the report you want from the Report List.
- ▶ Click the Screen Icon Bar button to display the highlighted report. A window will appear that will allow you to customize the report just selected. Because any needed customization has already been done for the files, simply click on the Ok button. For transaction reports or list reports, you may want to use the Filter option to limit the entries listed on the report. Refer to the Section titled "Using the Report Filter" for details on using that feature.
- ▶ To print the report, click on the Print Icon Bar button.
- ▶ Click on the Close Icon Bar button to exit from the currently displayed report.

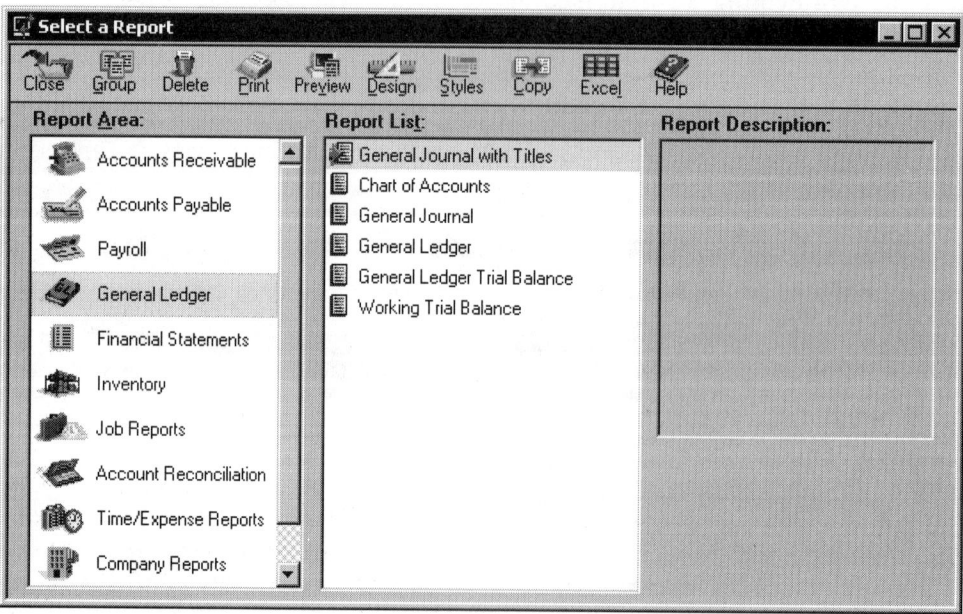

FIGURE 1.20 Select a Report Window

USING THE REPORT FILTER

The Report Filter option allows you to select which transactions or list items are to appear on the report. Follow the steps below to use this feature:

▶ **Select the Screen icon after you have selected the report. The Filter folder shown in Figure 1.21 will appear.**

Note: If you double-click on the report, the Filter window will be skipped.

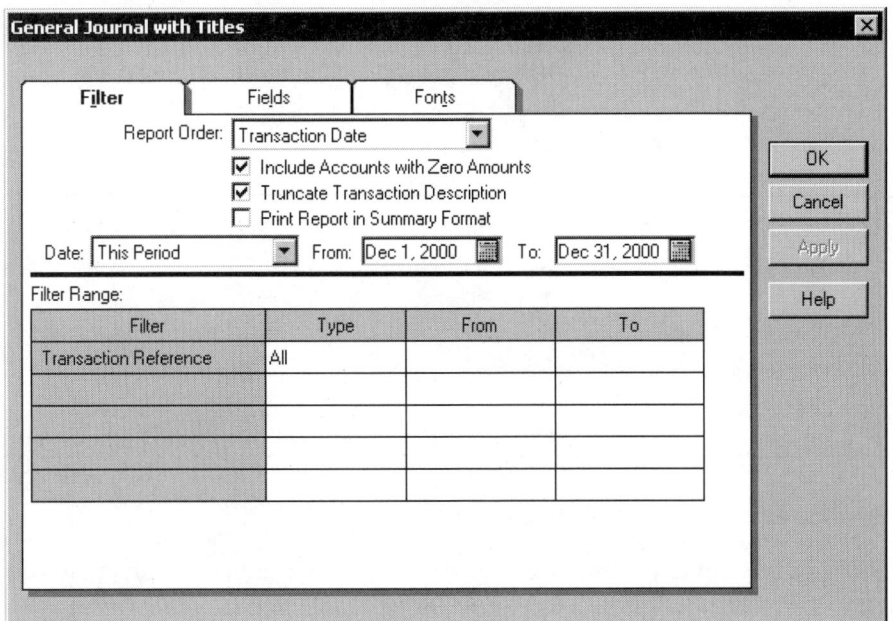

FIGURE 1.21 General Journal Filter Tab

▶ **To accept the defaults and display the report, just click on Ok.**
▶ **To filter the report entries, make any entries you want in the fields to establish the kind of information you want to include in the report and then click on Ok to display the report.**

Figure 1.21, for example, allows you to filter the general journal entries. You can restrict the general journal entries to a date range or restrict by transaction reference. In the example, only transactions in the December 15th to December 31st range will be displayed. An example of filtering by Transaction Reference field would be to list only transactions with references in the range of 1,000 to 1,100.

VIEWING REPORT DETAIL

When displayed on the screen, some areas on reports are outlined in a box and the cursor changes to a magnifying glass as illustrated in Figure 1.22 on the following page. This signifies that the drill-down feature is available for this data. This means you can access the transaction that resulted in this report entry and make changes and corrections to it. This is a very convenient way to make corrections to transactions. This means, for example, if you are viewing a general journal report and discover an error in a journal entry, you can access and correct that journal entry by simply double-clicking on the transaction within the report.

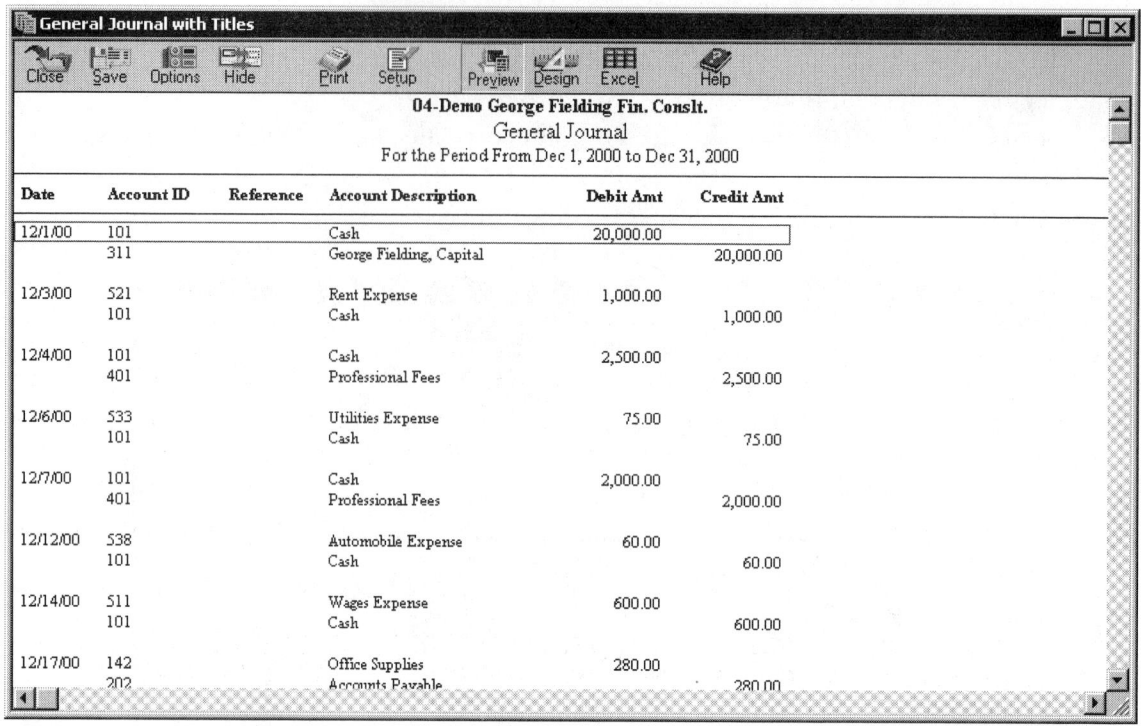

FIGURE 1.22 General Journal Report (Drill-Down Feature)

▶ Move the mouse pointer over a transaction outlined by the blue box. The cursor changes to a magnifying glass. Double-click the detail area you want to correct. The corresponding data entry window with the transaction display will appear as shown in Figure 1.23.

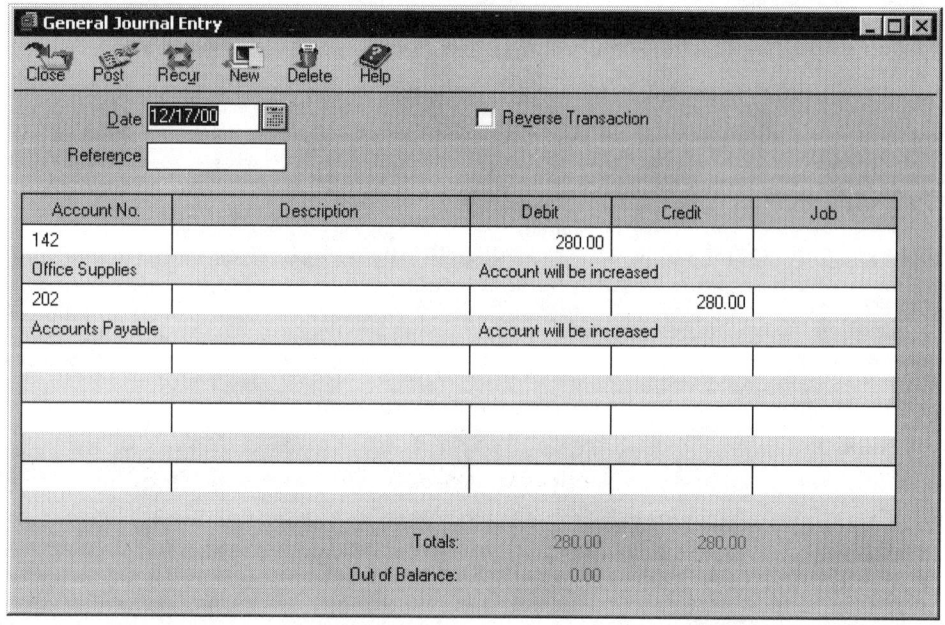

FIGURE 1.23 General Journal Entry (Making a Correction from Journal Report)

- ▶ Make any change you wish to make to the transaction.
- ▶ Click on the Post icon to save your changes.
- ▶ Click on the Close button.

CHANGING ACCOUNTING PERIODS

In Peachtree Accounting, accounting periods are established when the company is created. Each fiscal year is separated into anywhere from 1 to 13 accounting periods. You can have up to 26 periods or two fiscal years available at one time. This means you can have last year's history available for editing or adjusting throughout the current year. Before beginning processing for the next accounting period, you must change accounting periods. The process of changing accounting periods is identified in the following steps:

- ▶ From the Tasks menu, select System then Change Accounting Periods from the submenu. The Change Accounting Period window shown in Figure 1.24 will appear.
- ▶ Select the accounting period to which you want to change, and select Ok.
- ▶ A message box appears, reminding you to back up and to print applicable reports. If you have already printed reports, choose No.

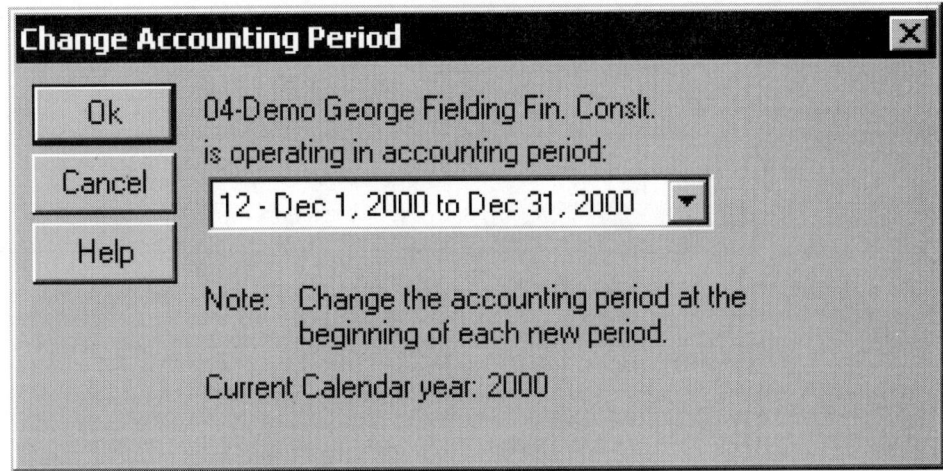

FIGURE 1.24 Change Accounting Periods Window

PAYROLL ENTRY

The Payroll Entry window allows you to select the employees to be paid this period and to enter hours and other pertinent information related to the current pay period. The computer will calculate and display earnings and withholdings data that you can modify if need be. Follow the steps listed below.

- ▶ From the Tasks menu, select the Payroll Entry option. The Payroll Entry windows shown in Figure 1.25 on the following page will appear.

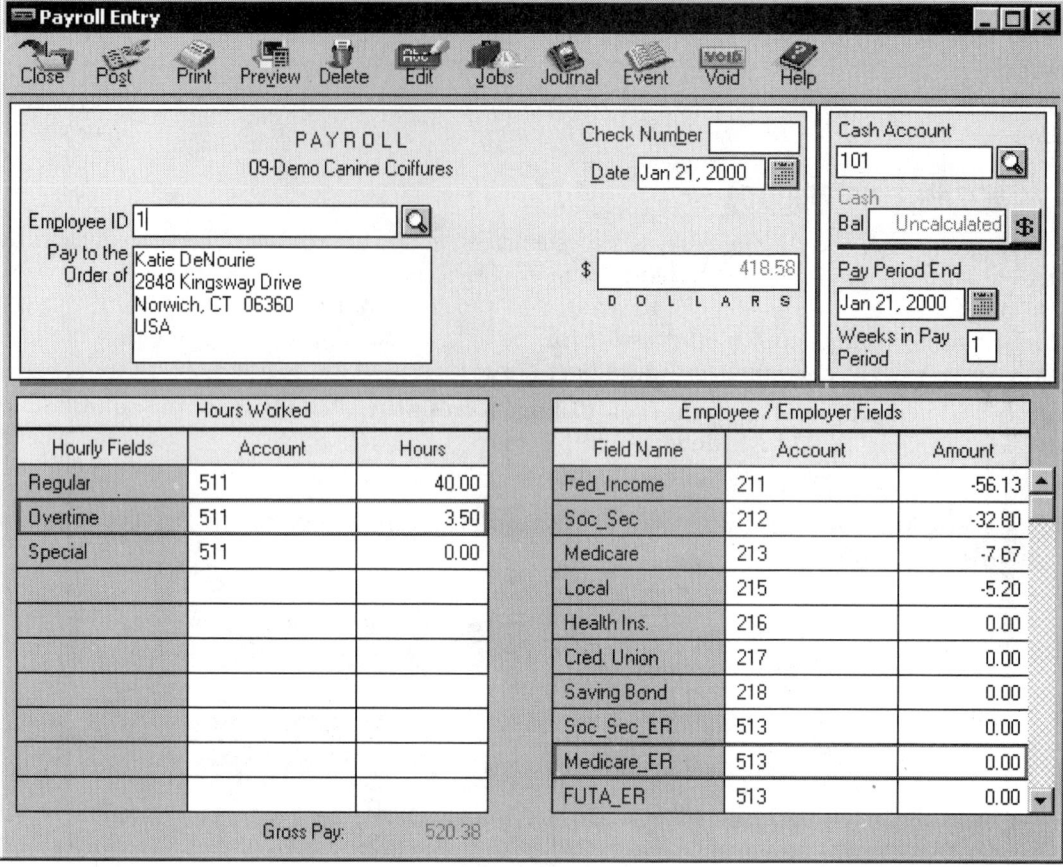

FIGURE 1.25 Payroll Entry Window

- Enter or select the Employee ID code.
- Enter the Check Number.
- Enter the Date of the check for this pay period.
- Enter the Pay Period Ended date if different from the Date of the check.
- Verify the Hourly or Salary amounts assigned. Make changes if necessary.
- You may click on the Journal Icon Bar button to view the journal entry that will be generated as a result of this entry. You can review the accounts affected and change the accounts if incorrect. The Accounting Behind the Screens journal window is illustrated in Figure 1.26 on the following page.
- Click on the Post Icon Bar button to save the transaction.

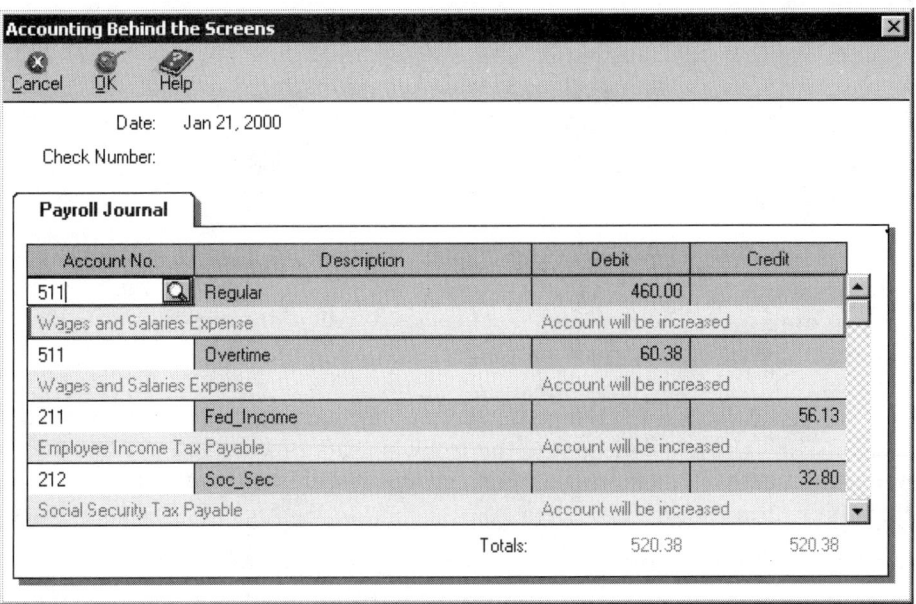

FIGURE 1.26 Accounting Behind the Screens Journal Window (Payroll Entry)

SALES/INVOICING WINDOW

Sales on account and credit memo transactions are entered into the Sales/Invoicing Window. The Sales/Invoicing Window is illustrated in Figure 1.27.

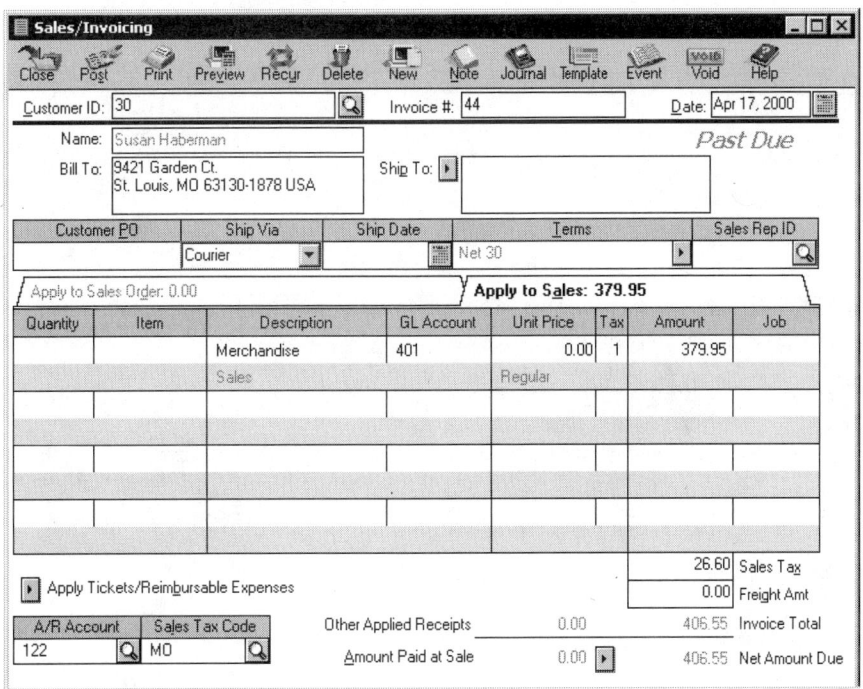

FIGURE 1.27 Sales/Invoicing Window (Sale on Account)

Sale on Account

▶ From the Tasks menu, select Sales/Invoicing.
▶ Enter or select the Customer ID. When the customer is selected, Peachtree supplies customer default information including sales account, payment terms, and sales tax code.
▶ Enter the Invoice Number.
▶ Enter the Date of the transaction.
▶ Peachtree uses the default terms for that customer. When a receipt that qualifies for an early payment discount is applied to the invoice, Peachtree will calculate the discount. Therefore, it is most important that the terms shown are correct.

You can select the Terms button to change the default discount dates or amounts for the invoice. Since the discount amount is recalculated each time the invoice amount changes, change the default discount information after you have finished entering all line items or it will be overwritten and recalculated with the customer default information.

▶ Enter the description.
▶ Enter the account number of the revenue account to be credited in the GL Account field.
▶ Accept the default Tax Code, or select a different one. Tax Code 1 indicates that the item is taxable. Tax Code 2 indicates that it is exempt from sales tax.
▶ Enter the amount sold for this item.
▶ Verify the Sales Tax Code displayed in the lower left corner of the window. If it is incorrect, select the applicable Sales Tax Code.
▶ You can view the journal entry resulting from this transaction by clicking on the Journal Icon Bar button. An example is shown in Figure 1.28.
▶ Post the invoice by clicking on the Post Icon Bar button.

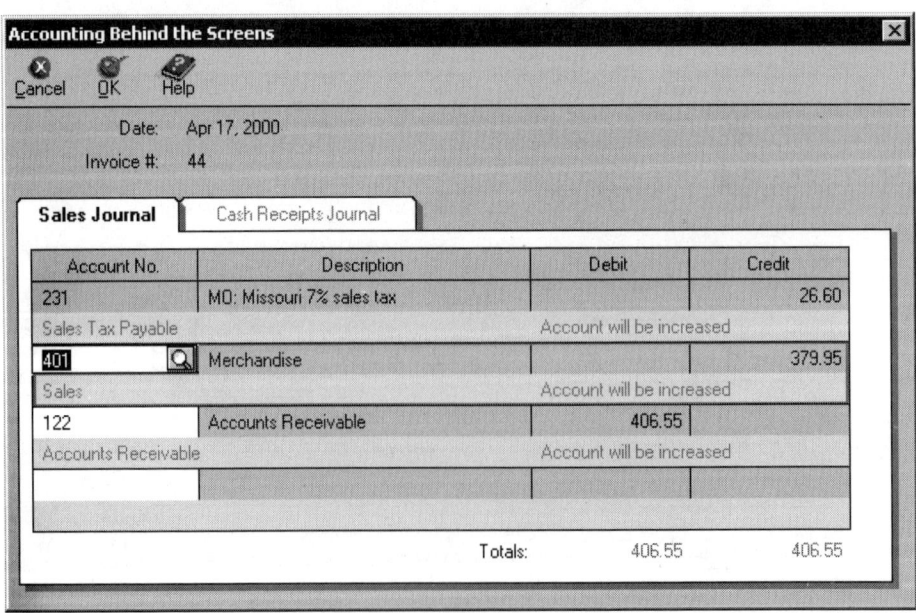

FIGURE 1.28 Accounting Behind the Screens (Sales Journal Entries)

Credit Memo

Credit Memos are entered in essentially the same way as normal invoices. The primary difference is that the amount is entered as a negative number. An example of a Credit Memo transaction is shown in the Sales/Invoicing window illustrated in Figure 1.29. The steps necessary for entering a sales return or allowance transaction follow the illustration.

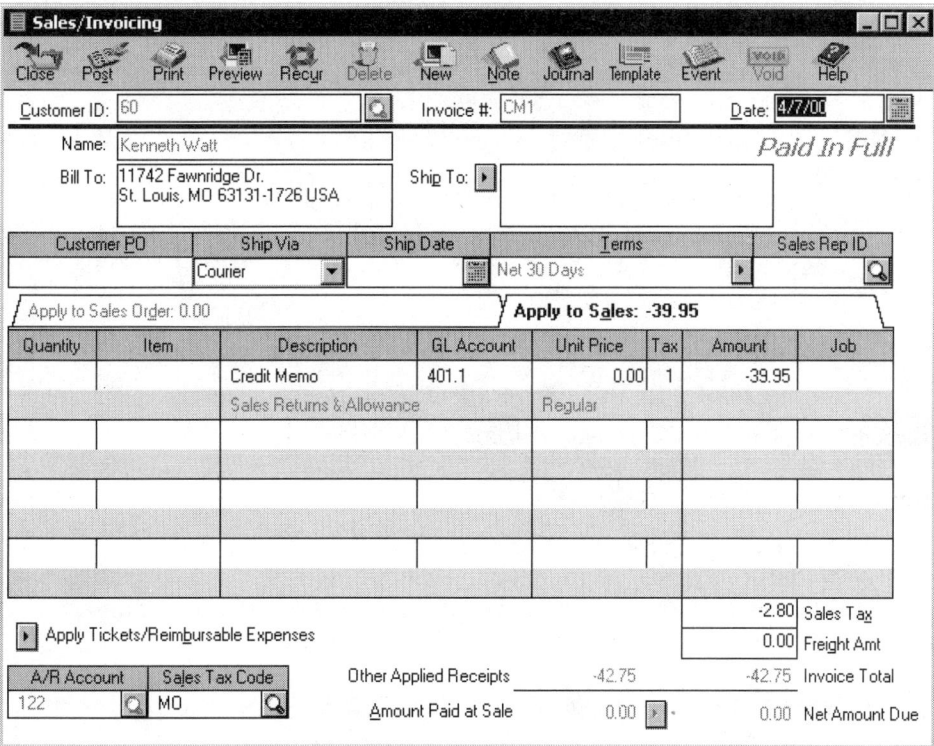

FIGURE 1.29 Sales/Invoicing Window (Credit Memo)

- ▶ From the Tasks menu, select Sales/Invoicing.
- ▶ Enter or select the Customer ID.
- ▶ Enter a credit memo identifier in the Invoice Number field. If a credit memo number is provided, enter it. If not, key CM plus the original invoice number (CM801, for example). If the original invoice number is not provided, key CM plus part of the customer name so the item is easily identifiable.
- ▶ Enter the Date of the credit memo. It is important that you enter the correct date, since Peachtree uses this date to determine whether partial discounts will be applied.
- ▶ Enter "Credit Memo" in the Description field.
- ▶ Enter the account number of the Sales Returns and Allowances account in the GL Account field.
- ▶ Accept or change the Tax Code (1=taxable, 2=exempt).
- ▶ Enter the amount of the credit memo as a negative number as illustrated in Figure 1.29.
- ▶ Verify that the correct Sales Tax Code is displayed in the lower left corner of the window. The Sales Tax Code is usually the name or abbreviation of the respective state. In the example in Figure 1.29, the code MO represents Missouri.
- ▶ You can view the journal entry resulting from this transaction by clicking on the Journal Icon Bar button. An example is shown in Figure 1.30 on the following page.
- ▶ Post the Credit Memo by clicking on the Post Icon Bar button.

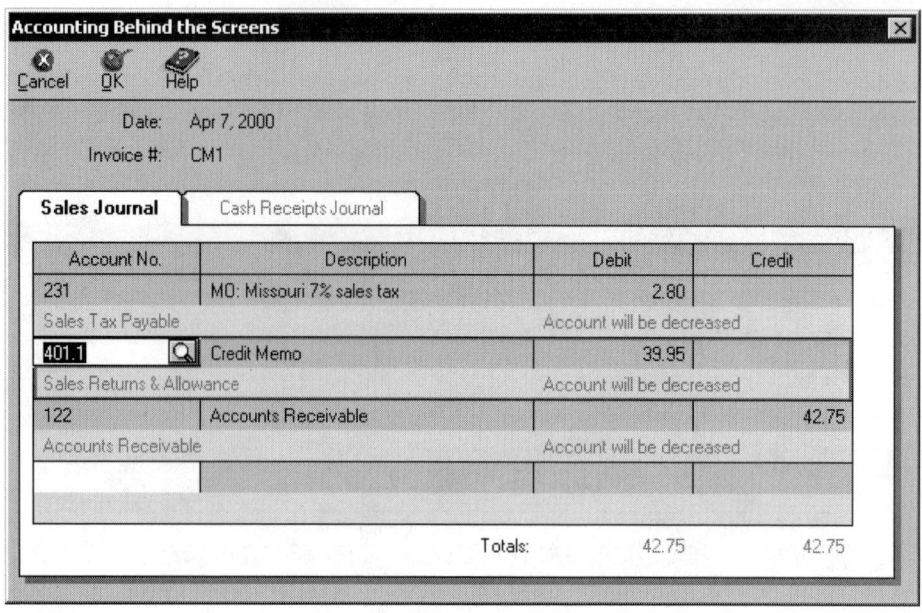

FIGURE 1.30 Accounting Behind the Screens (Credit Memo Journal Entry)

PURCHASE TRANSACTIONS

The Purchases/Receive Inventory task allows you to enter purchases on account and credit memo transactions. The Purchases/Receive Inventory window is illustrated in Figure 1.31.

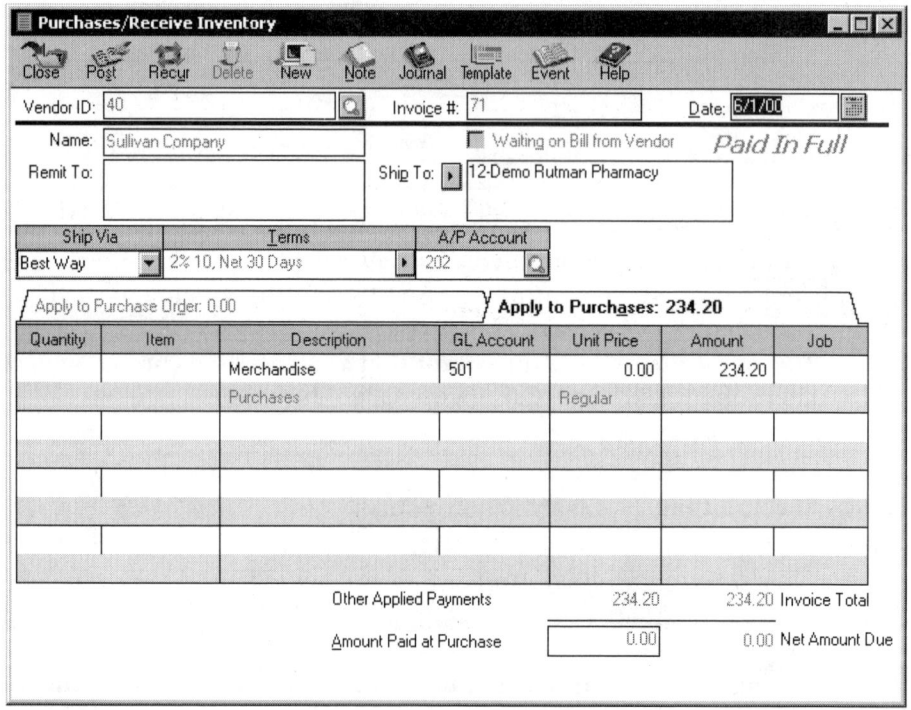

FIGURE 1.31 Purchases/Receive Inventory Window

Purchase on Account

▶ From the Task menu, select the Purchases/Receive Inventory option.
▶ Enter or select the Vendor ID code in the Vendor ID field.
▶ Enter the vendor's invoice number in the Invoice Number field.
▶ Enter the Date of the transaction.
▶ If the shipping instructions and terms of the invoice displayed are not correct, click on the right arrow button to make changes.
▶ If you are not using the Inventory system, leave the Quantity and Item fields blank.
▶ Enter a description of the transaction in the Description field.
▶ Enter or select the account number of the account to be debited. The default is the Purchases account.
▶ If you are not using the Inventory system, leave the Unit Price field blank.
▶ Enter the amount of the debit in the Amount field.
▶ Leave the Job number field blank.
▶ Continue entering transaction lines until the Invoice Total box equals the total balance of the vendor invoice.
▶ Click on Post to record the transaction.

Credit Memo (Purchases Returns and Allowances)

Purchases returns or allowances are entered in essentially the same way as normal invoices. The primary difference is that the amount is entered as a negative number. An example of a purchases allowance transaction is shown in the Purchases/Receive Inventory window illustrated in Figure 1.32. The steps necessary for entering a sales return or allowance transaction follow the illustration.

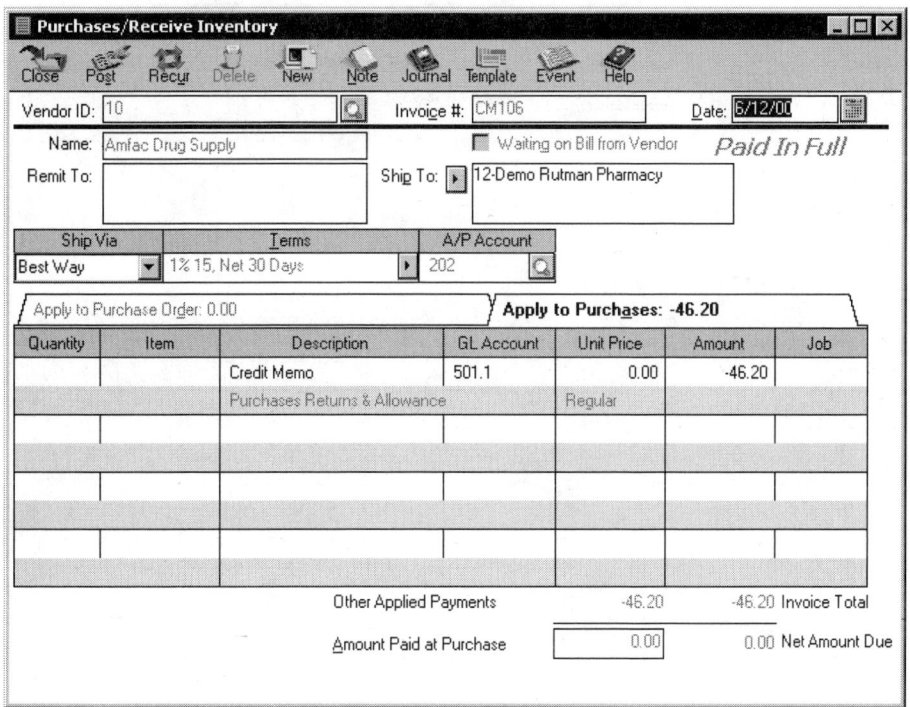

FIGURE 1.32 Purchases/Receive Inventory Window (Credit Memo)

▶ From the Task menu select the Purchases/Receive Inventory option.
▶ Enter or select the Vendor ID code in the Vendor ID field.
▶ Enter the CM followed by the original vendor's invoice number in the Invoice Number field (e.g., CM106).
▶ Enter the Date of the transaction.
▶ If the shipping instructions and terms of the invoice displayed are not correct, click on the right arrow button to make changes.
▶ If you are not using the Inventory system, leave the Quantity and Item fields blank.
▶ Enter a description of the transaction in the Description field.
▶ Enter or select the account number for Purchases Returns and Allowances.
▶ If you are not using the Inventory system, leave the Unit Price field blank.
▶ Enter the amount of the return or allowance in the Amount field as a negative number.
▶ Leave the Job number field blank.
▶ Click on Post to record the transaction.

PAYMENT TRANSACTIONS

The Payments window is illustrated in Figure 1.33. As you enter checks, a "stub" is displayed to the right of the check where you can select the cash account you want to use for the checks you are writing. The Payments window displays a check form at the top of the window in which you enter the Vendor information, Check Number, and Date. The bottom half of the window is divided into two tabs, Apply to Invoices and Apply to Expenses.

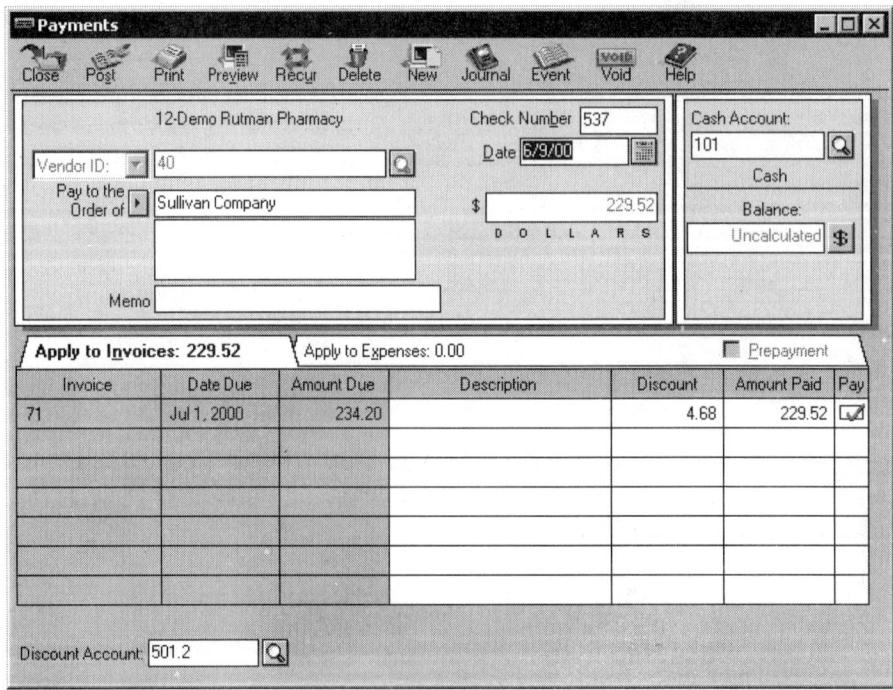

FIGURE 1.33 Payments Window

When you enter a Vendor ID, any open purchases invoices previously entered for that vendor display in the Apply to Invoices tab section as illustrated in Figure 1.33. You can then select the invoice(s) in the list. Next, either select the Pay box or enter the amount to apply against the invoice(s). If this is a cash purchase (direct payment as opposed to a previously-entered vendor invoice), the Apply to Expenses tab will be active.

Payment on Account

▶ From the Tasks menu, select Payments.

▶ Enter or select the Vendor ID code of the vendor you want to pay.

When you select a vendor with open invoices, the Apply to Invoices tab appears by default as illustrated in Figure 1.34. Notice that all the open invoices and credit memos for that particular vendor are listed.

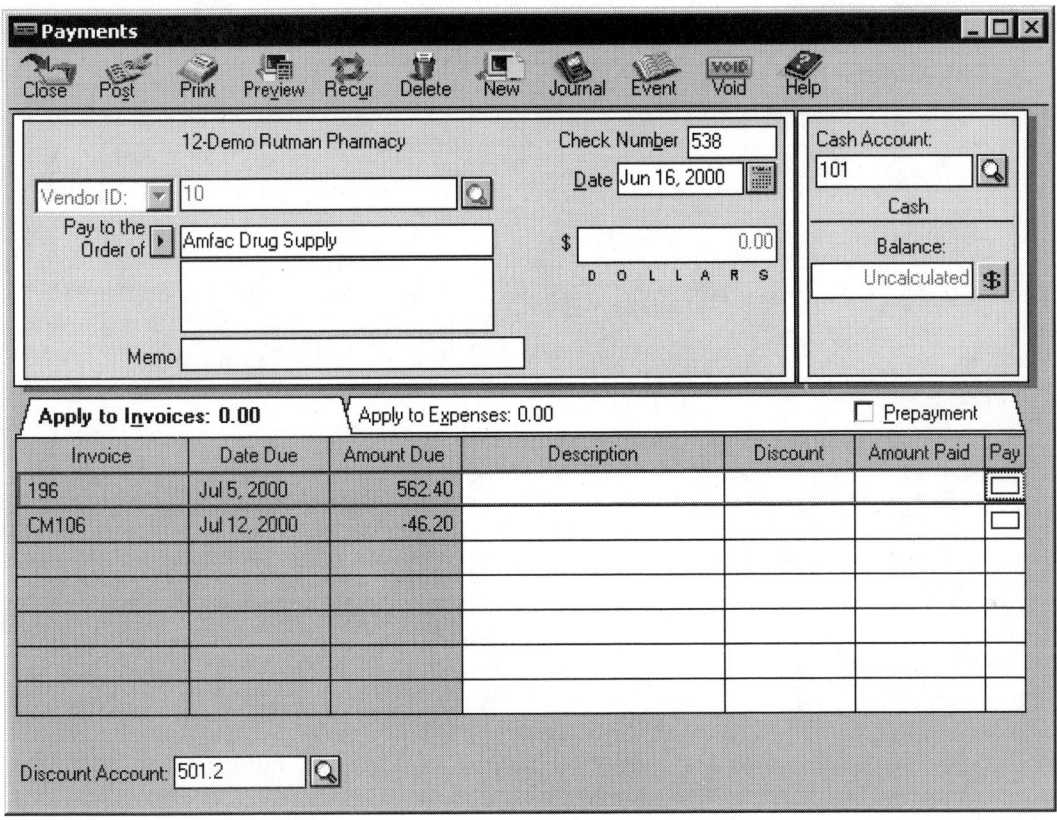

FIGURE 1.34 Payments Window (Apply to Invoices Tab)

▶ If you are entering a handwritten check, enter the check number in the Check Number box. If you want Peachtree Accounting to print the check, leave this field blank.

▶ Enter or select the Date of the check.

▶ Change the Cash Account if necessary.

▶ To pay the invoice in full, you can select the Pay box next to the invoice and the amount will be entered automatically and a red check will appear in the Pay box.

▶ Enter a description of the transaction in the Description field.

▶ If you want to change the discount amount, do so after you check the Pay box.

- The check window displays the amount to be paid on this check and updates the amount as you select the invoices.
- When you have completed paying invoices for a single check (the Check Amount box keeps a running total), select the Save or Post icon.
- Select the Journal Icon Bar button to display the Accounting Behind the Screens journal entries resulting from this transaction as illustrated in Figure 1.35.

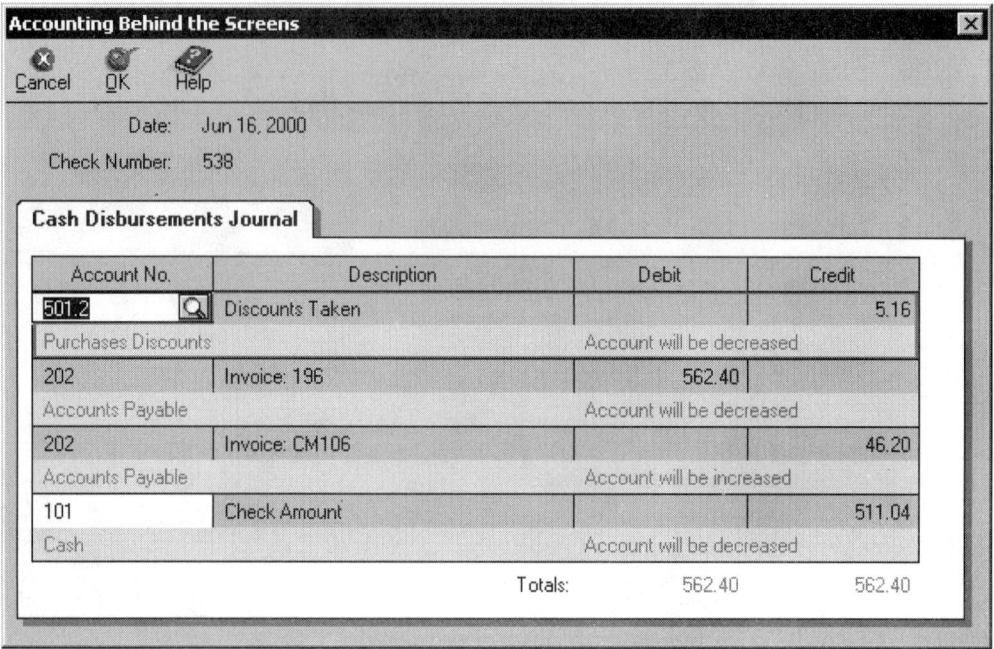

FIGURE 1.35 Accounting Behind the Screens (Payment on Account)

Cash Purchases (Direct Payment)

Instead of entering a Vendor ID, you can simply key the Payee into the Pay to the Order of field. In this case, the Apply to Expenses tab will be activated. This allows you to enter direct payments, such as rent payments, for which a vendor has not been set up. A direct payment is illustrated in Figure 1.36 on the following page.

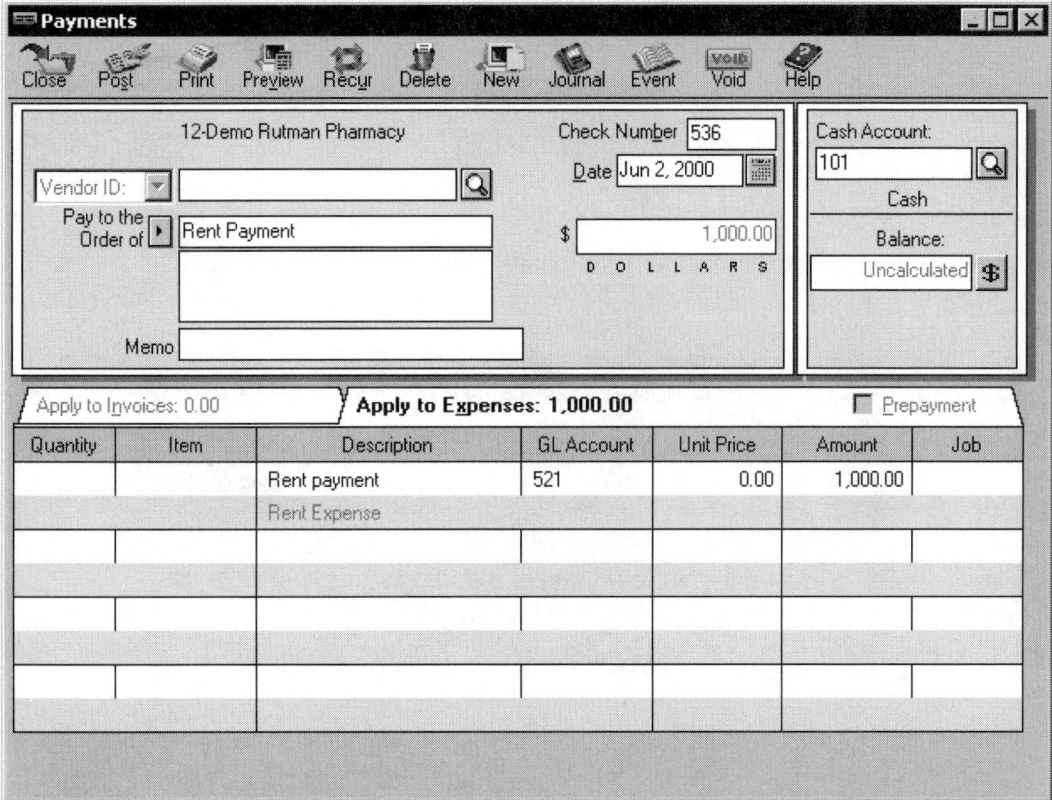

FIGURE 1.36 Payments Window (Direct Payment)

- Enter the Payee in the Pay to the Order of field.
- Enter the Check Number.
- Enter the Date of the transaction.
- Enter a description in the Description field.
- Enter the account number of the account to be debited in the GL Account field.
- Enter the amount to be paid in the Amount field.
- Click on the Post button to record the transaction.

Real-Time vs. Batch

The decision to process transactions in real-time or by batch is made at the time a company file is set up. All of the companies in these materials are set up to process transactions in real-time. When the batch posting mode is used, as transactions are entered they are stored in a temporary holding area where you can review them before posting the batch to the general ledger. In real-time posting, the transactions are posted immediately as they are recorded. The mode to be used is established on the Maintain Company Information window available from the Maintain menu.

BACKING UP AND RESTORING DATA FILES

Peachtree has the built-in capability to backup (make a copy of) a set of company data files. The backup option will make a mirror image copy of an existing set of data files on another drive and/or folder.

Backup

To backup or make a copy of the company data files that are currently open, complete the steps listed below:

▶ From the File menu select the Backup option. The Backup Company Data Files window shown in Figure 1.37 will appear.

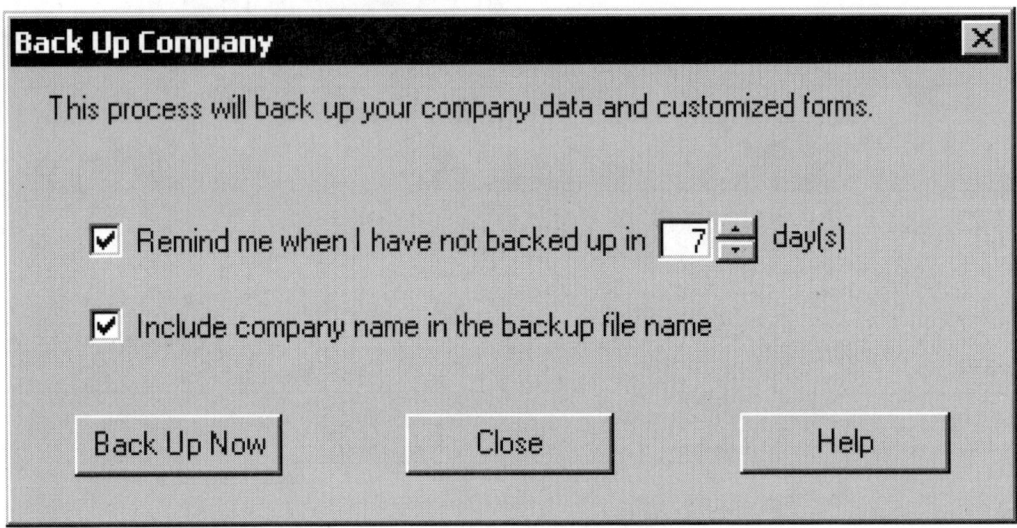

FIGURE 1.37 Backup Company Data Files Window

▶ Enter the path to the folder to which you wish to create the copy of the company data files. In the example, the current company files will be copied to the subfolder, "12-Demo" within the folder named "Allen". In this example, the folder named "Allen" would have to exist; however, the subfolder "12-Demo" would be created if necessary.
▶ Make sure that the "Simple copy (for small companies)" option button is selected.
▶ Click on the Backup button.

Restore

To restore the company data files for a company previously backup up with the backup procedure described above, complete the following steps:

▶ From the File menu select the Restore option. The Restore Company Data Files window shown in Figure 1.38 on the following page will appear.

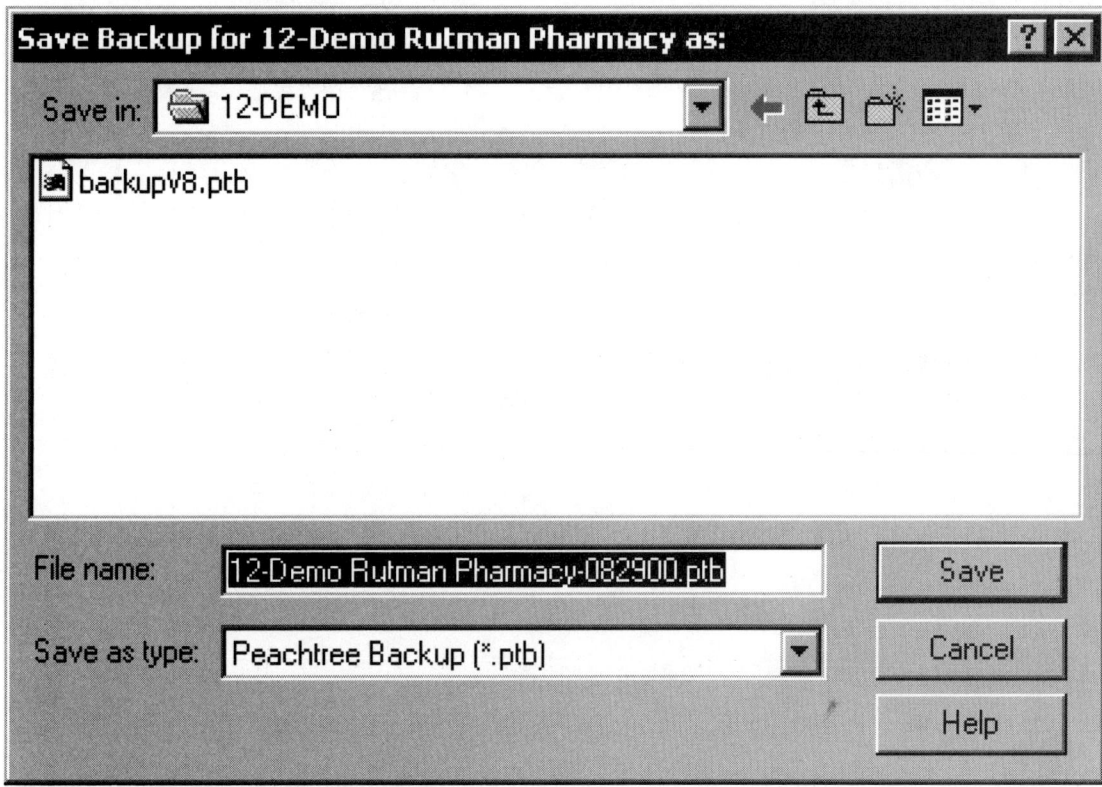

FIGURE 1.38 Restore Company Data Files Window

▶ **Enter the path to the folder that contains the previously backup up company data files that you wish to restore.**
▶ **Make sure that the "Simple copy (for small companies)" option button is selected.**
▶ **Click on the Backup button.**

SECTION 2

Instructions for Solving Selected Problems Using Peachtree Accounting Software

This section contains the instructions for solving problems using the Peachtree Accounting software. The beginning balance data for selected problems are included on the accompanying Peachtree Accounting install disk(s). The Install program stores a master copy of the Peachtree data files for the problems on your computer's hard drive. Without these data files, you would be required to enter the chart of accounts, vendor, customers, employees, and beginning balances for each problem before proceeding to solve it using Peachtree software.

When the beginning balance data was prepared, a specific accounting year was required. The year 2000 was used to establish these initial balances. Therefore, as you are solving the problems, you will reference the year 2000 even though the actual year may be after 2000.

CHAPTER 2 DEMONSTRATION PROBLEM (02-DEMO)

The Chapter 2 Demonstration Problem involves recording accounting transactions in the accounting equation and preparing financial statements for the company Home and Away Inspections. Because the Peachtree software does not have the capability of entering transactions into an accounting equation, you will instead utilize the software to create a chart of accounts, enter the account balances directly, and then display financial statements. The step-by-step instructions for solving the problem utilizing the Peachtree software are listed below:

STEP 1: Start up the Peachtree software.

Choose Peachtree Accounting from the Start button. When the screen titled Peachtree Accounting appears, choose the "Close this window" option. From the File Menu, choose the Open Company option. When the

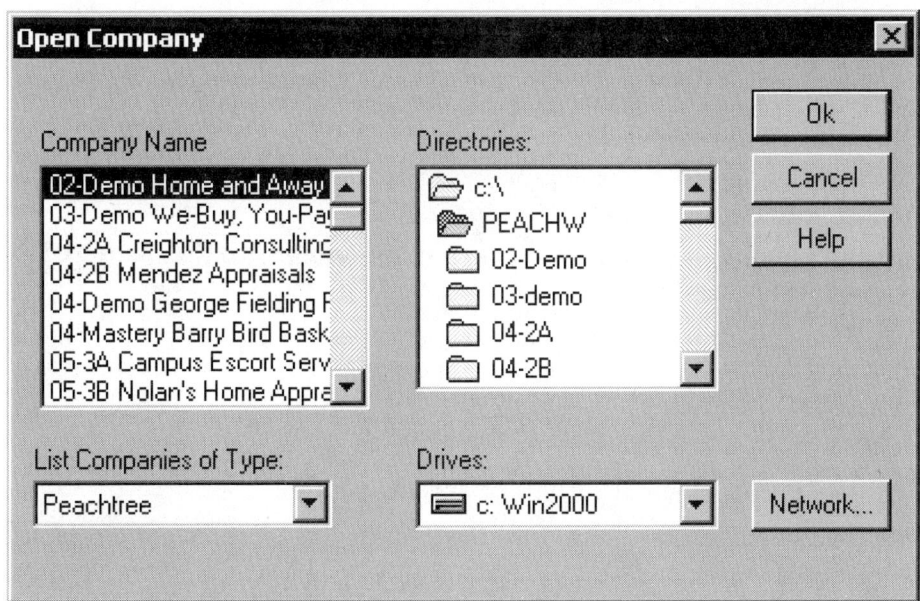

FIGURE 2.1 Open Company Dialog Box

Open Company dialog box shown in Figure 2.1 appears, select the directory in which you installed the Peachtree data files then choose the company named "02-Demo Home and Away." The Peachtree Today screen shown in Figure 2.2 will appear. Peachtree Today is the information center. The welcome page lets you browse product tips, open key areas of Peachtree Accounting, check for the latest updates, and get help on common tasks. All the program options available on the startup screen are also available via the Peachtree menus.

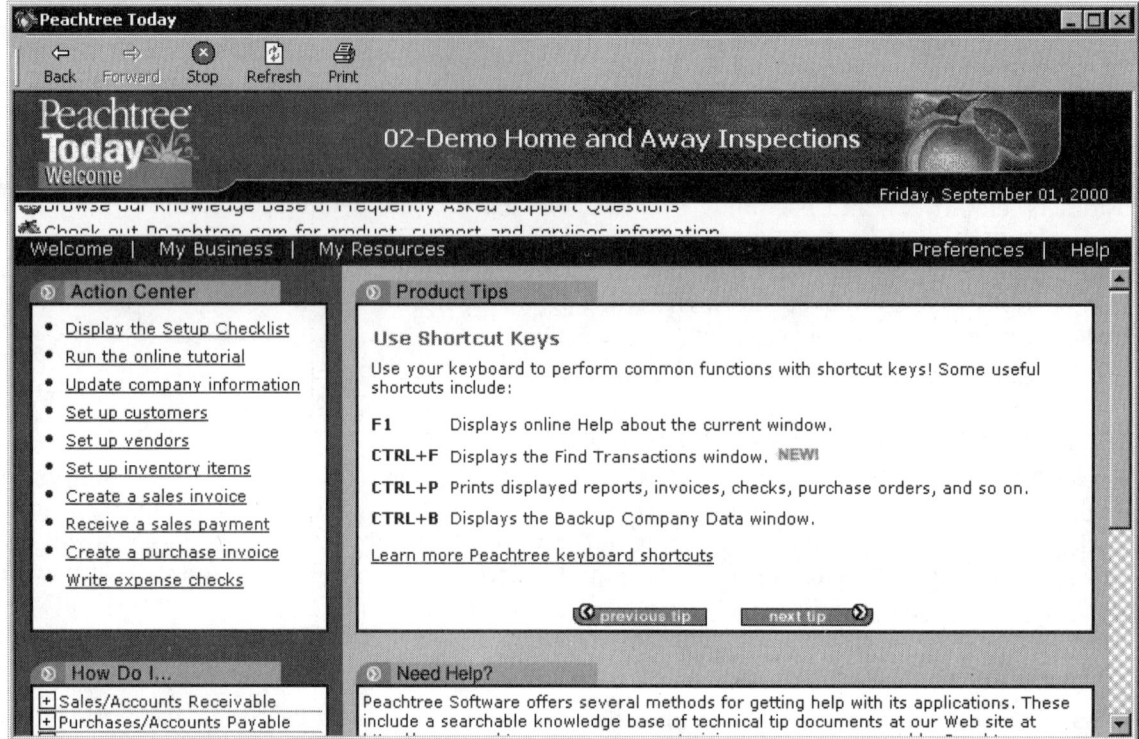

FIGURE 2.2 Peachtree Today Screen

STEP 2:   Restore the Opening Balance data for the Chapter 2 Demonstration Problem.

▶ From the File menu, choose Restore.
▶ When the Open Backup File window appears, select 02-Demo Opening Balances.
▶ When the Warning message appears, choose OK.
▶ When the Restore Options window appears, click the check box for Company Data and then click on the Restore button.

Restoring the opening balance data resets the Chapter 2 Demonstration Problem files so that you are ready to solve the problem from the beginning.

STEP 3:   Enter the chart of accounts entries shown below.

▶ From the Maintain menu, choose the Chart of Accounts option.

The Maintain Chart of Accounts window, with the first chart of accounts entry complete, is shown in Figure 2.3 on the following page.

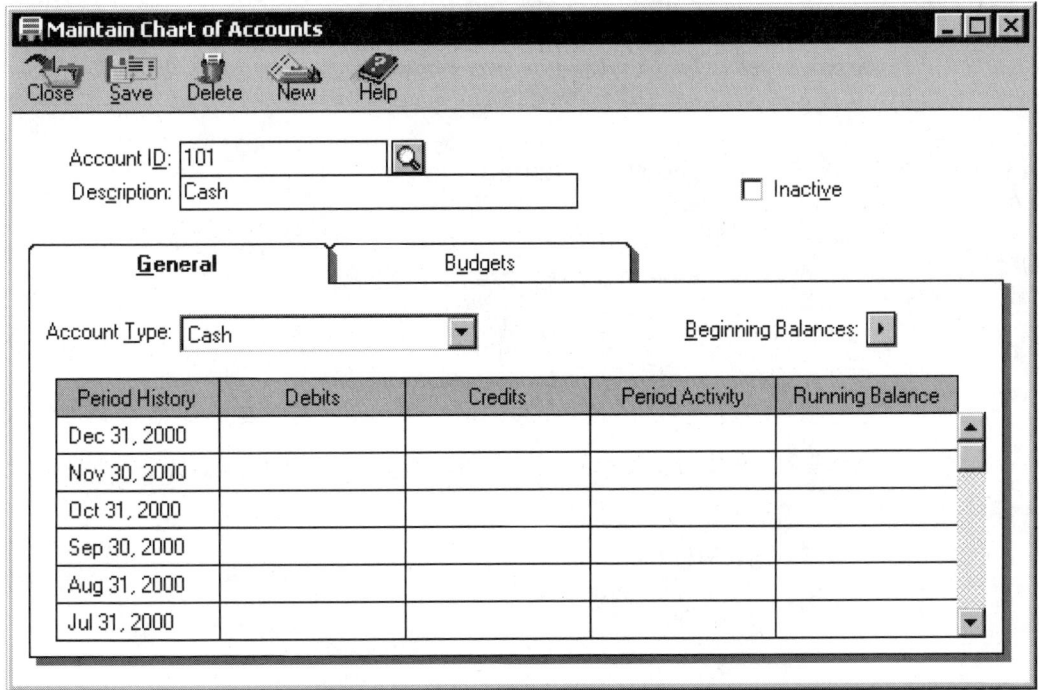

FIGURE 2.3 Maintain Chart of Accounts Window

- Enter the Account Number in the Account ID field.
- Enter the Account Title in the Description field.
- Select the Account Type from the drop-down list.
- Click on the Save button to record the account.

Account Number	Account Title	Account Type
101	Cash	Cash
102	Accounts Receivable	Accounts Receivable
103	Supplies	Other Current Asset
104	Prepaid Insurance	Other Current Asset
105	Tools	Fixed Asset
106	Truck	Fixed Asset
201	Accounts Payable	Accounts Payable
301	Damon Young, Capital	Equity-Retained Earnings
303	Damon Young, Drawing	Equity-Gets Closed
401	Inspection Fees	Income
501	Wages Expense	Expens
503	Rent Expense	Expense
505	Telephone Expense	Expense
507	Utilities Expense	Expense

STEP 4: Enter the account balances shown on the following page.

▶ Click on the right-arrow button labeled "Beginning Balances" on the Maintain Chart of Accounts window. The button is located near the center of the screen just to the right of the Account Type field.

▶ When the Select Period window shown in Figure 2.4 appears, choose "From 12/1/00 through 12/31/00" and click on Ok.

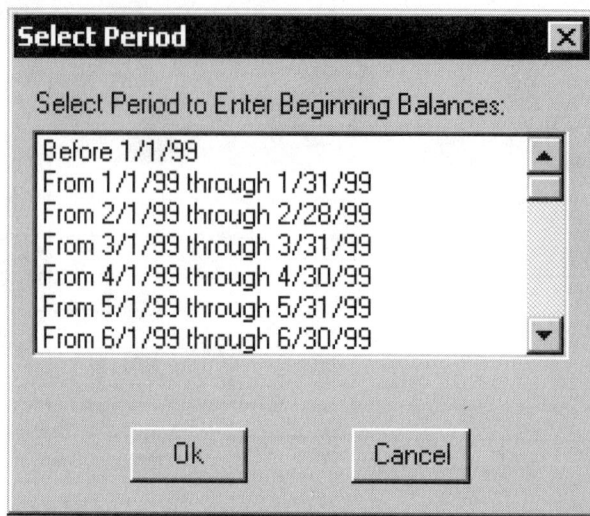

FIGURE 2.4 Select Period Window

▶ When the Chart of Accounts Beginning Balances window shown in Figure 2.5 on the following page appears, enter the account balances. Make sure that you enter the decimal point. After entering each account balance, press Tab to move to the next account.

▶ After all balances are entered, click on the Ok button.

Account Title	Account Balance	
Cash	7665.00	
Accounts Receivable	1300.00	
Supplies	300.00	
Prepaid Insurance	600.00	
Tools	3000.00	
Truck	8000.00	
Accounts Payable	2200.00	
Damon Young, Capital	15000.00	
Damon Young, Drawing	–500.00	(You must include the minus (–) sign.)
Inspection Fees	5000.00	
Wages Expense	450.00	
Rent Expense	300.00	
Telephone Expense	35.00	
Utilities Expense	50.00	

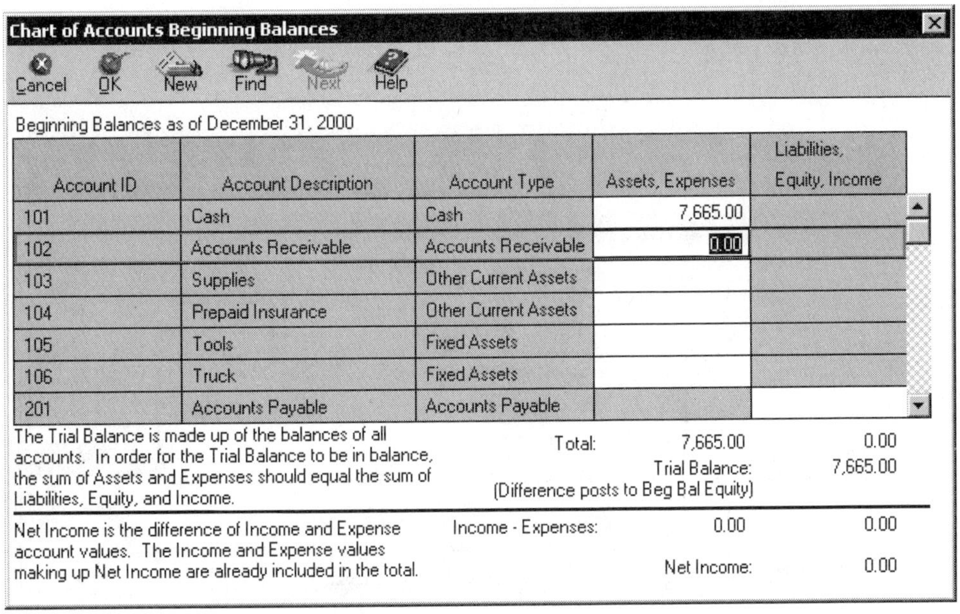

FIGURE 2.5 Chart of Accounts Beginning Balances

Notice that as you enter the account balances two totals are updated near the bottom of the window. The first is the total of Assets and Expenses and the second is the total of Liabilities, Equity, and Income. After all balances have been entered, the two totals must be equal. If they are not, you must find and fix any errors or the software will not allow you to proceed. Also, notice that the balance for drawing is negative and must be entered with a preceding minus sign (–500.00).

STEP 5: **Close the Maintain Chart of Accounts window by clicking on the Close button.**

STEP 6: **Display a Chart of Accounts Report.**

Click on the Reports menu and choose the General Ledger option.

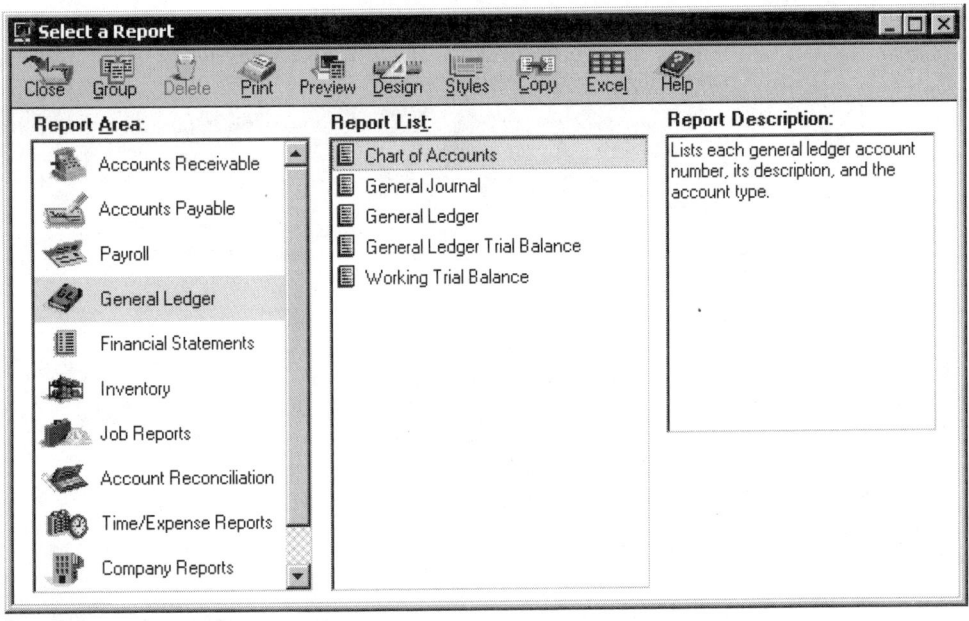

FIGURE 2.6 Select a Report Window

- When the In the Report List shown in Figure 2.6 on the previous page appears, click on Chart of Accounts under Report List.
- Click on the Preview button to display the report on the screen.
- When the Chart of Accounts filter shown in Figure 2.7 appears, click on Ok to display the chart of accounts report.

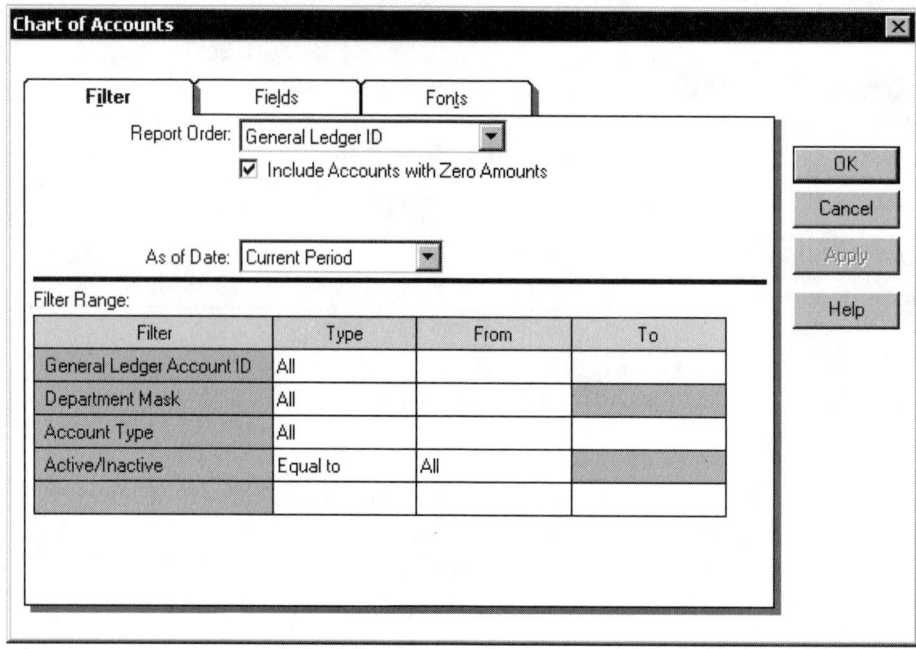

FIGURE 2.7 Chart of Accounts Report Filter

- When the Chart of Accounts Report shown in Figure 2.8 appears, click on Print to obtain a hard copy of the report.
- When the Print window appears, just click Ok to print the hard copy report.
- Click the Close button to dismiss the Chart of Accounts Report screen.

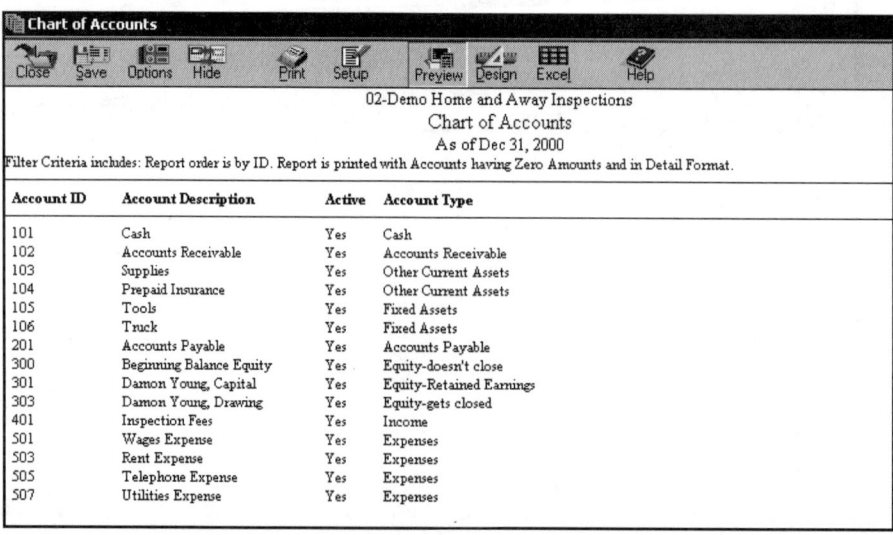

FIGURE 2.8 Chart of Accounts Report

STEP 7: Print the Financial Statements.

▶ Click on Financial Statements in the Report Area of the Select a Report window shown in Figure 2.6 on page 35.
▶ Display the Basic Balance Sheet.
▶ Display the Basic Income Statement.
▶ Display the Statement of Owner's Equity.

Compare your printouts to the solutions shown in the Demonstration Problem Solutions in Section 4 of this workbook.

CHAPTER 3 DEMONSTRATION PROBLEM (03-DEMO)

The Chapter 3 Demonstration Problem involves recording accounting transactions in T accounts and preparing financial statements. Because the Peachtree software does not have the capability of entering transactions into T accounts, you will utilize the software to enter the account balances directly and then display the financial statements. The step-by-step instructions for solving the problem utilizing the Peachtree software are listed as follows.

STEP 1: Start up the Peachtree software.

Choose Peachtree Accounting from the Start button.

STEP 2: Open the data file for the Chapter 3 Demonstration Problem.

STEP 3: Restore the Opening Balance data for the Chapter 3 Demonstration Problem.

▶ From the File menu, choose Restore.
▶ When the Open Backup File window appears, select 03-Demo Opening Balances.
▶ When the Warning message appears, choose OK.
▶ When the Restore Options window appears, click the check box for Company Data and then click on the Restore button.

STEP 4: Enter the account balances shown below.

▶ From the Maintain menu, choose the Chart of Accounts option.
▶ Click on the Beginning Balances on the Maintain Chart of Accounts window.
▶ When the Select Period Dialog appears, choose "From 12/1/00 through 12/31/00" and click on Ok. Be sure to select December of 2000 and not December of 1999.
▶ When the Chart of Accounts Beginning Balances window appears, enter the account balances. Make sure that you enter the decimal point. After entering each account balance, press Tab to move to the next account.

▶ After all balances are entered, click on the Ok button.

Account Title	Account Balance
Cash	20,010.00
Accounts Receivable	8,400.00
Office Equipment	10,000.00
Computer Equipment	4,800.00
Accounts Payable	6,000.00
Notes Payable	4,000.00
Celia Pints, Capital	30,000.00
Celia Pints, Drawing	–2,000.00
Shopping Fees	18,400.00
Rent Expense	500.00
Telephone Expense	90.00
Commissions Expense	10,500.00
Utilities Expense	600.00
Travel Expense	1,500.00

Notice that as you enter the account balances two totals are updated near the bottom of the window. The first is the total of Assets and Expenses and the second is the total of Liabilities, Equity, and Income. After all balances have been entered, the two totals must be equal. If they are not, you must find and fix any errors or the software will not allow you to proceed. Also, notice that the balance for drawing is negative and must be entered with a preceding minus sign (–2000.00).

STEP 5: Close the Maintain Chart of Accounts window by clicking on the Close button.

STEP 6: Display the Financial Statements. Click on Financial Statements in the Report Area of the Select a Report window.

▶ Display the Basic Balance Sheet.
▶ Display the Basic Income Statement.
▶ Display the Statement of Owner's Equity.

Compare your reports to the solutions shown in the Demonstration Problem Solutions in Section 4 of this workbook.

CHAPTER 4 DEMONSTRATION PROBLEM (04-DEMO)

George Fielding is a financial planning consultant. He provides budgeting, estate planning, tax planning, and investing advice for professional golfers. He developed the following chart of accounts for his business.

Assets
101　Cash
142　Office Supplies

Liabilities
202　Accounts Payable

Owner's Equity
311　George Fielding, Capital
312　George Fielding, Drawing

Revenues
401　Professional Fees

Expenses
511　Wages Expense
521　Rent Expense
525　Telephone Expense
533　Utilities Expense
534　Charitable Contributions Expense
538　Automobile Expense

The following transactions took place during the month of December of the current year.

Dec. 1 Fielding invested cash to start the business, $20,000.

3 Paid Bollhorst Real Estate for December office rent, $1,000.

4 Received cash from Aaron Patton, a client, for services, $2,500.

6 Paid T. Z. Anderson Electric for December heating and light, $75.

7 Received cash from Andrew Conder, a client, for services, $2,000.

12 Paid Fichter's Super Service for gasoline and oil purchases for the company car, $60.

14 Paid Hillenburg Staffing for temporary secretarial services during the past two weeks, $600.

17 Bought office supplies from Bowers Office Supply on account, $280.

20 Paid Mitchell Telephone Co. for business calls during the past month, $100.

21 Fielding withdrew cash for personal use, $1,100.

24 Made donation to the National Multiple Sclerosis Society, $100.

27 Received cash from Billy Walters, a client, for services, $2,000.

28 Paid Hillenburg Staffing for temporary secretarial services during the past two weeks, $600.

29 Made payment on account to Bowers Office Supply, $100.

The Chapter 4 Demonstration Problem involves entering general journal entries into the computer, displaying a general journal report, and displaying a general ledger trial balance report. Follow the step-by-step instructions below to complete the Chapter 4 Demonstration Problem.

STEP 1: Start up the Peachtree software.

Choose Peachtree Accounting from the Start button.

STEP 2: Open the data file for the Chapter 4 Demonstration Problem.

STEP 3: Restore the Opening Balance data for the Chapter 4 Demonstration Problem.

▶ From the File menu, choose Restore.
▶ When the Open Backup File window appears, select 04-Demo Opening Balances.
▶ When the Warning message appears, choose OK.
▶ When the Restore Options window appears, click the check box for Company Data and then click on the Restore button.

STEP 4: Enter the December transactions into the General Journal window.

From the Tasks menu, choose the General Journal Entry option. The first journal entry is illustrated in the General Journal Entry window shown in Figure 2.9 on the following page.

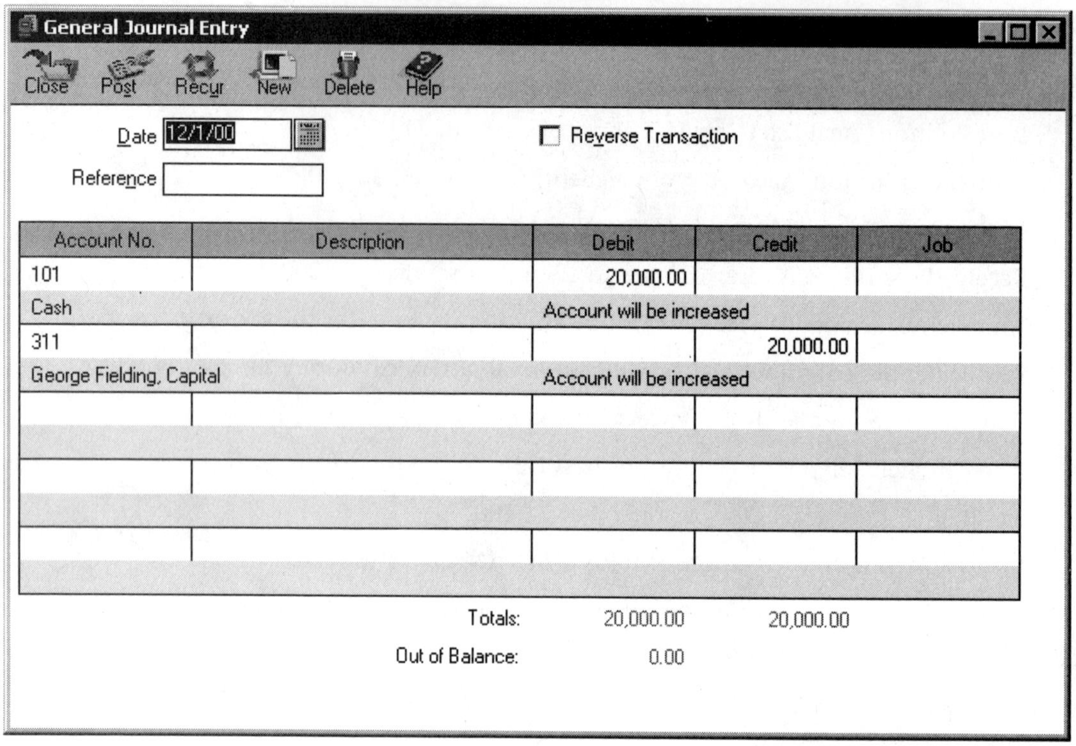

FIGURE 2.9 General Journal Entry Window

- Enter the transaction date.
- Since reference numbers are not provided in this problem, you may leave the Reference field blank. However, Peachtree will combine all journal entries with a blank reference and the same date. You can force the journal entries to print separately by assigning a unique Reference for each transaction of the same date (assigning each reference a letter, for example).
- For each leg of the transaction, enter the appropriate account number or select it from the drop-down Chart of Accounts list.
- Enter a description of the transaction.
- For each leg of the transaction, enter the debit or credit amount.
- When the transaction is complete, click on the Post button.

STEP 5:   Display a General Journal Report.

- Click on the Reports menu, and choose the General Ledger option.
- In the Report List, click on General Journal with Titles and click on Preview.

STEP 6:   If errors are detected on the General Journal Report, return to the General Journal window and make corrections.

- Click on the Edit Icon Bar button.
- Highlight the entry you wish to correct and click on Ok.
- Make corrections and click on Post.
- After all corrections are made, display another General Journal with Titles Report.

STEP 7:   Display a General Ledger Trial Balance Report.

- Display a trial balance report by double-clicking on the General Ledger Trial Balance in the Report List section of the Select a Report window.

STEP 8: Display a General Ledger Report.

▶ Double-click on General Ledger in the Report List section of the Select a Report window. Compare your report to the General Ledger Accounts shown in the Demonstration Problem.

▶ See the solution section of this workbook for the solution to the demonstration problem.

PROBLEM 4-2A

Annette Creighton opened Creighton Consulting. She rented a small office and paid a part-time worker to answer the telephone and make deliveries. Her chart of accounts is as follows:

Chart of Accounts

Assets
101 Cash
142 Office Supplies
181 Office Equipment

Liabilities
202 Accounts Payable

Owner's Equity
311 Annette Creighton, Capital
312 Annette Creighton, Drawing

Revenues
401 Consulting Fees

Expenses
511 Wages Expense
512 Advertising Expense
521 Rent Expense
525 Telephone Expense
526 Transportation Expense
533 Utilities Expense
549 Miscellaneous Expense

Creighton's transactions for the first month of business are as follows:

Jan. 1 Creighton invested cash in the business, $10,000.

1 Paid rent, $500.

2 Purchased office supplies on account, $300.

4 Purchased office equipment on account, $1,500.

6 Received cash for services rendered, $580.

7 Paid telephone bill, $42.

8 Paid utilities bill, $38.

10 Received cash for services rendered, $360.

12 Made payment on account, $50.

13 Paid for car rental while visiting an out-of-town client (transportation expense), $150.

15 Paid part-time worker, $360.

17 Received cash for services rendered, $420.

18 Creighton withdrew cash for personal use, $100.

20 Paid for a newspaper ad, $26.

22 Reimbursed part-time employee for cab fare incurred delivering materials to clients (transportation expense), $35.

24 Paid for books on consulting practices (miscellaneous expense), $28.

25 Received cash for services rendered, $320.

27 Made payment on account for office equipment purchased, $150.

29 Paid part-time worker, $360.

30 Received cash for services rendered, $180.

In Problem 4-2A, you will enter the general journal entries for the month of January for the year 2000, display a general journal report, display a general ledger trial balance, and display financial statements. Follow the step-by-step instructions below to complete Problem 4-2A.

STEP 1: Start up the Peachtree software.

Choose Peachtree Accounting from the Start button.

STEP 2: Open the data file for the Problem 4-2A (Creighton Consulting).

STEP 3: Restore the Opening Balance data for Problem 4-2A.

- From the File menu, choose Restore.
- When the Open Backup File window appears, select Problem 4-2A.
- When the Warning message appears, choose OK.
- When the Restore Options window appears, click the check box for Company Data and then click on the Restore button.

STEP 4: Enter the January transactions into the General Journal window.

STEP 5: Display a General Journal with Titles Report.

STEP 6: Display a General Ledger Trial Balance Report.

STEP 7: Display a Basic Income Statement.

STEP 8: Display a Statement of Owner's Equity.

STEP 9: Display a Basic Balance Sheet.

PROBLEM 4-2B

Benito Mendez opened Mendez Appraisals. He rented office space and has a part-time secretary to answer the telephone and make appraisal appointments. His chart of accounts is as follows:

Chart of Accounts

Assets
101 Cash
122 Accounts Receivable
142 Office Supplies
181 Office Equipment

Liabilities
202 Accounts Payable

Owner's Equity
311 Benito Mendez, Capital
312 Benito Mendez, Drawing

Revenues
401 Appraisal Fees

Expenses
511 Wages Expense
512 Advertising Expense
521 Rent Expense
525 Telephone Expense
526 Transportation Expense
533 Electricity Expense
549 Miscellaneous Expense

Mendez's transactions for the first month of business are as follows:

May 1 Mendez invested cash in the business, $5,000.

2 Paid rent, $500.

3 Purchased office supplies, $100.

4 Purchased office equipment on account, $2,000.

5 Received cash for services rendered, $280.

8 Paid telephone bill, $38.

9 Paid electric bill, $42.

10 Received cash for services rendered, $310.

13 Paid part-time employee, $500.

14 Paid car rental for out-of-town trip, $200.

15 Paid for newspaper ad, $30.

18 Received cash for services rendered, $620.

19 Paid mileage reimbursement for part-time employee's use of personal car for business deliveries (transportation expense), $22.

21 Mendez withdrew cash for personal use, $50.

23 Made payment on account for office equipment purchased earlier, $200.

24 Earned appraisal fee, which will be paid in a week, $500.

26 Paid for newspaper ad, $30.

27 Paid for local softball team sponsorship (miscellaneous expense), $15.

28 Paid part-time employee, $500.

29 Received cash on account, $250.

30 Received cash for services rendered, $280.

31 Paid cab fare (transportation expense), $13.

Problem 4-2B involves entering general journal entries for the month of May, displaying a general journal report, general ledger trial balance, and financial statements. Follow the step-by-step instructions below to complete the Problem 4-2B.

STEP 1: Start up the Peachtree software.

STEP 2: Open the data file for the Problem 4-2B (Mendez Appraisals).

STEP 3: Restore the Opening Balance data for Problem 4-2B.

- From the File menu, choose Restore.
- When the Open Backup File window appears, select Problem 4-2B.
- When the Warning message appears, choose OK.
- When the Restore Options window appears, click the check box for Company Data and then click on the Restore button.

STEP 4: Enter the May transactions into the General Journal window.

STEP 5: Display the General Journal with Titles Report.

STEP 6: Display a General Ledger Trial Balance Report.

STEP 7: Display a Basic Income Statement.

STEP 8: Display a Statement of Owner's Equity.

STEP 9: Display a Basic Balance Sheet.

CHAPTER 4 MASTERY PROBLEM

Barry Bird opened the Barry Bird Basketball Camp for children ages 10 through 18. Campers typically register for one week in June or July, arriving on Sunday and returning home the following Saturday. College players serve as cabin counselors and assist the local college and high school coaches who run the practice sessions. The registration fee includes a room, meals at a nearby restaurant, and basketball instruction. In the off-season, the facilities are used for weekend retreats and coaching clinics. Bird developed the following chart of accounts for his service business.

Chart of Accounts

Assets
101 Cash
142 Office Supplies
183 Athletic Equipment
184 Basketball Facilities

Liabilities
202 Accounts Payable

Owner's Equity
311 Barry Bird, Capital
312 Barry Bird, Drawing

Revenues
401 Registration Fees

Expenses
511 Wages Expense
512 Advertising Expense
524 Food Expense
525 Telephone Expense
533 Utilities Expense
536 Postage Expense

The following transactions took place during the month of June.

June 1 Bird invested cash in the business, $10,000.

1 Purchased basketballs and other athletic equipment, $3,000.

2 Paid Hite Advertising for fliers that had been mailed to prospective campers, $5,000.

2 Collected registration fees, $15,000.

2 Rogers Construction completed work on a new basketball court that cost $12,000. Arrangements were made to pay the bill in July.

5 Purchased office supplies on account from Gordon Office Supplies, $300.

6 Received bill from Magic's Restaurant for meals served to campers on account, $5,800.

7 Collected registration fees, $16,200.

10 Paid wages to camp counselors, $500.

14 Collected registration fees, $13,500.

14	Received bill from Magic's Restaurant for meals served to campers on account, $6,200.	
17	Paid wages to camp counselors, $500.	
18	Paid postage, $85.	
21	Collected registration fees, $15,200.	
22	Received bill from Magic's Restaurant for meals served to campers on account, $6,500.	
24	Paid wages to camp counselors, $500.	
28	Collected registration fees, $14,000.	
30	Received bill from Magic's Restaurant for meals served to campers on account, $7,200.	
30	Paid wages to camp counselors, $500.	
30	Paid Magic's Restaurant on account, $25,700.	
30	Paid utility bill, $500.	
30	Paid telephone bill, $120.	
30	Bird withdrew cash for personal use, $2,000.	

The Chapter 4 Mastery Problem involves entering general journal entries for the month of June, displaying a general journal report and a general ledger trial balance. Follow the step-by-step instructions below to complete the Chapter 4 Mastery Problem.

STEP 1: Start up the Peachtree software.

STEP 2: Open the data file for the Chapter 4 Mastery Problem.

STEP 3: Restore the Opening Balance data for the Chapter 4 Mastery Problem.

STEP 4: Enter the June transactions into the General Journal window.

STEP 5: Display the General Journal with Titles Report.

STEP 6: Display a General Ledger Trial Balance Report.

STEP 7: Display a Basic Income Statement.

STEP 8: Display a Statement of Owner's Equity.

STEP 9: Display a Basic Balance Sheet.

CHAPTER 5 DEMONSTRATION PROBLEM (05-DEMO)

Justin Park is a lawyer specializing in corporate tax law. He began his practice on January 1. A chart of accounts is shown in Figure 2.10 and a trial balance taken on December 31, 2000 is shown in Figure 2.11.

05-Demo Justin Park Legal Services
Chart of Accounts
As of Dec 31, 2000

Filter Criteria includes: Report order is by ID. Report is printed with Accounts having Zero Amounts and in Detail Format.

Account ID	Account Description	Active	Account Type
101	Cash	Yes	Cash
142	Office Supplies	Yes	Other Current Assets
145	Prepaid Insurance	Yes	Other Current Assets
181	Office Equipment	Yes	Fixed Assets
181.1	Accum. Depr.--Office Equipmen	Yes	Accumulated Depreciation
187	Computer Equipment	Yes	Fixed Assets
187.1	Accum. Depr.--Computer Equip.	Yes	Accumulated Depreciation
201	Notes Payable	Yes	Other Current Liabilities
202	Accounts Payable	Yes	Accounts Payable
219	Wages Payable	Yes	Other Current Liabilities
310	Beginning Balance Equity	Yes	Equity-doesn't close
311	Justin Park, Capital	Yes	Equity-Retained Earnings
312	Justin Park, Drawing	Yes	Equity-gets closed
401	Client Fees	Yes	Income
511	Wages Expense	Yes	Expenses
521	Rent Expense	Yes	Expenses
523	Office Supplies Expense	Yes	Expenses
525	Telephone Expense	Yes	Expenses
533	Utilities Expense	Yes	Expenses
535	Insurance Expense	Yes	Expenses
541	Depr. Expense--Office Equip.	Yes	Expenses
542	Depr. Expense--Computer Equi	Yes	Expenses

FIGURE 2.10 Justin Park Legal Services Chart of Accounts

05-Demo Justin Park Legal Services
General Ledger Trial Balance
As of Dec 31, 2000

Filter Criteria includes: Report order is by ID. Report is printed in Detail Format.

Account ID	Account Description	Debit Amt	Credit Amt
101	Cash	7,000.00	
142	Office Supplies	800.00	
145	Prepaid Insurance	1,200.00	
181	Office Equipment	15,000.00	
187	Computer Equipment	6,000.00	
201	Notes Payable		5,000.00
202	Accounts Payable		500.00
311	Justin Park, Capital		11,400.00
312	Justin Park, Drawing	5,000.00	
401	Client Fees		40,000.00
511	Wages Expense	12,000.00	
521	Rent Expense	5,000.00	
525	Telephone Expense	1,000.00	
533	Utilities Expense	3,900.00	
	Total:	56,900.00	56,900.00

FIGURE 2.11 Justin Park Legal Services Trial Balance

Information for year-end adjustments is as follows:

(a) Office supplies on hand at year end amounted to $300.

(b) On January 1, 2000, Park purchased office equipment costing $15,000 with an expected life of five years and no salvage value.

(c) Computer equipment costing $6,000 with an expected life of three years and no salvage value was purchased on July 1, 2000. Assume that Park computes depreciation to the nearest full month.

(d) A premium of $1,200 for a one-year insurance policy was paid on December 1, 2000.

(e) Wages earned by Park's part-time secretary, which have not yet been paid, amount to $300.

In the Chapter 5 Demonstration Problem, you will enter the adjusting entries, display the adjusting entries, and display the financial statements. A worksheet is not necessary in Peachtree. Follow the step-by-step instructions below to complete the Chapter 5 Demonstration Problem.

STEP 1: Start up the Peachtree software.

STEP 2: Open the data file for the Chapter 5 Demonstration Problem.

STEP 3: Restore the Opening Balance data.

STEP 4: Enter the adjusting entries into the General Journal window.

Enter each entry with a date of December 31, 2000, and enter "Adjusting Entry" as the description.

STEP 5: Display the adjusting entries using the General Journal with Titles Report.

STEP 6: Display a Basic Income Statement.

STEP 7: Display a Statement of Owner's Equity.

STEP 8: Display a Basic Balance Sheet.

See the solution section of this workbook for the solution to the demonstration problem.

PROBLEM 5-3A

Jason Armstrong started a business called Campus Escort Service. After the first month of operations, the trial balance as of November 30, 2000, is as shown below and on the next page.
Information needed to make month-end adjustments follows:

(a) Ending inventory of supplies on November 30, $185.

(b) Unexpired (remaining) insurance as of November 30, $800.

(c) Depreciation expense on van, $300.

(d) Wages earned, but not paid as of November 30, $190.

Account Name	Account Number	Balance in Account Before Adjusting Entry
Supplies	141	$ 575
Prepaid Insurance	145	1,300
Accum. Depr.—Van	185.1	0

Wages Payable	219	0
Wages Expense	511	1,800
Supplies Expense	523	0
Insurance Expense	535	0
Depr. Expense—Van	541	0

In Problem 5-3A, you will enter the adjusting entries, display adjusting entries, display a trial balance, and display the financial statements. Follow the step-by-step instructions below to complete Problem 5-3A.

STEP 1: Start up the Peachtree software.

STEP 2: Open the data file for Problem 5-3A.

STEP 3: Restore the Opening Balance data.

STEP 4: Enter the adjusting entries into the General Journal window.

STEP 5: Display the adjusting entries using the General Journal with Titles Report.

STEP 6: Display the General Ledger Trial Balance Report.

STEP 7: Display a Basic Income Statement.

STEP 8: Display a Statement of Owner's Equity.

STEP 9: Display a Basic Balance Sheet.

PROBLEM 5-3B

Val Nolan started a business called Nolan's Home Appraisals. The trial balance as of October 31, after the first month of operations, is shown below.

Information needed to make month-end adjustments follows:
(a) Supplies inventory as of October 31, $210.
(b) Unexpired (remaining) insurance as of October 31, $800.
(c) Depreciation of automobile, $250.
(d) Wages earned, but not paid as of October 31, $175.

Account Name	Account Number	Balance in Account Before Adjusting Entry
Supplies	141	$ 625
Prepaid Insurance	145	950
Accum. Depr.—Automobile	185.1	0
Wages Payable	219	0
Wages Expense	511	1,560
Supplies Expense	523	0
Insurance Expense	535	0
Depr. Expense—Automobile	541	0

In Problem 5-3B, you will enter the adjusting entries, display a trial balance, and display the financial statements. Follow the step-by-step instructions below to complete Problem 5-3B.

STEP 1: Start up the Peachtree software.

STEP 2: Open the data file for Problem 5-3B.

STEP 3: Restore the Opening Balance data.

STEP 4: Enter the adjusting entries into the General Journal window.

STEP 5: Display the adjusting entries using the General Journal with Titles Report.

STEP 6: Display the General Ledger Trial Balance Report.

STEP 7: Display a Basic Income Statement.

STEP 8: Display a Statement of Owner's Equity.

STEP 9: Display a Basic Balance Sheet.

CHAPTER 5 MASTERY PROBLEM

Kristi Williams offers family counseling services specializing in financial and marital problems. A chart of accounts and a trial balance taken on December 31, 2000, are provided on the next page.

Information for year-end adjustments:

(a) Office supplies on hand at year end amounted to $100.

(b) On January 1, 2000, Williams purchased office equipment that cost $18,000. It has an expected useful life of ten years and no salvage value.

(c) On July 1, 2000, Williams purchased computer equipment costing $6,000. It has an expected useful life of three years and no salvage value. Assume that Williams computes depreciation to the nearest full month.

(d) On December 1, 2000, Williams paid a premium of $600 for a six-month insurance policy.

In the Chapter 5 Mastery Problem, you will enter the adjusting entries, display a trial balance, and display the financial statements. Follow the step-by-step instructions below to complete the Chapter 5 Mastery Problem.

STEP 1: Start up the Peachtree software.

STEP 2: Open the data file for the Chapter 5 Mastery Problem. For this Peachtree project, the 2000 date on your data disk is correct.

STEP 3: Restore the Opening Balance data.

STEP 4: Enter the adjusting entries into the General Journal window.

STEP 5: Display the adjusting entries using the General Journal with Titles Report.

KRISTI WILLIAMS FAMILY COUNSELING SERVICES
CHART OF ACCOUNTS

Assets		Revenue	
101	Cash	401	Client Fees
142	Office Supplies		
145	Prepaid Insurance	**Expenses**	
181	Office Equipment	511	Wages Expense
181.1	Accumulated Depr.—	521	Rent Expense
	Office Equipment	523	Office Supplies Expense
187	Computer Equipment	533	Utilities Expense
187.1	Accumulated Depr.—	535	Insurance Expense
	Computer Equipment	541	Depr. Expense—
			Office Equipment
Liabilities		542	Depr. Expense—
201	Notes Payable		Computer Equipment
202	Accounts Payable	549	Miscellaneous Expense
Owner's Equity			
311	Kristi Williams, Capital		
312	Kristi Williams, Drawing		

Kristi Williams Family Counseling Services
Trial Balance
December 31, 20 - 1

ACCOUNT TITLE	ACCOUNT NO.	DEBIT BALANCE	CREDIT BALANCE
Cash	101	8 7 3 0 00	
Office Supplies	142	7 0 0 00	
Prepaid Insurance	145	6 0 0 00	
Office Equipment	181	18 0 0 0 00	
Computer Equipment	187	6 0 0 0 00	
Notes Payable	201		8 0 0 0 00
Accounts Payable	202		5 0 0 00
Kristi Williams, Capital	311		11 4 0 0 00
Kristi Williams, Drawing	312	3 0 0 0 00	
Client Fees	401		35 8 0 0 00
Wages Expense	511	9 5 0 0 00	
Rent Expense	521	6 0 0 0 00	
Utilities Expense	533	2 1 7 0 00	
Miscellaneous Expense	549	1 0 0 0 00	
		55 7 0 0 00	55 7 0 0 00

STEP 6: Display the General Ledger Trial Balance Report.

STEP 7: Display a Basic Income Statement.

STEP 8: Display a Statement of Owner's Equity.

STEP 9: Display a Basic Balance Sheet.

CHAPTER 6 DEMONSTRATION PROBLEM (06-DEMO)

In the Chapter 6 Demonstration Problem, you will display the financial statements and close the accounting period for Timothy Chang who owns and operates Hard Copy Printers. Follow the step-by-step instructions below to complete the Chapter 6 Demonstration Problem. Refer to the worksheet on the following page. Chang made no additional investments during the year.

STEP 1: Start up the Peachtree software.

STEP 2: Open the data file for the Chapter 6 Demonstration Problem.

STEP 3: Restore the Opening Balance data.

STEP 4: Enter the adjusting entries from the adjustment column of the worksheet.

STEP 5: Display a Statement of Owner's Equity.

STEP 6: Display a Basic Balance Sheet.

STEP 7: Display a Basic Income Statement.

STEP 8: Change the accounting period to January 1 of 2001.

▶ From the Tasks menu, select System, and then select Change Accounting Periods from the submenu.

▶ When the Change Accounting Period window appears, select January 1, 2001, to January 31, 2001, and click on Ok.

▶ A message box appears, asking if you would like to print reports before continuing. Since you just printed reports in the above steps, respond No.

Changing the accounting period to the next fiscal year will change the processing cycle from the year 2000 to the year 2001, in effect closing the year 2000. It is really a temporary closing. A permanent closing doesn't occur until the fiscal year is actually closed via the Close Fiscal Year option.

STEP 9: Display a trial balance report.

Because you changed to a new fiscal accounting year, the trial balance report should reflect the closing of the year 2000. If you should discover an error and wish to edit transactions from the previous period, simply change the accounting period back to December of 2000, make the corrections, display your reports, and again change the accounting period to January of 2001.

See the solution section of this workbook for the solution to the demonstration problem.

Hard Copy Printers
Work Sheet
For Year Ended December 31, 20--

	ACCOUNT TITLE	TRIAL BALANCE DEBIT	TRIAL BALANCE CREDIT	ADJUSTMENTS DEBIT	ADJUSTMENTS CREDIT	ADJUSTED TRIAL BALANCE DEBIT	ADJUSTED TRIAL BALANCE CREDIT	INCOME STATEMENT DEBIT	INCOME STATEMENT CREDIT	BALANCE SHEET DEBIT	BALANCE SHEET CREDIT	
1	Cash	11 8 0 0 00				11 8 0 0 00				11 8 0 0 00		1
2	Paper Supplies	3 6 0 0 00			(a) 3 5 5 0 00	5 0 00				5 0 00		2
3	Prepaid Insurance	1 0 0 0 00			(b) 5 0 5 00	4 9 5 00				4 9 5 00		3
4	Printing Equipment	5 8 0 0 00				5 8 0 0 00				5 8 0 0 00		4
5	Accum. Depr.—Printing Equipment				(d) 1 2 0 0 00		1 2 0 0 00				1 2 0 0 00	5
6	Accounts Payable		5 0 0 00				5 0 0 00				5 0 0 00	6
7	Wages Payable				(c) 3 0 00		3 0 00				3 0 00	7
8	Timothy Chang, Capital		10 0 0 0 00				10 0 0 0 00				10 0 0 0 00	8
9	Timothy Chang, Drawing	13 0 0 0 00				13 0 0 0 00				13 0 0 0 00		9
10	Printing Fees		35 1 0 0 00				35 1 0 0 00		35 1 0 0 00			10
11	Wages Expense	11 9 7 0 00		(c) 3 0 00		12 0 0 0 00		12 0 0 0 00				11
12	Rent Expense	7 5 0 0 00				7 5 0 0 00		7 5 0 0 00				12
13	Paper Supplies Expense			(a) 3 5 5 0 00		3 5 5 0 00		3 5 5 0 00				13
14	Telephone Expense	5 5 0 00				5 5 0 00		5 5 0 00				14
15	Utilities Expense	1 0 0 0 00				1 0 0 0 00		1 0 0 0 00				15
16	Insurance Expense			(b) 5 0 5 00		5 0 5 00		5 0 5 00				16
17	Depr. Expense—Printing Equipment			(d) 1 2 0 0 00		1 2 0 0 00		1 2 0 0 00				17
18		45 6 0 0 00	45 6 0 0 00	5 2 8 5 00	5 2 8 5 00	46 8 3 0 00	46 8 3 0 00	26 3 0 5 00	35 1 0 0 00	20 5 2 5 00	11 7 3 0 00	18
19	Net Income							8 7 9 5 00			8 7 9 5 00	19
20								35 1 0 0 00	35 1 0 0 00	20 5 2 5 00	20 5 2 5 00	20

PROBLEM 6-3A

A chart of accounts for Monte's Repairs is provided below.

Monte's Repairs
Chart of Accounts

Assets
101   Cash
122   Accounts Receivable
141   Supplies
145   Prepaid Insurance
185   Delivery Equipment
185.1 Accum. Depr.—Delivery Equip.

Liabilities
202   Accounts Payable
219   Wages Payable

Owner's Equity
311   Monte Eli, Capital
312   Monte Eli, Drawing
313   Income Summary

Revenues
401   Repair Fees

Expenses
511   Wages Expense
512   Advertising Expense
521   Rent Expense
523   Supplies Expense
525   Telephone Expense
535   Insurance Expense
538   Gas and Oil Expense
541   Depr. Exp.—Delivery Equip.
549   Miscellaneous Expense

In Problem 6-3A, you will enter the adjusting entries for Monte's Repairs, display reports, and enter closing entries. The processing for Problem 6-3A is somewhat different from the Chapter 6 Demonstration Problem because of a difference in the accounting period. The Demonstration Problem had a fiscal period of one year, whereas this problem has a fiscal period of one month. The Peachtree software assumes a fiscal period of one year. It allows for monthly accounting periods, but does not close until the end of the fiscal period. All this means is that, in order to close the accounting period at the end of a month, you must manually enter the closing journal entries. Follow the step-by-step procedures below to complete the processing for Problem 6-3A.

STEP 1:   Open the data file for Problem 6-3A.

STEP 2:   Enter the adjusting entries from the adjustment column of the worksheet shown on the following page.

STEP 3:   Restore the Opening Balance data.

STEP 4:   Display the adjusting entries with the General Journal with Titles Report.

STEP 5:   Display a Basic Income Statement.

STEP 6:   Display a Statement of Owner's Equity.

STEP 7:   Display a Basic Balance Sheet.

STEP 8:   Display a Trial Balance Report.

STEP 9:   Enter the closing entries into the General Journal window. Enter a transaction date of January 31, 2000, and a description of "Closing Entry."

STEP 10: Display the journal entries. Your report will include both adjusting and closing entries.

STEP 11: Display a post-closing trial balance, which is really just the normal trial balance report. It becomes post-closing because it was printed after closing entries were processed.

— 53 —

Monte's Repairs
Work Sheet
For Month Ended January 31, 20--

	ACCOUNT TITLE	TRIAL BALANCE DEBIT	TRIAL BALANCE CREDIT	ADJUSTMENTS DEBIT	ADJUSTMENTS CREDIT	ADJUSTED TRIAL BALANCE DEBIT	ADJUSTED TRIAL BALANCE CREDIT	INCOME STATEMENT DEBIT	INCOME STATEMENT CREDIT	BALANCE SHEET DEBIT	BALANCE SHEET CREDIT
1	Cash	3 0 8 0 00				3 0 8 0 00				3 0 8 0 00	
2	Accounts Receivable	1 2 0 0 00				1 2 0 0 00				1 2 0 0 00	
3	Supplies	8 0 0 00			(a) 2 0 0 00	6 0 0 00				6 0 0 00	
4	Prepaid Insurance	9 0 0 00			(b) 1 0 0 00	8 0 0 00				8 0 0 00	
5	Delivery Equipment	3 0 0 0 00				3 0 0 0 00				3 0 0 0 00	
6	Accum. Depr.—Delivery Equipment				(d) 30 00		30 00				30 00
7	Accounts Payable		1 1 0 0 00				1 1 0 0 00				1 1 0 0 00
8	Wages Payable				(c) 1 5 0 00		1 5 0 00				1 5 0 00
9	Monte Eli, Capital		7 0 0 0 00				7 0 0 0 00				7 0 0 0 00
10	Monte Eli, Drawing	1 0 0 0 00				1 0 0 0 00				1 0 0 0 00	
11	Repair Fees		4 2 3 0 00				4 2 3 0 00		4 2 3 0 00		
12	Wages Expense	1 6 5 0 00		(c) 1 5 0 00		1 8 0 0 00		1 8 0 0 00			
13	Advertising Expense	1 7 0 00				1 7 0 00		1 7 0 00			
14	Rent Expense	4 2 0 00				4 2 0 00		4 2 0 00			
15	Supplies Expense			(a) 2 0 0 00		2 0 0 00		2 0 0 00			
16	Telephone Expense	49 00				49 00		49 00			
17	Insurance Expense			(b) 1 0 0 00		1 0 0 00		1 0 0 00			
18	Gas and Oil Expense	33 00				33 00		33 00			
19	Depr. Expense—Delivery Equipment			(d) 30 00		30 00		30 00			
20	Miscellaneous Expense	28 00				28 00		28 00			
21		12 3 3 0 00	12 3 3 0 00	4 8 0 00	4 8 0 00	12 5 1 0 00	12 5 1 0 00	2 8 3 0 00	4 2 3 0 00	9 6 8 0 00	8 2 8 0 00
22	Net Income							1 4 0 0 00			1 4 0 0 00
23								4 2 3 0 00	4 2 3 0 00	9 6 8 0 00	9 6 8 0 00

PROBLEM 6-3B

A chart of accounts for Juanita's Consulting is provided below.

Juanita's Consulting
Chart of Accounts

Assets
- 101 Cash
- 122 Accounts Receivable
- 141 Supplies
- 145 Prepaid Insurance
- 181 Office Equipment
- 181.1 Accum. Depr.—Office Equip.

Liabilities
- 202 Accounts Payable
- 219 Wages Payable

Owner's Equity
- 311 Juanita Alvarez, Capital
- 312 Juanita Alvarez, Drawing
- 313 Income Summary

Revenues
- 401 Consulting Fees

Expense
- 511 Wages Expense
- 512 Advertising Expense
- 521 Rent Expense
- 523 Supplies Expense
- 525 Telephone Expense
- 533 Electricity Expense
- 535 Insurance Expense
- 538 Gas and Oil Expense
- 541 Depr. Exp.—Office Equip.
- 549 Miscellaneous Expense

In Problem 6-3B, you will enter the adjusting entries for Juanita's Consulting, display reports, and enter closing entries. This problem is similar to 6-3A in that the fiscal period is one month in duration, which means that you must close the period by actually entering the closing entries. Follow the step-by-step procedures below to complete the processing for Problem 6-3B.

STEP 1: Open the data file for Problem 6-3B.

STEP 2: Enter the adjusting entries from the adjustment column of the worksheet shown on the following page.

STEP 3: Restore the Opening Balance data.

STEP 4: Display the adjusting entries with the General Journal with Titles Report.

STEP 5: Display a Basic Income Statement.

STEP 6: Display a Statement of Owner's Equity.

STEP 7: Display a Basic Balance Sheet.

STEP 8: Display a Trial Balance Report.

STEP 9: Enter the closing entries into the General Journal window. Enter a transaction date of June 30, 2000, and a description of "Closing Entry."

STEP 10: Display the journal entries. Your report will include both adjusting and closing entries.

STEP 11: Display a post-closing trial balance, which is really just the normal trial balance report. It becomes post-closing because it was printed after closing entries were processed.

Juanita's Consulting
Work Sheet
For Month Ended June 30, 20--

	ACCOUNT TITLE	TRIAL BALANCE DEBIT	TRIAL BALANCE CREDIT	ADJUSTMENTS DEBIT	ADJUSTMENTS CREDIT	ADJUSTED TRIAL BALANCE DEBIT	ADJUSTED TRIAL BALANCE CREDIT	INCOME STATEMENT DEBIT	INCOME STATEMENT CREDIT	BALANCE SHEET DEBIT	BALANCE SHEET CREDIT	
1	Cash	5 2 8 5 00				5 2 8 5 00				5 2 8 5 00		1
2	Accounts Receivable	1 0 7 5 00				1 0 7 5 00				1 0 7 5 00		2
3	Supplies	7 5 0 00			(a) 2 5 0 00	5 0 0 00				5 0 0 00		3
4	Prepaid Insurance	5 0 0 00			(b) 1 0 0 00	4 0 0 00				4 0 0 00		4
5	Office Equipment	2 2 0 0 00				2 2 0 0 00				2 2 0 0 00		5
6	Accum. Depr.—Office Equipment				(d) 1 1 0 00		1 1 0 00				1 1 0 00	6
7	Accounts Payable		1 5 0 0 00				1 5 0 0 00				1 5 0 0 00	7
8	Wages Payable				(c) 2 0 0 00		2 0 0 00				2 0 0 00	8
9	Juanita Alvarez, Capital		7 0 0 0 00				7 0 0 0 00				7 0 0 0 00	9
10	Juanita Alvarez, Drawing	8 0 0 00				8 0 0 00				8 0 0 00		10
11	Consulting Fees		4 2 0 4 00				4 2 0 4 00		4 2 0 4 00			11
12	Wages Expense	1 4 0 0 00		(c) 2 0 0 00		1 6 0 0 00		1 6 0 0 00				12
13	Advertising Expense	6 0 00				6 0 00		6 0 00				13
14	Rent Expense	5 0 0 00				5 0 0 00		5 0 0 00				14
15	Supplies Expense			(a) 2 5 0 00		2 5 0 00		2 5 0 00				15
16	Telephone Expense	4 6 00				4 6 00		4 6 00				16
17	Electricity Expense	3 9 00				3 9 00		3 9 00				17
18	Insurance Expense			(b) 1 0 0 00		1 0 0 00		1 0 0 00				18
19	Gas and Oil Expense	2 8 00				2 8 00		2 8 00				19
20	Depr. Expense—Office Equipment			(d) 1 1 0 00		1 1 0 00		1 1 0 00				20
21	Miscellaneous Expense	2 1 00				2 1 00		2 1 00				21
22		12 7 0 4 00	12 7 0 4 00	6 6 0 00	6 6 0 00	13 0 1 4 00	13 0 1 4 00	2 7 5 4 00	4 2 0 4 00	10 2 6 0 00	8 8 1 0 00	22
23	Net Income							1 4 5 0 00			1 4 5 0 00	23
24								4 2 0 4 00	4 2 0 4 00	10 2 6 0 00	10 2 6 0 00	24

CHAPTER 6 MASTERY PROBLEM

In the Chapter 6 Mastery Problem, you will display the financial statements and close out the accounting period for Aunt Ibby's Styling Salon owned by Elizabeth Soltis. Follow the step-by-step instructions below to complete the Chapter 6 Mastery Problem.

STEP 1: Start up the Peachtree software.

STEP 2: Open the data file for the Chapter 6 Mastery Problem.

STEP 3: Restore the Opening Balance data.

STEP 4: Enter the adjusting entries from the adjustment column of the worksheet shown on the next page.

STEP 5: Display the adjusting entries with a General Journal with Titles Report.

STEP 6: Display a Statement of Owner's Equity.

STEP 7: Display a Basic Balance Sheet.

STEP 8: Display an Income Statement.

STEP 9: Change the accounting period to January 1 of 2001.

▶ From the Tasks menu, select System, then select Change Accounting Periods from the submenu.
▶ When the Change Accounting Period window appears, select January 1, 2001, to January 31, 2001, and click on Ok.
▶ A message box appears, asking if you would like to print reports before continuing. Since you just printed reports in the above steps, respond No.

Changing the accounting period to the next fiscal year will change the processing cycle from the year 2000 to the year 2001, in effect closing the year 2000.

STEP 10: Display a General Ledger Trial Balance Report.

Because you changed to a new fiscal accounting year, the General Ledger Trial Balance Report should reflect the closing of the year 2000. If you should discover an error and wish to edit transactions from the previous period, simply change the accounting period back to December of 2000, make the corrections, display your reports, and again change the accounting period to January of 2001.

Aunt Ibby's Styling Salon
Work Sheet
For Year Ended December 31, 20- -

	ACCOUNT TITLE	TRIAL BALANCE DEBIT	TRIAL BALANCE CREDIT	ADJUSTMENTS DEBIT	ADJUSTMENTS CREDIT	ADJUSTED TRIAL BALANCE DEBIT	ADJUSTED TRIAL BALANCE CREDIT	INCOME STATEMENT DEBIT	INCOME STATEMENT CREDIT	BALANCE SHEET DEBIT	BALANCE SHEET CREDIT	
1	Cash	9 4 0 00				9 4 0 00				9 4 0 00		1
2	Styling Supplies	1 5 0 0 00			(a) 1 4 5 0 00	5 0 00				5 0 00		2
3	Prepaid Insurance	8 0 0 00			(b) 6 5 0 00	1 5 0 00				1 5 0 00		3
4	Salon Equipment	4 5 0 0 00				4 5 0 0 00				4 5 0 0 00		4
5	Accum. Depr.—Salon Equipment				(d) 9 0 0 00		9 0 0 00				9 0 0 00	5
6	Accounts Payable		2 2 5 00				2 2 5 00				2 2 5 00	6
7	Wages Payable				(c) 4 0 00		4 0 00				4 0 00	7
8	Elizabeth Soltis, Capital		2 7 6 5 00				2 7 6 5 00				2 7 6 5 00	8
9	Elizabeth Soltis, Drawing	12 0 0 0 00				12 0 0 0 00				12 0 0 0 00		9
10	Styling Fees		32 0 0 0 00				32 0 0 0 00		32 0 0 0 00			10
11	Wages Expense	8 0 0 0 00		(c) 4 0 00		8 0 4 0 00		8 0 4 0 00				11
12	Rent Expense	6 0 0 0 00				6 0 0 0 00		6 0 0 0 00				12
13	Styling Supplies Expense			(a) 1 4 5 0 00		1 4 5 0 00		1 4 5 0 00				13
14	Telephone Expense	4 5 0 00				4 5 0 00		4 5 0 00				14
15	Utilities Expense	8 0 0 00				8 0 0 00		8 0 0 00				15
16	Insurance Expense			(b) 6 5 0 00		6 5 0 00		6 5 0 00				16
17	Depr. Expense—Salon Equipment			(d) 9 0 0 00		9 0 0 00		9 0 0 00				17
18		34 9 9 0 00	34 9 9 0 00	3 0 4 0 00	3 0 4 0 00	35 9 3 0 00	35 9 3 0 00	18 2 9 0 00	32 0 0 0 00	17 6 4 0 00	3 9 3 0 00	18
19	Net Income							13 7 1 0 00			13 7 1 0 00	19
20								32 0 0 0 00	32 0 0 0 00	17 6 4 0 00	17 6 4 0 00	20

COMPREHENSIVE PROBLEM 1

Bob Night opened The General's Favorite Fishing Hole. The fishing camp is open from April through September and attracts many famous college basketball coaches during the off-season. Guests typically register for one week, arriving on Sunday afternoon and returning home the following Saturday afternoon. The registration fee includes room and board, the use of fishing boats, and professional instruction in fishing techniques. The chart of accounts for the camping operation is provided below.

The General's Favorite Fishing Hole
Chart of Accounts

Assets
- 101 Cash
- 142 Office Supplies
- 144 Food Supplies
- 145 Prepaid Insurance
- 181 Fishing Boats
- 181.1 Accum. Depr.—Fishing Boats

Liabilities
- 202 Accounts Payable
- 219 Wages Payable

Owner's Equity
- 311 Bob Night, Capital
- 312 Bob Night, Drawing
- 313 Income Summary

Revenues
- 401 Registration Fees

Expenses
- 511 Wages Expense
- 521 Rent Expense
- 523 Office Supplies Expense
- 524 Food Supplies Expense
- 525 Telephone Expense
- 533 Utilities Expense
- 535 Insurance Expense
- 536 Postage Expense
- 542 Depr. Exp.—Fishing Boats

The following transactions took place during April 2000.

Apr.		
1	Night invested cash in business, $90,000.
1	Paid insurance premium for camping season, $9,000.
2	Paid rent for lodge and campgrounds for the month of April, $40,000.
2	Deposited registration fees, $35,000.
2	Purchased ten fishing boats on account for $60,000. The boats have estimated useful lives of five years, at which time they will be donated to a local day camp. Arrangements were made to pay for the boats in July.
3	Purchased food supplies from Acme Super Market on account, $7,000.
5	Purchased office supplies from Gordon Office Supplies on account, $500.
7	Deposited registration fees, $38,600.
10	Purchased food supplies from Acme Super Market on account, $8,200.
10	Paid wages to fishing guides, $10,000.
14	Deposited registration fees, $30,500.
16	Purchased food supplies from Acme Super Market on account, $9,000.
17	Paid wages to fishing guides, $10,000.
18	Paid postage, $150.
21	Deposited registration fees, $35,600.
24	Purchased food supplies from Acme Super Market on account, $8,500.
24	Paid wages to fishing guides, $10,000.

	28	Deposited registration fees, $32,000.
	29	Paid wages to fishing guides, $10,000.
	30	Purchased food supplies from Acme Super Market on account, $6,000.
	30	Paid Acme Super Market on account, $32,700.
	30	Paid utilities bill, $2,000.
	30	Paid telephone bill, $1,200.
	30	Bob Night withdrew cash for personal use, $6,000.

Adjustment information for the end of April is provided below.

(a) Office supplies remaining on hand, $100.

(b) Food supplies remaining on hand, $8,000.

(c) Insurance expired during the month of April, $1,500.

(d) Depreciation on the fishing boats for the month of April, $1,000.

(e) Wages earned, but not yet paid, at the end of April, $500.

Comprehensive Problem 1 involves processing the April transactions for The General's Favorite Fishing Hole, processing adjusting entries, generating financial statements, and changing the accounting period.

STEP 1: Open the data file for Comprehensive Problem 1.

STEP 2: Restore the Opening Balance data.

STEP 3: Enter the April transactions into the General Journal window.

STEP 4: Display the April transactions with the General Journal with Titles Report.

STEP 5: Display the a General Ledger Trial Balance Report.

STEP 6: Based on the trial balance created in Step 6, enter the adjusting entries.

STEP 7: Display the journal entries. Your report will include the monthly transactions plus the adjusting entries.

STEP 8: Display a Basic Income Statement.

STEP 9: Display a Statement of Owner's Equity.

STEP 10: Display a Basic Balance Sheet.

STEP 11: Display a General Ledger Trial Balance Report.

STEP 12: Change the accounting period to May 1, 2000, to May 31, 2000.

▶ From the Tasks menu, choose the System option, then, from the submenu, select the Change Accounting Period option.

▶ When the Change Accounting Period window appears, choose the May 1, 2000 to May 31, 2000 accounting period and click on Ok.

▶ When the message box appears asking if you wish to print reports, respond No.

STEP 13: Display a post-closing trial balance that is really just the normal General Ledger Trial Balance report. It becomes post-closing because it was printed after the accounting period was changed which, in effect, closes the period.

If you should discover an error and wish to edit transactions from the previous period, simply change the accounting period back to April 1, 2000, to April 30, 2000, then make the corrections, display your reports, and again change the accounting period to May 1, 2000, to May 31, 2000.

CHAPTER 7 DEMONSTRATION PROBLEM (07-DEMO)

Jason Kuhn's check stubs indicated a balance of $4,673.12 on March 31. This included a record of a deposit of $926.10 mailed to the bank on March 30 but not credited to Kuhn's account until April 1. In addition, the following checks were outstanding on March 31:

No. 462	$524.26
No. 465	$213.41
No. 473	$543.58
No. 476	$351.38
No. 477	$197.45

The bank statement showed a balance of $5,419.00 as of March 31. The bank statement included a service charge of $4.10 with the date of March 29. In matching the cancelled checks and record of deposits with the stubs, it was discovered that check no. 456, to Office Suppliers, Inc., for $93.00 was erroneously recorded on the stub for $39.00. This caused the bank balance on that stub and those following to be $54.00 too large. It was also discovered that an ATM withdrawal of $100.00 for personal use was not recorded on the books.

Kuhn maintains a $200.00 petty cash fund. His petty cash payments record showed the following totals at the end of March of the current year.

Automobile expense	$ 32.40
Postage expense	27.50
Charitable contributions expense	35.00
Telephone expense	6.20
Travel and entertainment expense	38.60
Miscellaneous expense	17.75
Jason Kuhn, Drawing	40.00
Total	$197.45

This left a balance of $2.55 in the petty cash fund.

In the Chapter 7 Demonstration Problem, you will reconcile the bank statement for Jason Kuhn as of March 31, 2000. When the problem is solved manually, the journal entry to record the replenishment of petty cash is recorded after reconciliation. In a computerized system, the entry to record the replenishment of petty cash must be made before reconciliation because it is one of the checks that must be stored in the computer so it can be included in the reconciliation. Therefore, in the opening balance data, the check has already been recorded and will appear in the list of checks in the Account Reconciliation window. In the manual problem, you are provided with a list of outstanding checks. The Peachtree Accounting software requires that you enter cleared checks; therefore, a list of cleared checks is provided below:

463	213.11
464	2,500.00
466	45.80
467	400.00

468	65.40
469	89.50
470	34.89
471	450.00
472	39.00
474	85.00
475	57.00

STEP 1: Open the data file for the Chapter 7 Demonstration Problem.

STEP 2: Restore the Opening Balance data.

STEP 3: Enter the account reconciliation data.

- From the Tasks menu, choose the Account Reconciliation option.
- When the Account Reconciliation window shown in Figure 2.12 appears, enter or select the cash account number 101 in the Account to Reconcile field.
- Enter a Statement Date of March 31, 2000.
- Enter the Statement Ending Balance in the lower right corner of the window.
- Click on the Adjust Icon Bar button, and enter the adjustments as shown in the Additional Transactions window in Figure 2.13 on the following page. Enter a date of March 31, 2000, for each entry. When completed, click on Ok.

Note: The computer will automatically generate the journal entries resulting from these adjustments. If you discover an error in your adjustments after you have clicked on Ok to record the entry, you must make corrections via the General Journal Entry window. To make corrections, select General Journal Entry from the Tasks menu, click on the Edit Icon Bar button, select the entry in error, make corrections, and click on Post to record the changes.

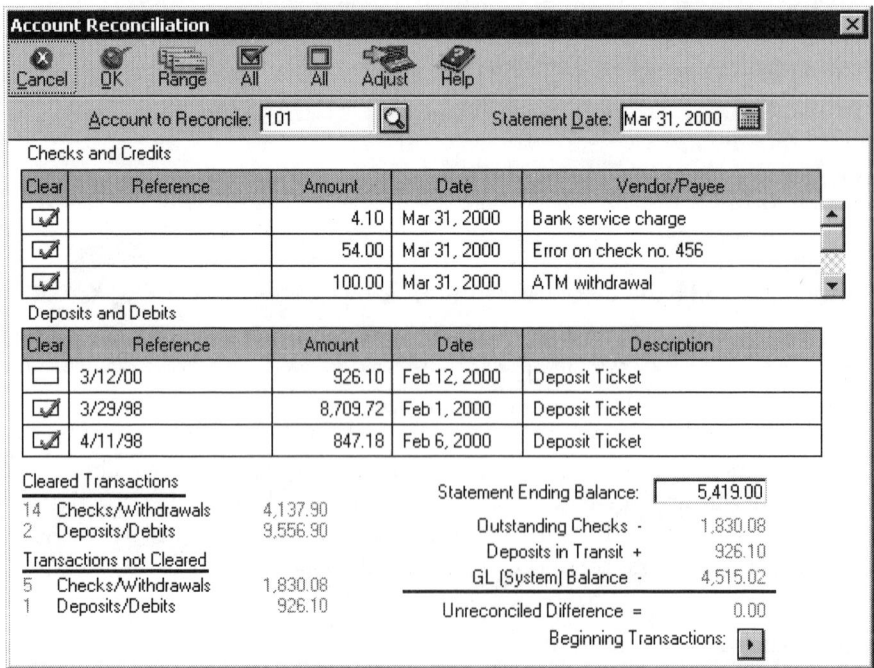

FIGURE 2.12 Account Reconciliation Window

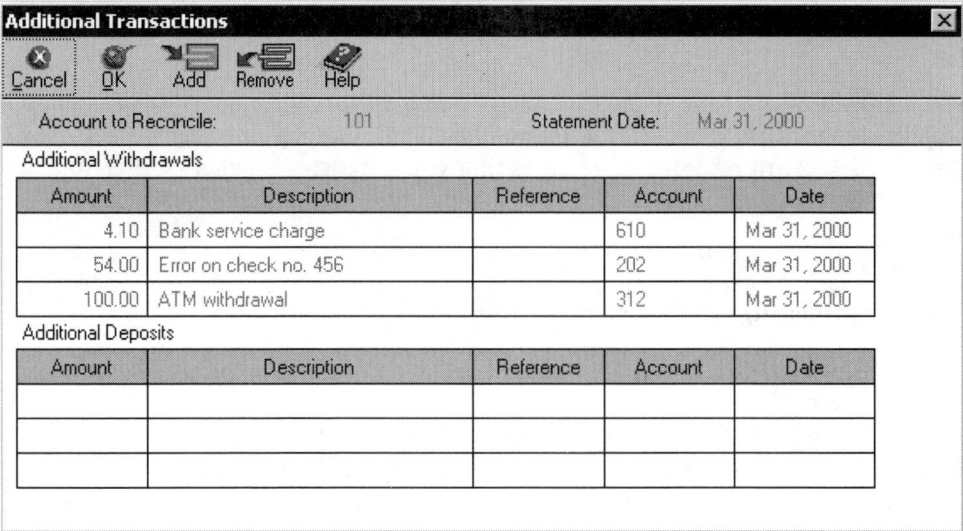

FIGURE 2.13 Additional Transactions Window

- In the Checks and Credits section of Account Reconciliation, mark the checks that have cleared by clicking on the rectangular boxes under the Clear column. In the problem, you are provided with a list of outstanding checks. In the software, you need to identify cleared checks. Therefore, you can assume that all checks not listed in the problem as outstanding have cleared.

- In the Deposits and Credits section, mark as cleared all deposits that are no longer outstanding as illustrated in the completed Account Reconciliation window in Figure 2.12 on the previous page.

- Make sure that the "Unreconciled Difference" is equal to zero, and then click on OK on the Icon bar to continue.

STEP 4: From the Reports menu, select the Account Reconciliation option. Display the Account Register and Account Reconciliation Reports.

See the solution section of this workbook for the solution to the demonstration problem.

PROBLEM 7-2A

The balance in the checking account of Lyle's Salon as of November 30 is $3,282.95. The bank statement shows an ending balance of $2,127.00. By examining last month's bank reconciliation, comparing the checks deposited and written per books and per bank in November, and noting the service charges and other debit and credit memos shown on the bank statement, the following were found:

(a) An ATM withdrawal of $150.00 on November 18 by Lyle for personal use was not recorded on the books.

(b) A bank debit memo issued for an NSFcheck from a customer of $19.50.

(c) A bank credit memo issued for interest of $19.00 earned during the month.

(d) On November 30, a deposit of $1,177.00 was made, which is not shown on the bank statement.

(e) A bank debit memo issued for $17.50 for bank service charges.

(f) Checks for the amounts of $185.00, $21.00, and $9.40 were written during November but have not yet been received by the bank.

(g) The reconciliation from the previous month showed outstanding checks of $271.95. One of those checks, for $18.65, has not yet been received by the bank.

(h) Check No. 523, written to a creditor in the amount of $372.90, was recorded in the books as $327.90.

In Problem 7-2A, you will reconcile the bank statement for Lyle's Salon as of November 30, 2000. Follow the step-by-step instructions provided. In the manual problem, you are provided with a list of outstanding checks. The Peachtree Accounting software requires that you enter cleared checks; therefore, a list of cleared checks is provided below:

523	327.90
524	32.00
525	2,300.00
526	56.00
527	400.00

STEP 1: Open the data file for Problem 7-2A.

STEP 2: Restore the Opening Balance data.

STEP 3: From the Tasks menu, choose the Account Reconciliation option.

▶ Enter the cash account number 101 in the Account to Reconcile field.
▶ Enter a Statement Date of November 30, 2000.
▶ Enter the Statement Ending Balance.
▶ Click on the Adjust Icon Bar button and enter the adjustments. When completed, click on Ok. If you discover an error in your adjustments after you have clicked on Ok to record the entry, you must make corrections via the General Journal Entry window. To make corrections, select General Journal Entry from the Tasks menu, click on the Edit Icon Bar button, select the entry in error, make corrections, and click on Post to record the changes.
▶ In the Checks and Credits section of Account Reconciliation, mark the checks that have cleared by clicking on the rectangular boxes under the Clear column. In the problem, you are provided with a list of outstanding checks. In the software, you need to identify cleared checks. Therefore, you can assume that all checks not listed in the problem as outstanding have cleared.
▶ In the Deposits and Credits section, mark as cleared all deposits that are no longer outstanding.

STEP 4: From the Reports menu, select the Account Reconciliation option. Display the Account Register and Account Reconciliation Reports.

PROBLEM 7-2B

The balance in the checking account of Tori's Health Center as of April 30 is $4,690.30. The bank statement shows an ending balance of $3,275.60. By examining last month's bank reconciliation, comparing the checks deposited and written per books and per bank in April, and noting the service charges and other debit and credit memos shown on the bank statement, the following were found:

(a) An ATM withdrawal of $200.00 on April 20 by Tori for personal use was not recorded on the books.

(b) A bank debit memo issued for an NSF check from a customer of $29.10.

(c) A bank credit memo issued for interest of $28.00 earned during the month.

(d) On April 30, a deposit of $1,592.00 was made, which is not shown on the bank statement.

e. A bank debit memo issued for $24.50 for bank service charges.

f. Checks for the amounts of $215.00, $71.00, and $24.30 were written during April but have not yet been received by the bank.

g. The reconciliation from the previous month showed outstanding checks of $418.25. One of these checks for $38.60 has not yet been received by the bank.

h. Check No. 422, written to a creditor in the amount of $217.90, was recorded in the books as $271.90.

REQUIRED 1. Prepare a bank reconciliation as of April 30.

2. Prepare the required journal entries.

In Problem 7-2B, you will reconcile the bank statement for Tori's Health Center as of April 30, 2000. Follow the step-by-step instructions provided. In the manual problem, you are provided with a list of outstanding checks. The Peachtree Accounting software requires that you enter cleared checks; therefore, a list of cleared checks is provided below:

422	271.90
425	540.00
427	71.20
429	870.00

STEP 1: Open the data file for Problem 7-2B.

STEP 2: Restore the Opening Balance data.

STEP 3: From the Tasks menu, choose the Account Reconciliation option.

▶ Enter the cash account number 101 in the Account to Reconcile field.
▶ Enter a Statement Date of April 30, 2000.
▶ Enter the Statement Ending Balance.
▶ Click on the Adjust Icon Bar button, and enter the adjustments. Leave the Reference field blank. Enter a date of April 30, 2000, for all adjustments. If you discover an error in your adjustments after you have clicked on Ok to record the entry, you must make corrections via the General Journal Entry window. To make corrections, select General Journal Entry from the Tasks menu, click on the Edit Icon Bar button, select the entry in error, make corrections, and click on Post to record the changes.
▶ In the Checks and Credits section of Account Reconciliation, mark the checks that have cleared by clicking on the rectangular boxes under the Clear column. In the problem, you are provided with a list of outstanding checks. In the software, you need to identify cleared checks. Therefore, you can assume that all checks not listed in the problem as outstanding have cleared.
▶ In the Deposits and Credits section, mark as cleared all deposits that are no longer outstanding.

STEP 4: From the Reports menu, select the Account Reconciliation option. Display the Account Register and Account Reconciliation Reports.

CHAPTER 8 DEMONSTRATION PROBLEM (08-DEMO)

Carole Vohsen operates a pet grooming salon called Canine Coiffures. She has five employees, all of whom are paid on a weekly basis. Canine Coiffures uses a payroll register, individual employee earnings records, a journal, and a general ledger.

The payroll data for each employee for the week ended January 21, 2000, are given below. Employees are paid 1½ times the regular rate for work over 40 hours a week and double-time for work on Sunday.

Name	Employee No.	No. of Allowances	Marital Status	Total Hours Worked Jan. 15–21	Rate	Total Earnings Jan. 1–14
DeNourie, Katie	1	2	S	44	$11.50	$1,058.00
Garriott, Pete	2	1	M	40	12.00	1,032.00
Martinez, Sheila	3	3	M	39	12.50	987.50
Parker, Nancy	4	4	M	42	11.00	957.00
Shapiro, John	5	2	S	40	11.50	931.50

Sheila Martinez is the manager of the Shampooing Department. Her Social Security number is 500-88-4189, and she was born April 12, 1969. She lives at 46 Darling Crossing; Norwich, CT 06360. Martinez was hired September 1 of last year.

Social Security tax is withheld at the rate of 6.2% of the first $76,200 earned. Medicare tax is withheld at the rate of 1.45%, and city earnings tax at the rate of 1%, both applied to gross pay. The computer makes these calculations automatically. Garriott and Parker each have $14.00 and Denourie and Martinez each have $4.00 withheld for health insurance. DeNourie, Martinez, and Shapiro each have $15.00 withheld to be invested in the groomers' credit union. Garriott and Shapiro each have $18.75 withheld under a savings bond purchase plan.

Canine Coiffures' payroll is met by drawing checks on its regular bank account. This week, the checks were issued in sequence, beginning with no. 811.

In the Chapter 8 Demonstration Problem, you will process the payroll for the week of January 21, 2000, for Canine Coiffures. The Peachtree Accounting software selects the tax table to use based on the year. At the time these materials were prepared, the Peachtree tax table available was for the year 2000. In order for the computer to calculate taxes correctly, it is imperative that a date in the year 2000 be used for the payroll problems. The step-by-step instructions for completing the Chapter 8 Demonstration Problem are listed below.

Note: The Peachtree Accounting software uses the percentage method of calculating the federal income tax withheld rather than a wage-bracket tax table.

STEP 1: Open the data file for the Chapter 8 Demonstration Problem.

STEP 2: Restore the Opening Balance data.

STEP 3: From the Options menu, select the Change System Date option and set the system date to January 21, 2000.

STEP 4: Enter the weekly payroll transactions.

From the Tasks menu, select the Payroll Entry option.
- Enter the Employee ID code of the employee you wish to pay (or click on the magnifying glass button and select the employee to pay from the list).
- For the first employee, enter a check number of 811. Thereafter, the computer will increment by 1 for each employee.
- Enter a Check Date of January 21, 2000.
- Enter the hours worked. Any hours worked in excess of 40 should be recorded as overtime.

- Enter the health insurance, credit union, and savings bond deductions. The deductions must be entered with a preceding minus sign (e.g., –4.00).
- You may click on the Journal Icon Bar button to view the journal entry that will be generated as a result of this entry.
- Click on the Post Icon Bar button to save the transaction.
  A Payroll Entry window with the first entry completed is illustrated in Figure 2.14.

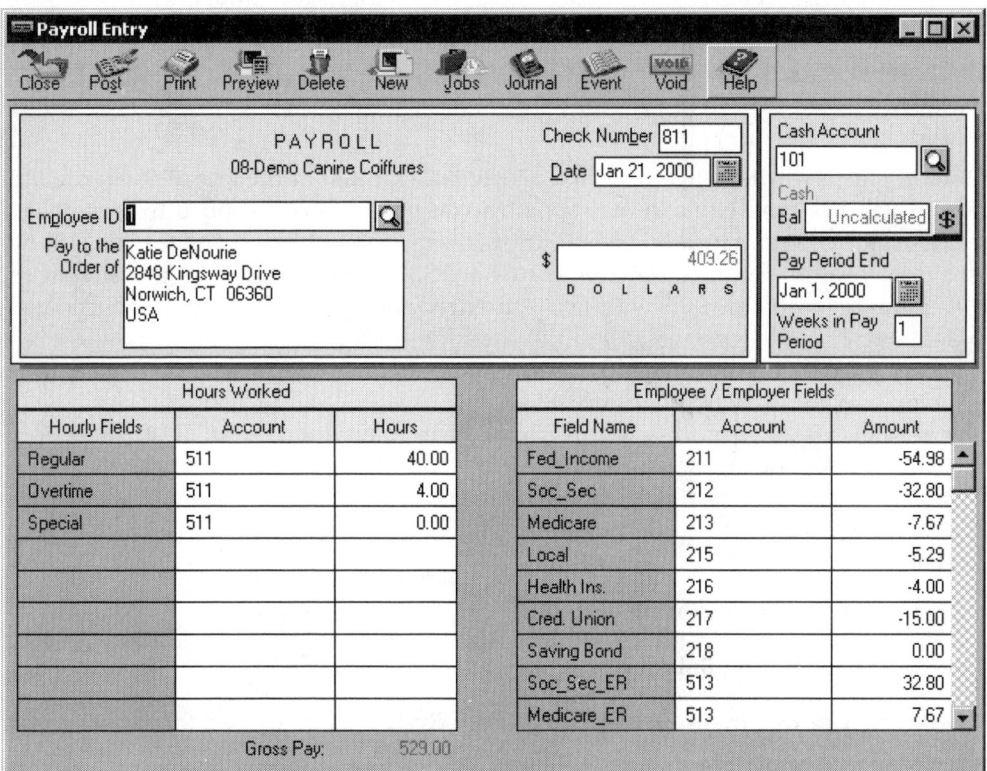

FIGURE 2.14 Payroll Entry Window

STEP 5: Display the payroll reports.

- From the Reports menu, select the Payroll option and click on Check Register.
- When the Check Register filter window appears, choose a date range of January 15, 2000, to January 21, 2000.
- Click on Payroll Journal (choose a date range of January 15, 2000, to January 21, 2000).
- Click on Payroll Register (choose a date range of January 15, 2000, to January 21, 2000).
  See the solution section of this workbook for the solution to the demonstration problem.

PROBLEM 8-2A

Don McCullum operates a travel agency called Don's Luxury Travel. He has five employees, all of whom are paid on a weekly basis. The travel agency uses a payroll register, individual employee earnings records, and a general journal.

Don's Luxury Travel uses a weekly federal income tax withholding table. The payroll data for each employee for the week ended March 22, 2000, are given below. Employees are paid 1½ times the regular rate for working over 40 hours per week.

Name	No. of Allowances	Marital Status	Total Hours Worked Mar. 16–22	Rate	Total Earnings Jan. 1–Mar. 15
Ali, Loren	4	M	45	$11.00	$5,280.00
Carson, Judy	1	S	40	12.00	5,760.00
Hernandez, Maria	3	M	43	9.50	4,560.00
Knox, Wayne	1	S	39	11.00	5,125.50
Paglione, Jim	2	M	40	10.50	4,720.50

Social Security tax is withheld from the first $76,200 of earnings at the rate of 6.2%. Medicare tax is withheld at the rate of 1.45%, and city earnings tax at the rate of 1%, both applied to gross pay. The computer makes these calculations automatically. Ali and Knox have $15.00 withheld and Carson and Hernandez have $5.00 withheld for health insurance. Ali and Knox have $20.00 withheld to be invested in the travel agencies' credit union. Carson has $38.75 withheld and Hernandez has $18.75 withheld under a savings bond purchase plan.

Don's Luxury Travel's payroll is met by drawing checks on its regular bank account. The checks were issued in sequence, beginning with check no. 423.

In Problem 8-2A, you will process the payroll for the week ended March 22, 2000, for Don's Luxury Travel. The Peachtree Accounting software selects the tax table to use based on the year. At the time these materials were prepared, the tax table available was for the year 2000. Therefore, it is imperative that a date in the year 2000 be used for the payroll problems. The step-by-step instructions for completing Problem 8-2A are listed below.

STEP 1: Open the data file for Problem 8-2A.

STEP 2: Restore the Opening Balance data.

STEP 3: From the Options menu, select the Change System Date option and set the system date to March 22, 2000.

STEP 4: Enter the weekly payroll transactions.

▶ From the Tasks menu, select the Payroll Entry option.

▶ Enter the Employee ID code for the employee you wish to pay.

▶ For the first employee, enter a check number of 423. Thereafter, the computer will increment by 1 for each employee.

▶ Enter a Check Date of March 22, 2000.

▶ Enter the hours worked. Any hours worked in excess of 40 should be recorded as overtime.

▶ Enter the health insurance, credit union, and savings bond deductions. The deductions must be entered with a preceding minus sign (e.g., –4.00).

▶ You may click on the Journal Icon Bar button to view the journal entry that will be generated as a result of this entry.

▶ Click on the Post Icon Bar button to save the transaction.

STEP 5: Display the payroll reports.

▶ From the Reports menu, select the Payroll option and click on Check Register.

▶ When the Check Register filter window appears, choose a date range of March 16, 2000, to March 22, 2000.

- Click on Payroll Journal (choose a date range March 16, 2000, to March 22, 2000). The computer-generated journal entries appear somewhat different from those prepared manually. This is because the computer generates a journal entry for each employee, whereas manually one journal entry is prepared to record the entire payroll. In addition, the computer generates the entries to record the employer's share of payroll as well.
- Click on Payroll Register (choose a date range of March 16, 2000 to March 22, 2000).
- Note: The Peachtree Accounting software uses the percentage method of calculating the federal income tax withheld rather than a wage-bracket tax table.

PROBLEM 8-2B

Karen Jolly operates a bakery called Karen's Cupcakes. She has five employees, all of whom are paid on a weekly basis. Karen's Cupcakes uses a payroll register, individual employee earnings records, and a general journal. The payroll data for each employee for the week ended February 15, 2000, are given below. Employees are paid 1½ times the regular rate for working over 40 hours per week.

Name	No. of Allowances	Marital Status	Total Hours Worked Feb. 9–15	Rate	Total Earnings Jan. 1–Feb. 15
Barone, William	1	S	40	$10.00	$2,400.00
Hastings, Gene	4	M	45	12.00	3,360.00
Nitobe, Isako	3	M	46	8.75	2,935.00
Smith, Judy	4	M	42	11.00	2,745.00
Tarshis, Dolores	1	S	39	10.50	2,650.75

Social Security tax is withheld from the first $76,200 of earnings at the rate of 6.2%. Medicare tax is withheld at the rate of 1.45%, and city earnings tax at the rate of 1%, both applied to gross pay. Withholding tax calculations are made automatically by the computer. Hastings and Smith have $35.00 withheld and Nitobe and Tarshis have $15.00 withheld for health insurance. Nitobe and Tarshis have $25.00 withheld to be invested in the bakers' credit union. Hastings has $18.75 withheld and Smith has $43.75 withheld under a savings bond purchase plan.

Karen's Cupcakes' payroll is met by drawing checks on its regular bank account. The checks were issued in sequence, beginning with no. 365.

In Problem 8-2B, you will process the payroll for the week ended February 15, 2000, for Karen's Cupcakes. The Peachtree Accounting software selects the tax table to use based on the year. At the time these materials were prepared, the tax table available was for the year 2000. Therefore, it is imperative that a date in the year 2000 be used for the payroll problems. The step-by-step instructions for completing Problem 8-2B are listed below.

STEP 1: Open the data file for Problem 8-2B.

STEP 2: Restore the Opening Balance data.

STEP 3: From the Options menu, select the Change System Date option and set the system date to February 15, 2000.

STEP 4: Enter the weekly payroll transactions.

- From the Tasks menu, select the Payroll Entry option.
- Enter the Employee ID code for the employee you wish to pay.
- For the first employee, enter a check number of 365. Thereafter, the computer will increment by 1 for each employee.

- Enter a Check Date of February 15, 2000.
- Enter the hours worked. Any hours worked in excess of 40 should be recorded as overtime.
- Enter the health insurance, credit union, and savings bond deductions. The deductions must be entered with a preceding minus sign (e.g., –4.00).
- You may click on the Journal Icon Bar button to view the journal entry that will be generated as a result of this entry.
- Click on the Post Icon Bar button to save the transaction.

STEP 5: Display the payroll reports.

- From the Reports menu, select the Payroll option and click on Check Register.
- When the Check Register filter window appears, choose a date range of February 8, 2000, to February 15, 2000.
- Click on Payroll Journal (choose a date range of February 8, 2000, to February 15, 2000)
- Click on Payroll Register (choose a date range of February 8, 2000, to February 15, 2000).

Note: The Peachtree Accounting software uses the percentage method of calculating the federal income tax withheld rather than a wage-bracket tax table.

CHAPTER 8 MASTERY PROBLEM

Abigail Trenkamp owns and operates the Trenkamp Collection Agency. Listed below are the name, number of allowances claimed, marital status, information from time cards on hours worked each day, and the hourly rate of each employee. All hours worked in excess of 40 hours for Monday through Friday are paid at 1½ times the regular rate. All weekend hours are paid at double the regular rate.

Social Security tax is withheld at the rate of 6.2% for the first $76,200 earned. Medicare tax is withheld at 1.45% and state income tax at 3.5%. Each employee has $5.00 withheld for health insurance. All employees use payroll deduction to the credit union for varying amounts as listed on the next page.

Trenkamp Collection Agency
Payroll Information for the Week Ended November 18, 2000

Name	Employee No.	No. of Allow.	Marital Status	Regular Hours Worked							Hourly Rate	Credit Union Deposit	Total Earnings 1/1–11/11
				S	S	M	T	W	T	F			
Berling, James	1	3	M	2	2	9	8	8	9	10	$12.00	$149.60	$24,525.00
Merz, Linda	2	4	M	4	3	8	8	8	8	11	10.00	117.00	20,480.00
Goetz, Ken	3	5	M	0	0	6	7	8	9	10	11.00	91.30	21,500.00
Menick, Judd	4	2	M	8	8	0	0	8	8	9	11.00	126.50	22,625.00
Morales, Eva	5	3	M	0	0	8	8	8	6	8	13.00	117.05	24,730.00
Heimbrock, Jacob	6	2	S	0	0	8	8	8	8	8	30.00	154.25	67,600.00
Townsley, Sarah	7	2	M	4	0	6	6	6	6	4	9.00	83.05	21,425.00
Salzman, Ben	8	4	M	6	2	8	8	6	6	6	11.00	130.00	6,635.00
Layton, Esther	9	4	M	0	0	8	8	8	8	8	11.00	88.00	5,635.00
Thompson, David	10	5	M	0	2	10	9	7	7	10	11.00	128.90	21,635.00
Vadillo, Carmen	11	2	S	8	0	4	8	8	8	9	13.00	139.11	24,115.00

The Trenkamp Collection Agency follows the practice of drawing a single check for the net amount of the payroll and depositing the check in a special payroll account at the bank. Individual checks issued were numbered consecutively, beginning with no. 331.

In the Chapter 8 Mastery Problem, you will process the payroll for the week ended November 18, 2000, for Trenkamp Collection. The step-by-step instructions for completing the Problem are listed below.

STEP 1: Open the data file for Chapter 8 Mastery Problem.

STEP 2: Restore the Opening Balance data.

STEP 3: From the Options menu, select the Change System Date option and set the system date to November 18, 2000.

STEP 4: Enter the weekly payroll transactions.

- From the Tasks menu, select the Payroll Entry option.
- Enter the Employee ID code.
- For the first employee, enter a check number of 331. Thereafter, the computer will increment by 1 for each employee.
- Enter a Check Date of November 18, 2000.
- Enter the hours worked. Any hours worked in excess of 40 during the workweek should be recorded as overtime. All weekend hours are recorded as special hours and are paid double the regular rate.
- Enter the health insurance and credit union deductions. The deductions must be entered with a preceding minus sign (e.g., –4.00).
- You may click on the Journal Icon Bar button to view the journal entry that will be generated as a result of this entry.
- Click on the Post Icon Bar button to save the transaction.

STEP 5: Display the payroll reports.

- From the Reports menu, select the Payroll option, click on Check Register and then click on the Preview Icon Bar button.
- When the Check Register filter window appears, choose a date range of November 12, 2000, to November 18, 2000.
- Click on Payroll Journal (choose a date range of November 12, 2000, to November 18, 2000).
- Click on Payroll Register (choose a date range of November 12, 2000, to November 18, 2000).

Note: The Peachtree Accounting software uses the percentage method of calculating the federal income tax withheld rather than a wage-bracket tax table.

CHAPTER 9 DEMONSTRATION PROBLEM (09-DEMO)

The totals from Hart Company's payroll register for the week ended December 31, 2000, is as follows:
  Total earnings, $3,800
  Taxable Earnings:
    Unemployment compensation, $400
    Social Securioty, $3,800
  Federal Income Tax, $380
  Social Security Tax, $235.60
  Medicare Tax, $55.10
  Health Insurance, $50.00
  United Way, $100
Net Pay, $2,979.30

Payroll taxes are imposed as follows: Social Security, 6.2%; Medicare, 1.45%; FUTA, 0.8%; and SUTA, 5.4%.

REQUIRED
1. a. Prepare the journal entry for payment of this payroll on December 31, 2000.

   b. Prepare the journal entry for the employer's payroll taxes for the period ended December 31, 2000.

2. Hart Company had the following balances in its general ledger after the entries for Requirement 1 were made:

Employee Income Tax Payable	$1,520.00
Social Security Tax Payable	1,847.00
Medicare Tax Payable	433.00
FUTA Tax Payable	27.20
SUTA Tax Payable	183.60

   a. Prepare the journal entry for payment of the liabilities for employee federal income taxes and Social Security and Medicare taxes on January 15, 2000.

   b. Prepare the journal entry for payment of the liability for FUTA tax on January 31, 2000

   c. Prepare the journal entry for payment of the liability for SUTA tax on January 31, 2000.

3. Hart Company paid a premium of $280 for workers' compensation insurance based on estimated payroll as of the beginning of the year. Based on actual payroll as of the end of the year, the premium is $298. Prepare the adjusting entry to reflect the underpayment of the insurance premium.

In the Chapter 9 Demonstration Problem you will enter the journal entries to record the payroll, the employer's payroll taxes, and the payment of payroll withholding liabilities. Follow the steps listed to complete the Chapter 9 Demonstration Problem.

STEP 1: Open the data file for the Chapter 9 Demonstration Problem.

STEP 2: Restore the Opening Balance data.

STEP 3: Enter the December general journal entries. December journal entries include Requirement 1 parts (a) and (b) as well as the workers' compensation adjustment in Requirement 3.

STEP 4: Select the General Journal with Titles Report to display the December journal entries.

STEP 5: Change the accounting period to be January 1, 2001, to January 31, 2001.

▶ From the Tasks menu, choose the System option, and then select Change Accounting Period from the submenu.

▶ When the Change Accounting Period window appears, select January 1, 2001, to January 31, 2001.

▶ Click on the Ok button.

STEP 6: Enter the January journal entries.

STEP 7: Use the General Journal with Titles Report to display the January journal entries.

STEP 8: Display a General Ledger Trial Balance Report.

Note: If you need to make corrections to your journal entries using the Edit option, you will need to change the Period in the upper right portion of the Select Journal Entry window to reflect the correct period. The Select Journal Entry window appears when you click on the Edit Icon Bar button to make corrections from the General Journal window. If you want to change a December transaction, change it to December. If you want to change a January transaction, change the period to January.

See the solution section of this workbook for the solution to the demonstration problem.

PROBLEM 9-2A

The Cascade Company has four employees. All are paid on a monthly basis. The fiscal year of the business is July 1 to June 30. Payroll taxes are imposed as follows:

1. Social Security tax of 6.2% withheld from employees' wages on the first $76,200 of earnings and Medicare tax withheld at 1.45% of gross earnings.

2. Social Security tax of 6.2% imposed on the employer on the first $76,200 of earnings and Medicare tax of 1.45% on gross earnings.

3. SUTA tax of 5.4% imposed on the employer on the first $7,000 of earnings.

4. FUTA tax of 0.8% imposed on the employer on the first $7,000 of earnings.

The accounts kept by Cascade include the following:

Account Number	Title	Balance on July 1
101	Cash	$50,200
211	Employee Income Tax Payable	1,015
212	Social Security Tax Payable	1,458
213	Medicare Tax Payable	342
218	Savings Bond Deductions Payable	350
221	FUTA Tax Payable	164
222	SUTA Tax Payable	810
511	Wages and Salaries Expense	0
530	Payroll Taxes Expense	0

The following transactions relating to payrolls and payroll taxes occurred during July and August.

July 15 Paid $2,815 covering the following June taxes:
Social Security tax .... $ 1,458
Medicare tax 342
Employee income tax withheld 1,015
Total .... $ 2,815

31 July payroll:
Total wages and salaries expense $12,000
Less amounts withheld:
Social Security tax .... $ 744
Medicare tax 174
Employee income tax 1,020
Savings bond deductions 350   2,288
Net amount paid .... $ 9,712

31 Purchased savings bonds for employees, $700

	31	Data for completing employer's payroll taxes expense for July:	
		Social Security taxable wages	$12,000
		Unemployment taxable wages	3,000
Aug.	15	Paid $2,856 covering the following July taxes:	
		Social Security tax	$ 1,488
		Medicare tax	348
		Employee income tax withheld	1,020
		Total	$ 2,856
	15	Paid SUTA tax for the quarter, $972	
	15	Paid FUTA tax, $188	

In Problem 9-2A, you will enter the journal entries to record the payroll, the employer's payroll taxes, and the payment of payroll withholding liabilities. Follow the steps listed to complete the Problem 9-2A.

STEP 1: Open the data file for the Problem 9-2A.

STEP 2: Restore the Opening Balance data.

STEP 3: Enter the July general journal entries.

STEP 4: Use the General Journal with Titles Report to display the July journal entries.

STEP 5: Change the accounting period to August.

▶ From the Tasks menu, choose the System option, then select Change Accounting Period from the submenu.
▶ When the Change Accounting Period window appears, select August 1, 2000, to August 31, 2000.
▶ Click on the Ok button.

STEP 6: Enter the August journal entries.

STEP 7: Use the General Journal with Titles Report to display the August journal entries.

STEP 8: Display the General Ledger Report. Make sure that you change the filter date to include both July and August, or the report will only list August transactions.

STEP 9: Display a General Ledger Trial Balance Report.

Note: If you need to make corrections to your journal entries using the Edit option, you will need to change the Period in the upper right portion of the Select Journal Entry screen to reflect the correct period. If you want to change a July transaction, change it to July. If you want to change an August transaction, change the period to August.

PROBLEM 9-2B

The Oxford Company has five employees. All are paid on a monthly basis. The fiscal year of the business is June 1 to May 31. Payroll taxes are imposed as follows:

1. Social Security tax of 6.2% to be withheld from employees' wages on the first $76,200 of earnings and Medicare tax of 1.45% on gross earnings.

2. Social Security tax of 6.2% imposed on the employer on the first $76,200 of earnings and Medicare tax of 1.45% on gross earnings.

3. SUTA tax of 5.4% imposed on the employer on the first $7,000 of earnings.

4. FUTA tax of 0.8% imposed on the employer on the first $7,000 of earnings.

The accounts kept by the Oxford Company include the following:

Account Number	Title	Balance on June 1
101	Cash	$48,650
211	Employee Income Tax Payable	1,345
212	Social Security Tax Payable	1,823
213	Medicare Tax Payable	427
218	Savings Bond Deductions Payable	525
221	FUTA Tax Payable	360
222	SUTA Tax Payable	920
511	Wages and Salaries Expense	0
530	Payroll Taxes Expense	0

The following transactions relating to payrolls and payroll taxes occurred during June and July.

June 15   Paid $3,595.00 covering the following May taxes:

Social Security tax		$ 1,823.00
Medicare tax		427.00
Employee income tax withheld		1,345.00
Total		$ 3,595.00

30   June payroll:

Total wages and salaries expense		$14,700.00
Less amounts withheld:		
Social Security tax	$ 911.40	
Medicare tax	213.15	
Employee income tax	1,280.00	
Savings bond deductions	525.00	2,929.55
Net amount paid		$11,770.45

30   Purchased savings bonds for employees, $1,050.00

30   Data for completing employer's payroll taxes expense for June:

Social Security taxable wages	$14,700.00
Unemployment taxable wages	4,500.00

July 15   Paid $3,529.10 covering the following June taxes:

Social Security tax	$ 1,822.80
Medicare tax	426.30
Employee income tax withheld	1,280.00
Total	$ 3,529.10

15   Paid SUTA tax for the quarter, $1,163.00

15   Paid FUTA tax, $396.00

— 75 —

In Problem 9-2B, you will enter the journal entries to record the payroll, the employer's payroll taxes, and the payment of payroll withholding liabilities. Follow the steps listed to complete the problem.

STEP 1: Open the data file for Problem 9-2B.

STEP 2: Restore the Opening Balance data.

STEP 3: Enter the June general journal entries.

STEP 4: Use the General Journal with Titles Report to display the June journal entries.

STEP 5: Change the accounting period to July.

▶ From the Tasks menu, choose the System option, and then select Change Accounting Period from the submenu.
▶ When the Change Accounting Period window appears, select July 1, 2000, to July 31, 2000.
▶ Click on the Ok button.

STEP 6: Enter the July journal entries.

STEP 7: Use the General Journal with Titles Report to display the July journal entries.

STEP 8: Display the General Ledger Report. Make sure that you change the filter date to include both June and July or the report will only list July transactions.

STEP 9: Display a General Ledger Trial Balance Report.

Note: If you need to make corrections to your journal entries using the Edit option, you will need to change the Period in the upper right portion of the Select Journal Entry screen to reflect the correct period. If you want to change a June transaction, change it to June. If you want to change a July transaction, change the period to July.

CHAPTER 9 MASTERY PROBLEM

The totals from Nix Company's payroll register for the week ended March 31, 2000 is as follows:
Earnings, $5500
Taxable Earnings:
    Unemployment compensation, $5,000
    Social Security, $5,500
Federal Income Tax, $500
Social Security Tax, $341
Medicare Tax, $79.75
Health Insurance, $165
Life Insurance, $200
Net Pay, $4,214.25

Payroll taxes are imposed as follows: Social Security tax, 6.2%; Medicare tax, 1.45%; FUTA tax, 0.8%; and SUTA tax, 5.4%.

REQUIRED   1. a. Prepare the journal entry for payment of this payroll on March 31, 2000.

b. Prepare the journal entry for the employer's payroll taxes for the period ended March 31, 2000.

2. Nix Company had the following balances in its general ledger before the entries for Requirement 1 were made:

Employee income tax payable	$2,500
Social Security tax payable	2,008
Medicare tax payable	470
FUTA tax payable	520
SUTA tax payable	3,510

   a. Prepare the journal entry for payment of the liabilities for federal income taxes and Social Security and Medicare taxes on April 15, 2000.

   b. Prepare the journal entry for payment of the liability for FUTA tax on April 30, 2000.

   c. Prepare the journal entry for payment of the liability for SUTA tax on April 30, 2000.

3. Nix Company paid a premium of $420 for workers' compensation insurance based on the estimated payroll as of the beginning of the year. Based on actual payroll as of the end of the year, the premium is only $400. Prepare the adjusting entry to reflect the overpayment of the insurance premium at the end of the year (December 31, 2000).

In the Chapter 9 Mastery Problem, you will enter the journal entries to record the payroll, the employer's payroll taxes, and the payment of payroll withholding liabilities. Follow the steps listed to complete the problem:

STEP 1: Open the data file for the Chapter 9 Mastery Problem.

STEP 2: Restore the Opening Balance data.

STEP 3: Enter the March general journal entries.

STEP 4: Use the General Journal with Titles Report to display the March journal entries.

STEP 5: Change the accounting period to be April 1, 2000, to April 30, 2000.

STEP 6: Enter the April journal entries.

STEP 7: Use the General Journal with Titles Report to display the April journal entries.

STEP 8: Change the accounting period to be December 1, 2000, to December 31, 2000.

STEP 9: Enter the December journal entry.

STEP 10: Use the General Journal with Titles Report to display the December journal entry.

STEP 11: Display a General Ledger Trial Balance Report.

Note: If you need to make corrections to your journal entries using the Edit option, you will need to change the Period in the upper right portion of the Select Journal Entry screen to reflect the correct period.

CHAPTER 10 DEMONSTRATION PROBLEM (10-DEMO)

Maria Vietor is a financial planning consultant. She developed the following chart of accounts for her business.

Vietor Financial Planning
Chart of Accounts

Assets
101   Cash
142   Office Supplies

Liabilities
202   Accounts Payable

Owner's Equity
311   Maria Vietor, Capital
312   Maria Vietor, Drawing
313   Income Summary

Revenues
401   Professional Fees

Expenses
511   Wages Expense
521   Rent Expense
523   Office Supplies Expense
525   Telephone Expense
526   Automobile Expense
533   Utilities Expense
534   Charitable Contributions Expense

Vietor completed the following transactions during the month of December of the current year:

Dec. 1   Vietor invested cash to start a consulting business, $20,000.
      3   Paid December office rent, $1,000.
      4   Received a check from Aaron Bisno, a client, for services, $2,500.
      6   Paid Union Electric for December heating and light, $75.
      7   Received a check from Will Carter, a client, for services, $2,000.
     12   Paid Smith's Super Service for gasoline and oil purchases, $60.
     14   Paid Comphelp for temporary secretarial services obtained through them during the past two weeks, $600.
     17   Purchased office supplies on account from Cleat Office Supply, $280.
     20   Paid Cress Telephone Co. for local and long-distance business calls during the past month, $100.
     21   Vietor withdrew cash for personal use, $1,100.
     24   Made donation to the National Multiple Sclerosis Society, $100.
     27   Received a check from Ellen Thaler, a client, for services, $2,000.
     28   Paid Comphelp for temporary secretarial services obtained through them during the past two weeks, $600.
     29   Made payment on account to Cleat Office Supply, $100.

When solved manually, the Chapter 10 Demonstration Problem involves entering transactions in a combination journal. Since the Peachtree Accounting software does not support a combination journal, you will enter the transactions in the general journal. In addition, you will display a journal report and a trial balance report. Follow the step-by-step instructions below to complete the problem.

STEP 1:   Open the data file for the Chapter 10 Demonstration Problem.

STEP 2:   Restore the Opening Balance data.

STEP 3:   Enter the December transactions into the General Journal window.

STEP 4:   Display a General Journal with Titles Report.

STEP 5:   Display a trial balance report.

See the solution section of this workbook for the solution to the demonstration problem.

PROBLEM 10-2A

Sue Reyton owns a suit tailoring shop. She opened her business in September. She rents a small work space and has an assistant to receive job orders and process claim tickets. Her trial balance on the next page shows her account balances for the first two months of business (September and October). No adjustments were made in September or October.

Sue Reyton Tailors
Trial Balance
As Of 10/31/00

Acct. Number	Account Title	Debit	Credit
101	Cash	5711.00	
141	Tailoring Supplies	1000.00	
142	Office Supplies	485.00	
145	Prepaid Insurance	100.00	
188	Tailoring Equipment	3800.00	
202	Accounts Payable		4125.00
311	Sue Reyton, Capital		5430.00
312	Sue Reyton, Drawing	500.00	
401	Tailoring Fees		3600.00
511	Wages Expense	800.00	
512	Advertising Expense 3	3.00	
521	Rent Expense	600.00	
525	Telephone Expense	60.00	
533	Electricity Expense	44.00	
549	Miscellaneous Expense	22.00	
	Totals	13155.00	13155.00

Reyton's transactions for November are as follows:

Nov. 1 Paid November rent, $300.
  2 Purchased tailoring supplies on account from Sew Easy Supplies, $150.
  3 Purchased a new buttonhole machine on account from Seam's Sewing Machines, $3,000.
  5 Earned first week's revenue: $400 in cash.
  8 Paid for newspaper advertising, $13.
  9 Paid telephone bill, $28.
  10 Paid electricity bill, $21.
  12 Earned second week's revenue: $200 in cash, $300 on account.
  15 Paid part-time worker, $400.
  16 Made payment on account for tailoring supplies, $100.
  17 Paid for magazine subscription (miscellaneous expense), $12.
  19 Earned third week's revenue: $450 in cash.
  21 Paid for prepaid insurance for the year, $500.
  23 Received cash from customers (previously owed), $300.
  24 Paid for newspaper advertising, $13.
  26 Paid for special delivery fee (miscellaneous expense), $12.
  29 Earned fourth week's revenue: $600 in cash.

Additional accounts needed are as follows:

Nov. 30 Adjustments:

(a) Tailoring supplies on hand, $450.

(b) Office supplies on hand, $285.

(c) Prepaid insurance expired over past three months, $150.

(d) Depreciation on tailoring equipment for the last three months, $300.

Problem 10-2A involves entering the November transactions for Sue Reyton Tailors in the general journal, processing adjusting entries, generating financial statements, and changing the accounting period.

STEP 1: Open the data file for Problem 10-2A.

STEP 2: Restore the Opening Balance data.

STEP 3: Since the Peachtree Accounting software does not support the combination journal, enter the November transactions into the General Journal window.

STEP 4: Display the General Journal with Titles Report.

STEP 5: Display a General Ledger Trial Balance Report.

STEP 6: Based on the trial balance created in Step 4, enter the adjusting entries.

STEP 7: Display the journal entries. Your report will include the monthly transactions plus the adjusting entries.

STEP 8: Display a Basic Income Statement.

STEP 9: Display a Statement of Owner's Equity.

STEP 10: Display a Basic Balance Sheet.

STEP 11: Display a General Ledger Trial Balance Report.

STEP 12: Change the accounting period to be December 1, 2000, to December 31, 2000.

▶ From the Tasks menu, choose the System option, then, from the submenu, select the Change Accounting Period option.

▶ When the Change Accounting Period window appears, choose the December 1, 2000 to December 31, 2000 accounting period and click on Ok.

▶ When the dialog box appears asking if you wish to print reports, respond No.

STEP 13: Display a post-closing trial balance, which is really just the normal General Ledger Trial Balance Report. It becomes post-closing because it was printed after the accounting period was changed which, in effect, closes the period.

If you should discover an error and wish to edit transactions from the previous period, simply change the accounting period back to November of 2000, make the corrections, display your reports, and again change the accounting period to December of 2000.

PROBLEM 10-2B

Molly Claussen owns a lawn care business. She opened her business in April. She rents a small shop area where she stores her equipment and has an assistant to receive orders and process accounts. Her trial balance shows her account balances for the first two months of business (April and May). No adjustments were made at the end of April or May.

Claussen's Green Thumb
Trial Balance
As Of 06/30/00

Acct. Number	Account Title	Debit	Credit
101	Cash	4604.00	
141	Lawn Care Supplies	588.00	
142	Office Supplies	243.00	
145	Prepaid Insurance	150.00	
189	Lawn Care Equipment	2408.00	
202	Accounts Payable		1080.00
311	Molly Claussen, Capital		5000.00
312	Molly Claussen, Drawing	800.00	
401	Lawn Care Fees		4033.00
511	Wages Expense	600.00	
521	Rent Expense	400.00	
525	Telephone Expense	88.00	
533	Electricity Expense	62.00	
537	Repair Expense	50.00	
538	Gas and Oil Expense	120.00	
	Totals	10113.00	10113.00

Transactions for June are as follows:

June 1 Paid shop rent, $200.
  2 Purchased office supplies, $230.
  3 Purchased new landscaping equipment on account from Earth Care, Inc., $1,000.
  5 Paid telephone bill, $31.
  6 Received cash for lawn care fees, $640.
  8 Paid electricity bill, $31.
  10 Paid part-time worker, $300.
  11 Received cash for lawn care fees, $580.
  12 Paid for a one-year insurance policy, $200.
  14 Made payment on account for landscaping equipment previously purchased, $100.
  15 Paid for gas and oil, $40.
  19 Paid for mower repairs, $25.
  21 Received $310 cash for lawn care fees and earned $480 on account.
  24 Withdrew cash for personal use, $100.
  26 Paid for edging equipment repairs, $20.
  28 Received cash from customers (previously owed), $480.
  29 Paid part-time worker, $300.

June 30 Adjustments:

(a) Office supplies on hand, $273.

(b) Lawn care supplies on hand, $300.

(c) Prepaid insurance expired over past three months, $100.

(d) Depreciation on lawn care equipment for past three months, $260.

Problem 10-2B involves entering the June transactions for Claussen's Green Thumb in the general journal, processing adjusting entries, generating financial statements, and changing the accounting period.

STEP 1: Open the data file for Problem 10-2B.

STEP 2: Restore the Opening Balance data.

STEP 3 Since the Peachtree Accounting software does not support the combination journal, enter the November transactions into the General Journal window.

STEP 4: Display the General Journal with Titles Report.

STEP 5: Display a General Ledger Trial Balance Report.

STEP 6: Based on the trial balance created in Step 4, enter the adjusting entries.

STEP 7: Display the journal entries. Your report will include the monthly transactions plus the adjusting entries.

STEP 8: Display a Basic Income Statement.

STEP 9: Display a Statement of Owner's Equity.

STEP 10: Display a Basic Balance Sheet.

STEP 11: Display a General Ledger Trial Balance Report.

STEP 12: Change the accounting period to July 1, 2000 to July 31, 2000.

▶ From the Tasks menu, choose the System option, then, from the submenu, select the Change Accounting Period option.

▶ When the Change Accounting Period window appears, choose the July 1, 2000 to July 31, 2000 accounting period and click on Ok.

▶ When the dialog box appears asking if you wish to print reports, respond No.

STEP 13: Display a post-closing trial balance, which is really just the normal General Ledger Trial Balance Report. It becomes post-closing because it was printed after the accounting period was changed which, in effect, closes the period.

CHAPTER 10 MASTERY PROBLEM

John McRoe opened a tennis resort in June 2000. Most guests register for one week, arriving on Sunday afternoon and returning home the following Saturday afternoon. Guests stay at an adjacent hotel. The tennis resort provides lunch and dinner. Dining and exercise facilities are provided in a building rented by McRoe. A dietitian, masseuse, physical therapist, and athletic trainers are on call to assure the proper combination of diet and exercise. The chart of accounts and transactions for the month of June are provided below. McRoe uses the modified cash basis of accounting.

McRoe Tennis Resort

McRoe Tennis Resort
Chart of Accounts

Assets
101 Cash
142 Office Supplies
144 Food Supplies
184 Tennis Facilities
184.1 Accum. Depr.—Tennis Facilities
186 Exercise Equipment
186.1 Accum. Depr.—Exercise Equip.

Liabilities
202 Accounts Payable

Owner's Equity
311 John McRoe, Capital
312 John McRoe, Drawing
313 Income Summary

Revenues
401 Registration Fees

Expenses
511 Wages Expense
521 Rent Expense
523 Office Supplies Expense
524 Food Supplies Expense
525 Telephone Expense
533 Utilities Expense
535 Insurance Expense
536 Postage Expense
541 Depr. Exp.—Tennis Facilities
542 Depr. Exp.—Exercise Equip.

June	1	McRoe invested cash in the business, $90,000.
	1	Paid for new exercise equipment, $9,000.
	2	Deposited registration fees in the bank, $15,000.
	2	Paid rent for month of June on building and land, $2,500.
	2	Rogers Construction completed work on new tennis courts that cost $70,000. The estimated useful life of the facility is five years, at which time the courts will have to be resurfaced. Arrangements were made to pay the bill in July.
	3	Purchased food supplies on account from Au Naturel Foods, $5,000.
	5	Purchased office supplies on account from Gordon Office Supplies, $300.
	7	Deposited registration fees in the bank, $16,200.
	10	Purchased food supplies on account from Au Naturel Foods, $6,200.
	10	Paid wages to staff, $500.
	14	Deposited registration fees in the bank, $13,500.
	16	Purchased food supplies on account from Au Naturel Foods, $4,000.
	17	Paid wages to staff, $500.
	18	Paid postage, $85.
	21	Deposited registration fees in the bank, $15,200.
	24	Purchased food supplies on account from Au Naturel Foods, $5,500.
	24	Paid wages to staff, $500.
	28	Deposited registration fees in the bank, $14,000.

30 Purchased food supplies on account from Au Naturel Foods, $6,000.

30 Paid wages to staff, $500.

30 Paid Au Naturel Foods on account, $28,700.

30 Paid utility bill, $500.

30 Paid telephone bill, $120.

30 McRoe withdrew cash for personal use, $1,500.

The Chapter 10 Mastery Problem involves entering transactions in the general journal, displaying a journal report, and displaying a trial balance report. Follow the step-by-step instructions below to complete the problem.

STEP 1: Open the data file for the Chapter 10 Mastery Problem.

STEP 2: Restore the Opening Balance data.

STEP 3: Enter the June transactions into the General Journal window.

STEP 4: Display a General Journal with Titles Report.

STEP 5: Display a Trial Balance Report.

CHAPTER 11 DEMONSTRATION PROBLEM (11-DEMO)

Karen Hunt operates Hunt's Audio-Video Store. The following transactions related to sales on account and cash receipts occurred during April 2000.

April 3 Sold merchandise on account to Susan Haberman, $159.50 plus tax of $11.17. Sale no. 41.

4 Sold merchandise on account to Goro Kimura, $299.95 plus tax of $21.00. Sale no. 42.

6 Received payment from Tera Scherrer on account, $69.50.

7 Issued a credit memo to Kenneth Watt for merchandise returned that had been sold on account, $42.75 including tax of $2.80.

10 Received payment from Kellie Cokley on account, $99.95.

11 Sold merchandise on account to Victor Cardona, $499.95 plus tax of $35.00. Sale no. 43.

14 Received payment from Kenneth Watt in full settlement of account, $157.00.

17 Sold merchandise on account to Susan Haberman, $379.95 plus tax of $26.60. Sale no. 44.

19 Sold merchandise on account to Tera Scherrer, $59.95 plus tax of $4.20. Sale no. 45.

21 Issued a credit memo to Goro Kimura for merchandise returned that had been sold on account, $53.45 including tax of $3.50.

24 Received payment from Victor Cardona on account, $299.95.

25 Sold merchandise on account to Kellie Cokley, $179.50 plus tax of $12.57. Sale no. 46.

26 Received payment from Susan Haberman on account, $250.65.

28 Sold merchandise on account to Kenneth Watt, $49.95 plus tax of $3.50. Sale no. 47.

30 Bank credit card sales for the month, $1,220.00 plus tax of $85.40. Bank credit card expense on these sales, $65.27.

30 Cash sales for the month, $2,000.00 plus tax of $140.00.

Hunt had the following general ledger account balances as of April 1:

Account Title	Account No.	General Ledger Balance on April 1
Cash	101	$5,000.00
Accounts Receivable	122	1,208.63
Sales Tax Payable	231	72.52
Sales	401	8,421.49
Sales Returns and Allowances	401.1	168.43
Bank Credit Card Expense	513	215.00

Hunt also had the following accounts receivable ledger account balances as of April 1:

Customer	Accounts Receivable Balance
Victor Cardona 6300 Washington Blvd. St. Louis, MO 63130-9523	$299.95
Kellie Cokley 4220 Kingsbury Blvd. St. Louis, MO 63130-1645	$99.95
Susan Haberman 9421 Garden Ct. Kirkwood, MO 63122-1878	$79.98
Goro Kimura 6612 Arundel Pl. Clayton, MO 63150-9266	$379.50
Tera Scherrer 315 W. Linden St. Webster Groves, MO 63119-9881	$149.50
Kenneth Watt 11742 Fawnridge Dr. St. Louis, MO 63131-1726	$199.75

In the Chapter 11 Demonstration Problem, you will use the Peachtree Accounting software to process sales, cash receipts, and credit memos. In addition, you will display the invoice register, sales journal, cash receipts journal, and customer accounts receivable ledger. Follow the steps listed to complete the problem.

STEP 1: Open the data file for the Chapter 11 Demonstration Problem.

STEP 2: Restore the Opening Balance data.

STEP 3: From the Tasks menu, select the Sales/Invoicing option and enter the sales on account and credit memo transactions.

Sales on Account Transactions:

▶ Enter or select the Customer ID.
▶ Enter the Sale No. into the Invoice Number field.
▶ Enter the Date of the transaction.

- In the Description field, enter "Merchandise."
- Accept the default GL Account of 401 and Tax Code of 1.
  Note: If the GL Account field does not appear, this indicates that someone has chosen the option to hide General Ledger Accounts in the Maintain Global Options under the Options menu. Since the default is 401, the solution will come the same even if the General Ledger Accounts columns have been hidden.
- Enter the amount of the credit to Sales.
- Verify that the sales tax is calculated correctly. If not, select the correct Sales Tax Code of MO near the lower left corner of the window. If you enter the Sales Tax Code rather than select it from the list, it must be keyed in upper case.
- Click on the Journal Icon Bar button to verify that the correct journal entry is being generated. Click Ok to return to the Sales/Invoicing screen.
- Click on Post to record the transaction.
  A completed Sales/Invoicing window is illustrated in Figure 2.15.

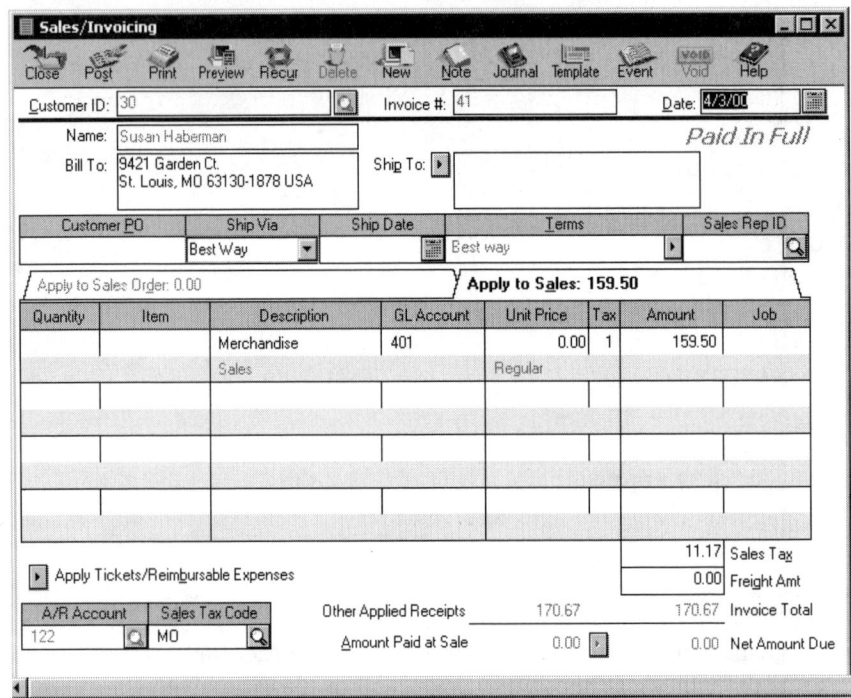

FIGURE 2.15 Sales/Invoicing Window (Sales on Account)

Credit Memo Transactions:

- Enter or select the Customer ID.
- Enter CM followed by a consecutively assigned number beginning with 1 (e.g., CM1).
- Enter the Date of the credit memo.
- In the Description field, enter "Credit Memo."
- Enter the Sales Returns and Allowance account number in the GL Account column.
- Accept the default Tax Code of 1.
- Enter the amount of the sales return or allowance as a negative number.
- Verify that the A/R Account and Sales Tax Code fields in the lower left corner of the screen have been selected.

▶ Click on the Journal Icon Bar button to verify that the correct journal entry is being generated. Click Ok to return to the Sales/Invoicing screen.
▶ Click on Post to record the transaction.

The recording of the first credit memo transaction is illustrated in the Sales/Invoicing window shown in Figure 2.16.

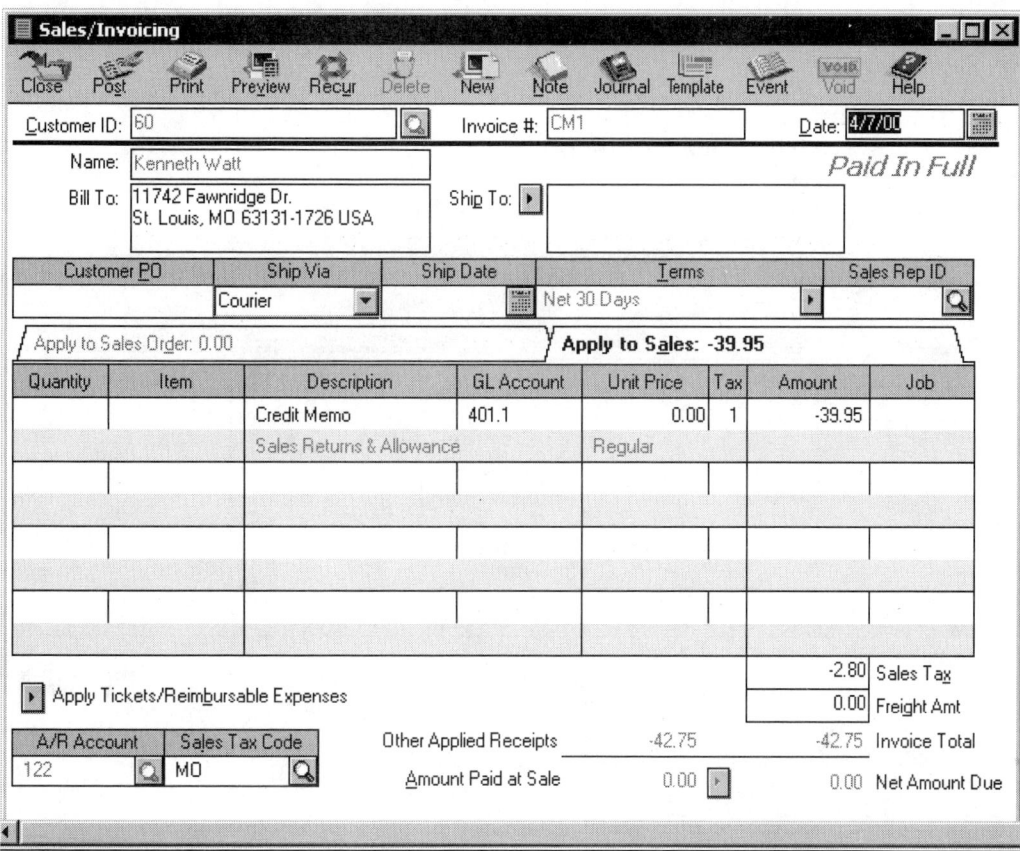

FIGURE 2.16 Sales/Invoicing Window (Credit Memo)

STEP 4: From the Tasks menu, select the Receipts option and enter the cash receipts on account, credit card sales, and cash sales transactions.

Cash Received on Account Transactions:

▶ Enter 04/30/00 as the Deposit ticket ID. (This provides a deposit ticket reference for bank reconciliation.)
▶ Enter or select the customer number.
▶ A Reference number is required. Since none is provided, either number the transactions consecutively beginning with 1 or simply record a reference of "Cash" for each.
▶ Enter the transaction Date.
▶ Select a payment method of Cash.

- Select Cash as the G/L Account.
- Click on the Apply to Invoices Tab.
- If more than one invoice is displayed, move the cursor to the Description column for the invoice you wish to pay. Enter "On account" as the description. If the payment covers more than one invoice, you must split it among the applicable invoices or it may be applied to the balance forward. If the entire invoice is being paid, simply click on the Pay box and a red check mark will appear and the amount paid will also appear. If it is a partial payment, enter the amount of cash received into the Amount Paid column that is to be applied to that invoice. If a credit memo applies to an invoice being paid, click on the Pay box for the credit memo to apply it to the invoice being paid.
- Click on Post to record the transaction.

An example of a cash receipt on account transaction with the first cash receipt transaction completed is illustrated in Figure 2.17.

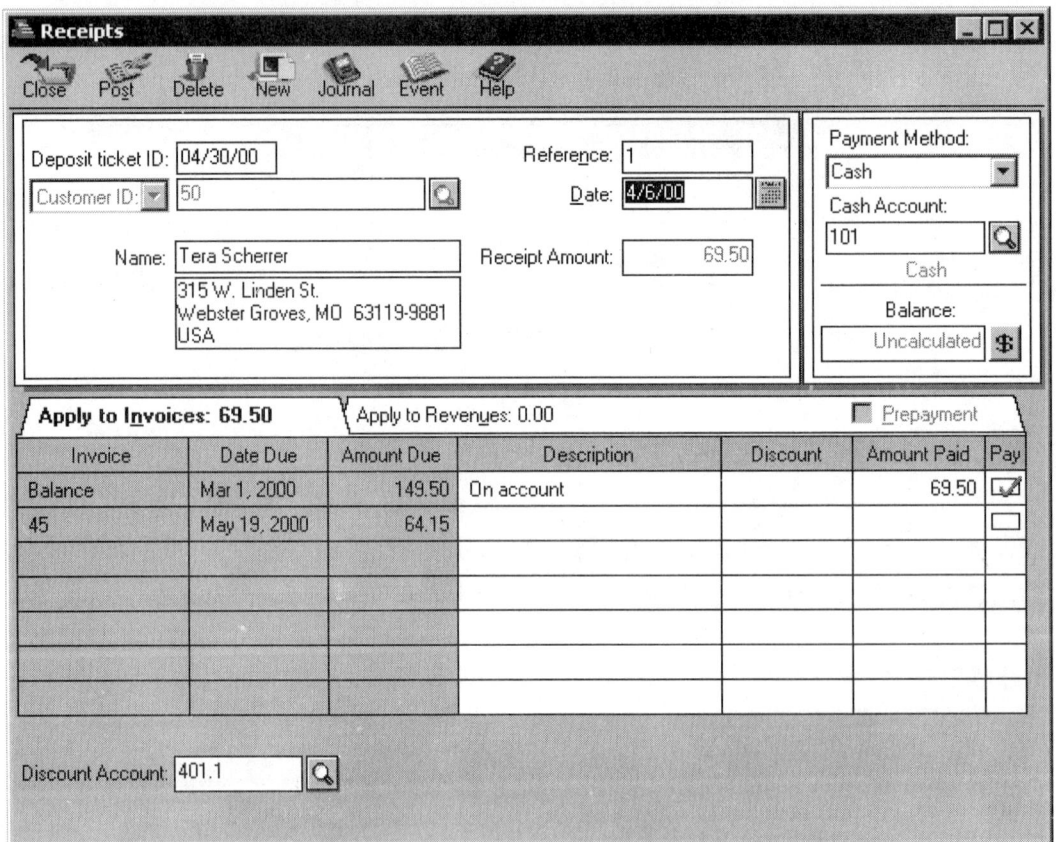

FIGURE 2.17 Receipts Window (Cash Received on Account)

Figure 2.18 illustrates the transaction on April 14th for Kenneth Watt. In this example, cash was received on account where an invoice is paid that has a credit memo applied.

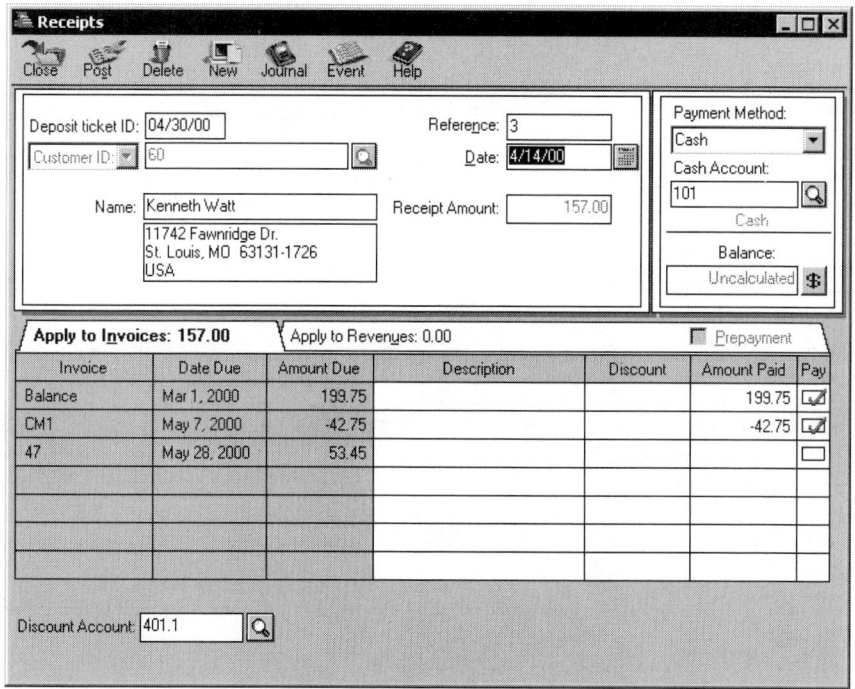

FIGURE 2.18 Receipts Window (Cash on Account for Invoice with Credit Memo Applied)

Credit Card Sales Transactions:

▶ Enter VISA as the Deposit ticket ID.
▶ Leave the Customer ID blank.
▶ Enter "Credit card receipts" in the Name field.
▶ Enter either the next consecutive number or "Credit card" as the Reference.
▶ Enter the Date of the transaction.
▶ Select a payment method of VISA.
▶ Select Cash as the G/L Account.
▶ Click on the Apply to Revenues tab.
▶ Leave the Quantity and Item fields blank.
▶ On the first line, enter "Credit card receipts" in the Description column, the Sales account number in the GL Account column, 1 as the Tax code and the Sales Credit amount in the Amount Column.
▶ Verify that the sales tax is calculated correctly. If not, select the correct Sales Tax Code of MO near the lower left corner of the window. If you enter the Sales Tax Code rather than select it from the list, it must be keyed in upper case.
▶ On the second line, enter "Credit card expense" in the Description column, the Credit Card Expense account number in the GL Account column, 2 as the Tax Code, and the amount of the credit card expense in the Amount column as a negative number.
▶ Click on Post to record the transaction.

A completed Receipts window illustrating credit card receipts is illustrated in Figure 2.19 on the following page.

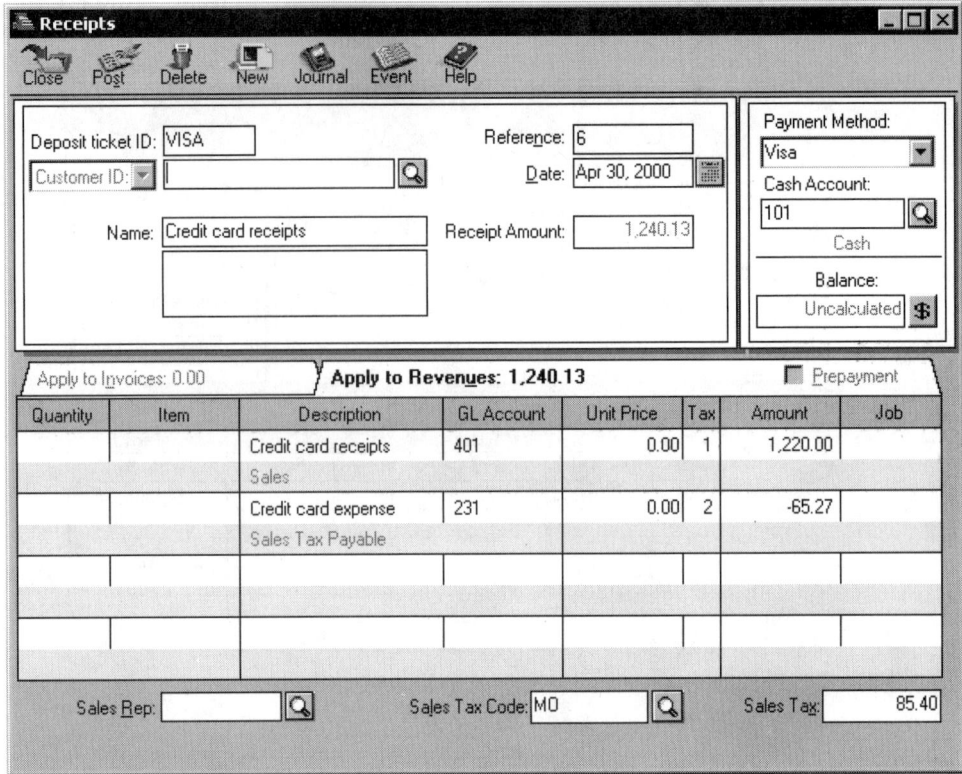

FIGURE 2.19 Receipts Window (Credit Card Receipts)

Cash Sales:

▶ Enter 04/30/00 as the Deposit ticket ID.
▶ Leave the Customer ID blank.
▶ Enter "Cash sales" in the Name field.
▶ Enter the day of the month as the Reference.
▶ Enter the Date of the transaction.
▶ Select a payment method of Cash.
▶ Select Cash as the G/L Account.
▶ Click on the Apply to Revenues tab.
▶ Leave the Quantity and Item fields blank.
▶ On the first line, enter "Cash sales" in the Description column, enter the Sales Account number in the GL Account column, enter 1 as the Tax Code, and enter the Sales Credit amount in the Amount Column.
▶ Verify that the Sales Tax Code shown near the bottom of the screen contains "MO." If not, select it from the list. The sales tax amount should appear in the Sales Tax field in the lower right corner of the window. If you enter the Sales Tax Code rather than select it from the list, it must be keyed as shown, that is, all upper case.
▶ Click on Post to record the transaction.
A completed cash sale transaction is illustrated in Figure 2.20 on the following page.

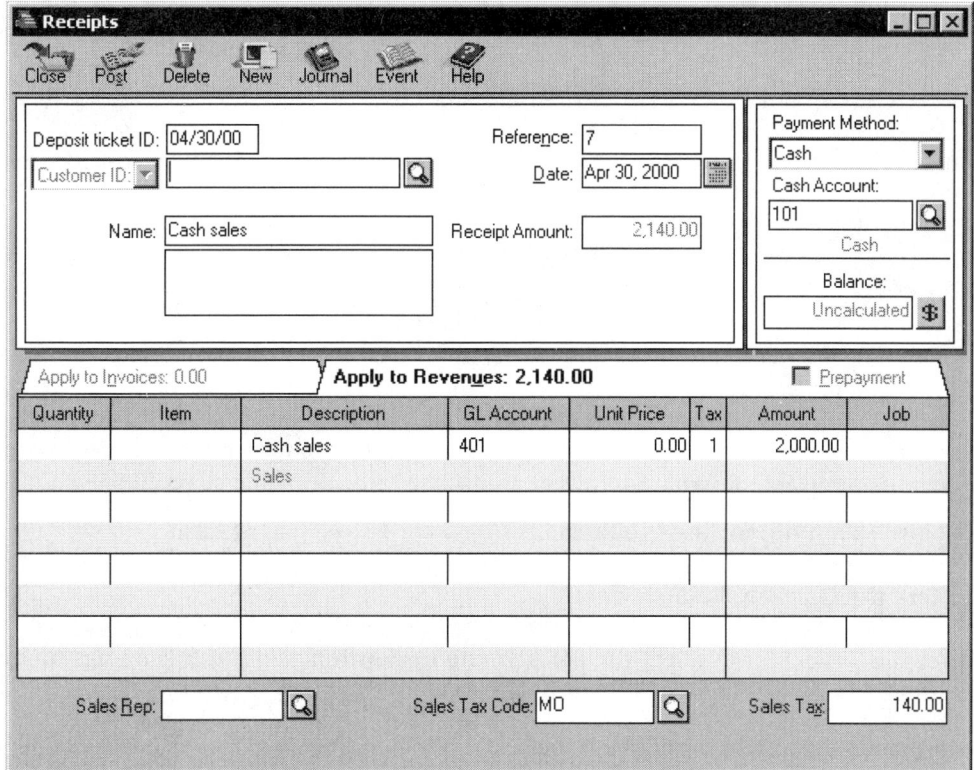

FIGURE 2.20 Receipts Windows (Cash Sales)

STEP 5: Display the accounts receivable reports.

▶ From the Reports menu, select the Accounts Receivable option.
▶ Display the Sales Journal with Titles.
▶ Display the Cash Receipts Journal with Titles.
▶ Display the Invoice Register.
▶ Display the Customer Ledgers report.

STEP 6: If errors are detected on the reports, return to the appropriate data-entry window (Sales/Invoicing or Receipts) and use the Edit Icon Bar button to select the transaction in error and make corrections.

See the solution section of this workbook for the solution to the demonstration problem.

PROBLEM 11-3A

Owens Distributors is a retail business. The following sales, returns, and cash receipts occurred during March 2000. There is an 8% sales tax. Beginning general ledger account balances were: Cash, $9,741.00; and Accounts Receivable, $1,058.25. Beginning customer account balances were: Thompson Group, $1,058.25.

March 1 Sale no. 33C to Able & Co., $1,800 plus sales tax.
3 Sale no. 33D to R. J. Kalas, Inc., $2,240 plus sales tax.
5 Able & Co. returned merchandise from sale no. 33C for a credit (credit memo no. 66), $30 plus sales tax.

7	Cash sales for the week, $3,160 plus sales tax.
10	Received payment from Able & Co. for sale no. 33C less credit memo no. 66.
11	Sale no. 33E to Blevins Bakery, $1,210 plus sales tax.
13	Received payment from R. J. Kalas for sale no. 33D.
14	Cash sales for the week, $4,200 plus sales tax.
16	Blevins Bakery returned merchandise from sale no. 33E for a credit (credit memo no. 67), $44 plus sales tax.
18	Sale no. 33F to R. J. Kalas, Inc., $2,620 plus sales tax.
20	Received payment from Blevins Bakery for sale no. 33E less credit memo no. 67.
21	Cash sales for the week, $2,400 plus sales tax.
25	Sale no. 33G to Blevins Bakery, $1,915 plus sales tax.
27	Sale no. 33H to Thompson Group, $2,016 plus sales tax.
28	Cash sales for the week, $3,500 plus sales tax.

In Problem 11-3A, you will use the Peachtree Accounting software to process sales and cash receipts and display the accounts receivable reports. Follow the steps listed to complete the problem.

STEP 1: Open the data file for the Problem 11-3A.

STEP 2: Restore the Opening Balance data.

STEP 3: From the Tasks Menu, select the Sales/Invoicing option and enter the sales on account transactions into the Sales/Invoicing window.

▶ Enter "Merchandise" in the Description field.
▶ Verify that "Indiana" is selected for the Sales Tax Code in the lower left portion of the window.

STEP 4: Enter the credit memo transactions into the Sales/Invoicing window.

▶ Enter CM followed by the credit memo number into the Invoice No. field (e.g., CM66).
▶ Enter "Credit Memo" in the Description field.
▶ Enter the account number for Sales Returns and Allowance in the GL Account field.
▶ Enter the credit memo amount as a negative number.

STEP 5: From the Tasks menu, select the Receipts option and enter the cash receipts on account transactions.

▶ Enter Deposit ticket ID of "03/31/00."
▶ Enter the invoice number provided as the reference.
▶ Enter "On account" in the Description Field.
▶ Be sure to apply any applicable credit memos.

STEP 6: Enter the cash sales into the Receipts window.

▶ Enter "Cash sales" in the Name field; enter "Cash sales" in the Description field.
▶ Enter the credit to sales in the Amount field.
▶ Select "Indiana" in the Sales Tax Code field near the bottom of the screen.

STEP 7: Display the accounts receivable reports.

From the Reports menu, select the Accounts Receivable option.
▶ Display the Sales Journal with Titles.
▶ Display the Cash Receipts Journal with Titles.

▶ Display the Invoice Register.
▶ Display the Customer Ledgers Report.
▶ Display a Trial Balance Report.

STEP 8: If errors are detected on the reports, return to the appropriate data entry window (Sales/Invoicing or Receipts) and use the Edit Icon Bar button to select the transaction in error and make corrections.

PROBLEM 11-3B

Paul Jackson owns a retail business. The following sales, returns, and cash receipts are for April 2000. There is a 7% sales tax.

April 1   Sale no. 111 to O. L. Meyers, $2,100 plus sales tax.
    3   Sale no. 112 to Andrew Plaa, $1,000 plus sales tax.
    6   O. L. Meyers returned merchandise from sale no. 111 for a credit (credit memo no. 42), $50 plus sales tax.
    7   Cash sales for the week, $3,240 plus sales tax.
    9   Received payment from O. L. Meyers for sale no. 111 less credit memo no. 42.
    12 Sale no. 113 to Melissa Richfield, $980 plus sales tax.
    14 Cash sales for the week, $2,180 plus sales tax.
    17 Melissa Richfield returned merchandise from sale no. 113 for a credit (credit memo no. 43), $40 plus sales tax.
    19 Sale no. 114 to Kelsay Munkres, $1,020 plus sales tax.
    21 Cash sales for the week, $2,600 plus sales tax.
    24 Sale no. 115 to O. L. Meyers, $920 plus sales tax.
    27 Sale no. 116 to Andrew Plaa, $1,320 plus sales tax.
    28 Cash sales for the week, $2,800 plus sales tax.

Beginning general ledger account balances:
Cash $2,864.54
Accounts Receivable   2,726.25
Beginning customer account balances:
O. L. Meyers $2,186.00
K. Munkres   482.00
M. Richfield   58.25

In Problem 11-3B, you will use the Peachtree Accounting software to process sales and cash receipts and display the accounts receivable reports. Follow the steps listed to complete the problem.

STEP 1: Open the data file for Problem 11-3B.

STEP 2: Restore the Opening Balance data.

STEP 3: From the Tasks Menu, select the Sales/Invoicing option and enter the sales on account transactions into the Sales/Invoicing window.

▶ Enter "Merchandise" in the Description field.
▶ Verify that "Indiana" is selected for the Sales Tax Code in the lower left portion of the window.

STEP 4: Enter the credit memo transactions into the Sales/Invoicing window.

▶ Enter CM followed by the credit memo number into the Invoice No. field (e.g., CM33).
▶ Enter "Credit Memo" in the Description field.

- Enter the account number for Sales Returns and Allowance in the GL Account field.
- Enter the credit memo amount as a negative number.

STEP 5: From the Tasks menu, select the Receipts option and enter the cash receipts on account transactions.

- Enter Deposit ticket ID of "04/30/00."
- Enter the invoice number provided as the reference.
- Enter "On account" in the Description Field.
- Be sure to apply in applicable credit memos.

STEP 6: Enter the cash sales into the Receipts window.

- Enter "Cash sales" in the Name field; enter "Cash sales" in the Description field.
- Enter the credit to sales in the Amount field.
- Select "CT" in the Sales Tax Code field near the bottom of the screen.

STEP 7: Display the accounts receivable reports.

- From the Reports menu, select the Accounts Receivable option.
- Display the Sales Journal with Titles.
- Display the Cash Receipts Journal with Titles.
- Display the Invoice Register.
- Display the Customer Ledgers Report.
- Display a Trial Balance Report.

STEP 8: If errors are detected on the reports, return to the appropriate data entry window (Sales/Invoicing or Receipts) and use the Edit Icon Bar button to select the transaction in error and make corrections.

CHAPTER 11 MASTERY PROBLEM

Geoff and Sandy Harland own and operate Wayward Kennel and Pet Supply. Their motto is, "If your pet is not becoming to you, he should be coming to us." The Harlands maintain a sales tax payable account throughout the month to account for the 6% sales tax. They use a sales journal, a cash receipts journal, and a general journal. The following sales and cash collections took place during the month of September.

Sept. 2 Sold a fish aquarium on account to Ken Shank, $125.00 plus tax of $7.50, terms n/30. Sale no. 101.
    3 Sold dog food on account to Nancy Truelove, $68.25 plus tax of $4.10, terms n/30. Sale no. 102.
    5 Sold a bird cage on account to Jean Warkentin, $43.95 plus tax of $2.64, terms n/30. Sale no. 103.
    8 Cash sales for the week, $2,332.45 plus tax of $139.95.
    10 Received cash for boarding and grooming services, $625.00 plus tax of $37.50.
    11 Jean Warkentin stopped by the store to point out a minor defect in the bird cage purchased in sale no. 103. The Harlands offered a sales allowance of $10.00 plus tax on the price of the cage, which satisfied Warkentin.
    12 Sold a cockatoo on account to Tully Shaw, $1,200.00 plus tax of $72.00, terms n/30. Sale no. 104.
    14 Received cash on account from Rosa Alanso, $256.00.
    15 Rosa Alanso returned merchandise, $93.28 including tax of $5.28.
    15 Cash sales for the week, $2,656.85 plus tax of $159.41.
    16 Received cash on account from Nancy Truelove, $58.25.
    18 Received cash for boarding and grooming services, $535.00 plus tax of $32.10.
    19 Received cash on account from Ed Cochran, $63.25.

20	Sold pet supplies on account to Susan Hays, $83.33 plus tax of $5.00, terms n/30. Sale no. 105.
21	Sold three Labrador Retriever puppies to All American Day Camp, $375.00 plus tax of $22.50, terms n/30. Sale no. 106.
22	Cash sales for the week, $3,122.45 plus tax of $187.35.
23	Received cash for boarding and grooming services, $515.00 plus tax of $30.90.
25	Received cash on account from Ken Shank, $132.50.
26	Received cash on account from Nancy Truelove, $72.35.
27	Received cash on account from Joe Gloy, $273.25.
28	Borrowed cash to purchase a pet limousine, $11,000.00.
29	Cash sales for the week, $2,835.45 plus tax of $170.13.
30	Received cash for boarding and grooming services, $488.00 plus tax of $29.28.

Wayward had the following general ledger account balances as of September 1:

Account Title	Account No.	General Ledger Balance on Sept. 1
Cash	101	$23,500.25
Accounts Receivable	122	850.75
Notes Payable	201	2,500.00
Sales Tax Payable	231	909.90
Sales	401	13,050.48
Sales Returns and Allowances	401.1	86.00
Boarding and Grooming Revenue	402	2,115.00

Wayward also had the following accounts receivable ledger balances as of September 1:

Customer	Accounts Receivable Balance
Rosa Alanso 2541 East 2nd Street Bloomington, IN 47401-5356	$456.00
Ed Cochran 2669 Windcrest Drive Bloomington, IN 47401-5446	$63.25
Joe Gloy 1458 Parnell Avenue Muncie, IN 47304-2682	$273.25
Nancy Truelove 2300 E. National Road Cumberland, IN 46229-4824	$58.25

New customers opening accounts during September were:

All American Day Camp
3025 Old Mill Run
Bloomington, IN 47408-1080

Susan Hays
1424 Jackson Creek Road
Nashville, IN 47448-2245

Ken Shank
6422 E. Bender Road
Bloomington, IN 47401-7756

Tully Shaw
3315 Longview Avenue
Bloomington, IN 47401-7223

Jean Warkentin
1813 Deep Well Court
Bloomington, IN 47401-5124

In the Chapter 11 Mastery Problem, you will use the Peachtree Accounting software to process sales and cash receipts, and to display the invoice register, sales journal, cash receipts journal, and customer accounts receivable ledger. Follow the steps listed to complete the problem.

STEP 1: Open the data file for the Chapter 11 Mastery Problem.

STEP 2: Restore the Opening Balance data.

STEP 3: From the Tasks menu, select the Sales/Invoicing option and enter the sales on account transactions into the Sales/Invoicing window.

▶ Enter a description of the merchandise sold in the Description field.

▶ Verify that "Indiana" is selected for the Sales Tax Code in the lower left portion of the window.

STEP 4: Enter the credit memo transactions into the Sales/Invoicing window.

▶ Enter CM followed by the original invoice number into the Invoice No. field (e.g., CM103). If the return applies to the balance forward for that customer, enter "CMBalance."

▶ Enter "Credit Memo" in the Description field.

▶ Enter the account number for Sales Returns and Allowance in the GL Account field.

▶ Enter the credit memo amount as a negative number.

STEP 5: From the Tasks menu, select the Receipts option and enter the cash receipts on account transactions.

▶ Enter Deposit ticket ID of "09/30/00."

▶ Enter the invoice number provided as the reference. If a specific invoice does not apply, enter "Balance" to indicate that it applies to the balance forward for that customer.

▶ Enter "On account" in the Description Field.

▶ Be sure to apply in applicable credit memos.

STEP 6: Enter the cash sales into the Receipts window.

▶ Enter Deposit ticket ID of "09/30/00".

▶ Enter the day of the month as the Reference.

▶ Enter "Cash sales" in the Name field; enter "Cash sales" in the Description field.

▶ Enter or select the correct revenue account in the GL Account field (either Sales or Board and Groom Revenue).

▶ Enter the credit to sales in the Amount field.

▶ Select "Indiana" in the Sales Tax Code field near the bottom of the screen.

Note: When entering the transaction involving borrowed cash, enter "Borrowed Cash" as the Description, enter "Notes Payable" as the GL Account number, and enter a Tax Code of 2 which indicates that there is no sales tax.

STEP 7: Display the accounts receivable reports.

▶ From the Reports menu, select the Accounts Receivable option.

▶ Display the Sales Journal with Titles.

▶ Display the Cash Receipts Journal with Titles.

▶ Display the Invoice Register.

▶ Display the Customer Ledgers Report.

▶ Display a Trial Balance Report.

STEP 8: If errors are detected on the reports, return to the appropriate data entry window (Sales/Invoicing or Receipts) and use the Edit Icon Bar button to select the transaction in error and make corrections.

CHAPTER 12 DEMONSTRATION PROBLEM (12-DEMO)

Jodi Rutman operates a retail pharmacy called Rutman Pharmacy. The following are the transactions related to purchases and cash payments for the month of June 2000.

June 1 Purchased merchandise from Sullivan Co. on account, $234.20. Invoice no. 71 dated June 1, terms 2/10, n/30.
2 Issued check no. 536 for payment of June rent (Rent Expense), $1,000.00.
5 Purchased merchandise from Amfac Drug Supply on account, $562.40. Invoice no. 196 dated June 2, terms 1/15, n/30.
7 Purchased merchandise from University Drug Co. on account, $367.35. Invoice no. 914A dated June 5, terms 3/10 eom, n/30.
9 Issued check no. 537 to Sullivan Co. in payment of invoice no. 71 less 2% discount.
12 Received a credit memo from Amfac Drug Supply for merchandise returned that was purchased on June 5, $46.20.
14 Purchased merchandise from Mutual Drug Co. on account, $479.40. Invoice no. 745 dated June 14, terms 2/10, n/30.
15 Received a credit memo from University Drug Co. for merchandise returned that was purchased on June 7, $53.70.
16 Issued check no. 538 to Amfac Drug Supply in payment of invoice no. 196 less the credit memo of June 12 and less 1% discount.
23 Issued check no. 539 to Mutual Drug Co. in payment of invoice no. 745 less 2% discount.
27 Purchased merchandise from Flites Pharmaceuticals on account, $638.47. Invoice no. 675 dated June 27, terms 2/10 eom, n/30.
29 Issued check no. 540 to Dolgin Candy Co. for a cash purchase of merchandise, $270.20.
30 Issued check no. 541 to Vashon Medical Supply in payment of invoice no. 416, $1,217.69. No discount allowed.

In the Chapter 12 Demonstration Problem, you will use the Peachtree Accounting software to process purchases and cash payments, and to display a trial balance, schedule of accounts payable, purchases journal, check register, and cash disbursements journal. Follow the steps listed to complete the Chapter 12 Demonstration Problem.

STEP 1: Open the data file for the Chapter 12 Demonstration Problem.

STEP 2: Restore the Opening Balance data.

STEP 3: From the Tasks menu, select the Purchases/Receive Inventory option and enter the purchases on account and returns and allowance transactions.

Entering Purchases Transactions:

▶ Enter or select the Vendor ID number.
▶ Enter the Invoice Number.
▶ Enter the Date of the transaction.
▶ Verify that the terms of the sale are correctly indicated. If not, click on the right arrow button at the end of the Terms field and a Term Information window will appear allowing you to enter the pertinent discount data.

- On the Apply to Purchases tab, enter "Merchandise" in the Description field.
- Enter the amount of the purchase in the Amount field.
- Click on Post to record the transaction.

An example of the recording of a purchase of merchandise on account is illustrated in the Purchases/Receive Inventory window shown in Figure 2.21.

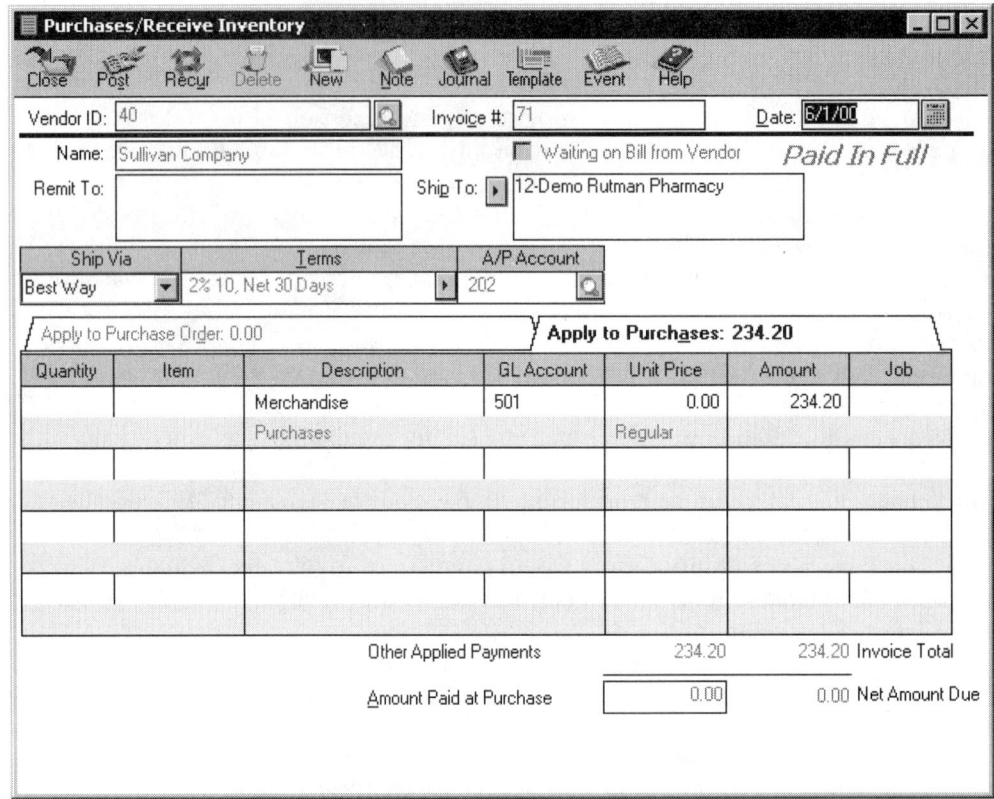

FIGURE 2.21 Purchases/Receive Inventory (Purchase on Account)

Entering Purchases Returns and Allowance Transactions:
- Enter or select the Vendor ID number.
- Enter an Invoice Number consisting of CM plus the original invoice number.
- Verify that the terms of the sale are correct; if not, click on the right arrow button in the Terms field and enter correct terms.
- Enter "Credit memo" as the Description.
- Enter the Purchases Returns and Allowances Account Number in the GL Account field.
- Enter the amount of the credit memo received as a negative number.
- Click on Post to record the transaction.
  The recording of a Purchase Return transaction is illustrated in the Purchases/Receive Inventory window shown in Figure 2.22 on the following page.

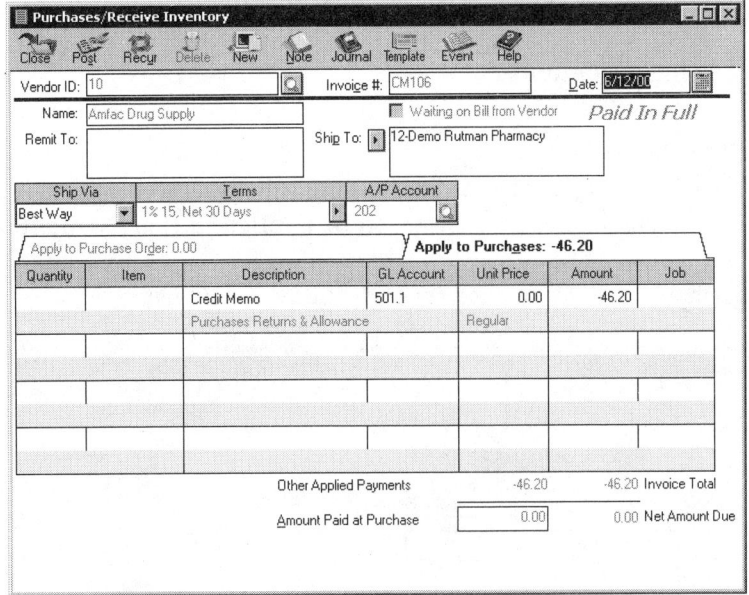

FIGURE 2.22 Purchases/Receive Inventory (Purchases Return)

STEP 4: From the Tasks menu, select the Payments option and enter the cash payment transactions.

There are two types of cash payments: (1) payments on account and (2) direct payments. Payments on account require a vendor number and must be applied to the applicable invoice(s). Direct payments do not require a vendor number and are applied to expenses.

Direct payments require that a name be entered in the Pay to the Order of field. If none is provided in the transaction, you will have to be creative and come up with one as the software will not allow you to proceed without entering a name.

When entering payments on account, you must select the invoices you wish to pay and apply the appropriate credit memos to the invoice(s). An example of a completed Payments window illustrating the payment of an invoice and applying a credit memo is shown in Figure 2.23.

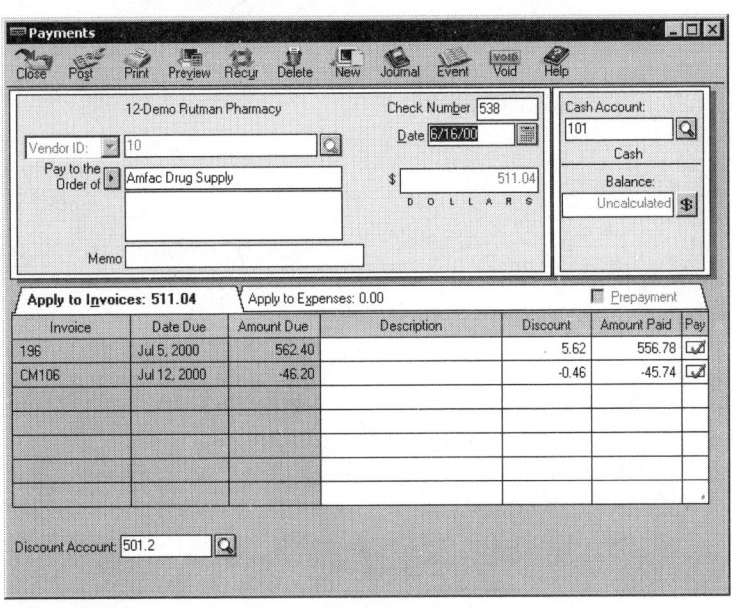

FIGURE 2.23 Payment Windows (Applying a Credit Memo to Payment)

Payment on Account (Apply to Invoices Tab):

▶ Enter or select the Vendor ID number.
▶ Enter the Check Number.
▶ Enter the Date of the check.
▶ Under the Apply to Invoices tab, click on the Pay box for the invoice or invoices to be paid. Click on the Pay box for any credit memos that are to be applied to this payment.
▶ Click on Post to record the payment.

An example of a payment on account transaction is illustrated in Figure 2.24.

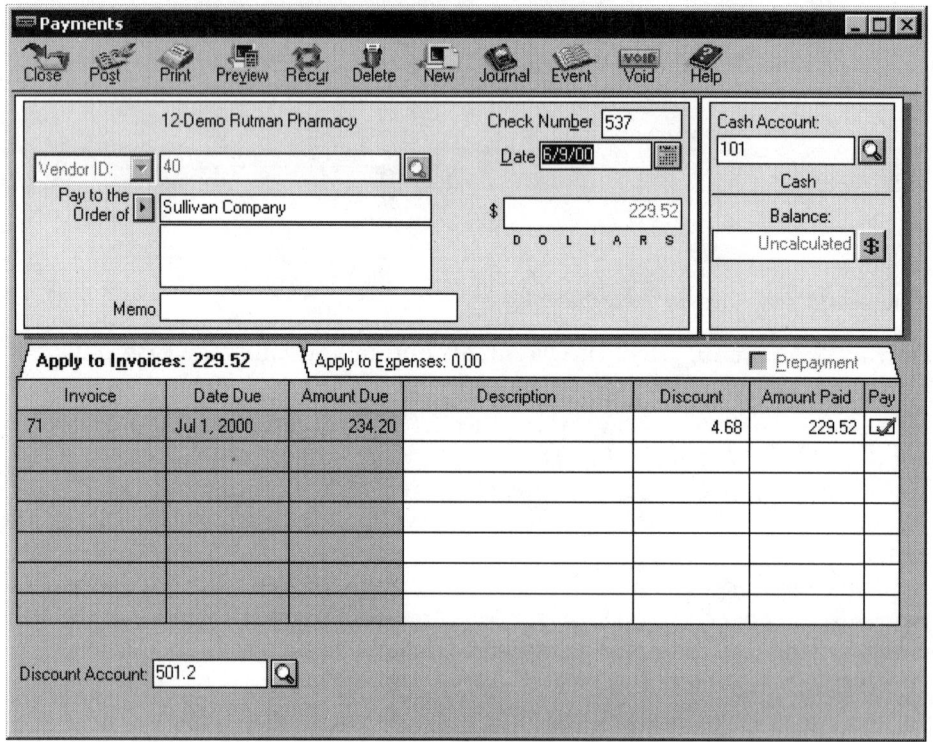

FIGURE 2.24 Payments Window (Payment on Account)

Direct Payment (Apply to Expenses Tab):

▶ Enter the payee in the Pay to the Order of field. If none is available in the transaction statement, create one. For example, if the check is for rent, enter "Rent payment."
▶ Enter the Check Number.
▶ Enter the Date.
▶ Under the Apply to Expenses tab, enter a description of the transaction, the account number of the account to be debited, and the amount of the payment.
▶ Click Post to record the transaction.

A Payments window illustrating the recording of a direct payment for rent is illustrated in Figure 2.25 on the following page.

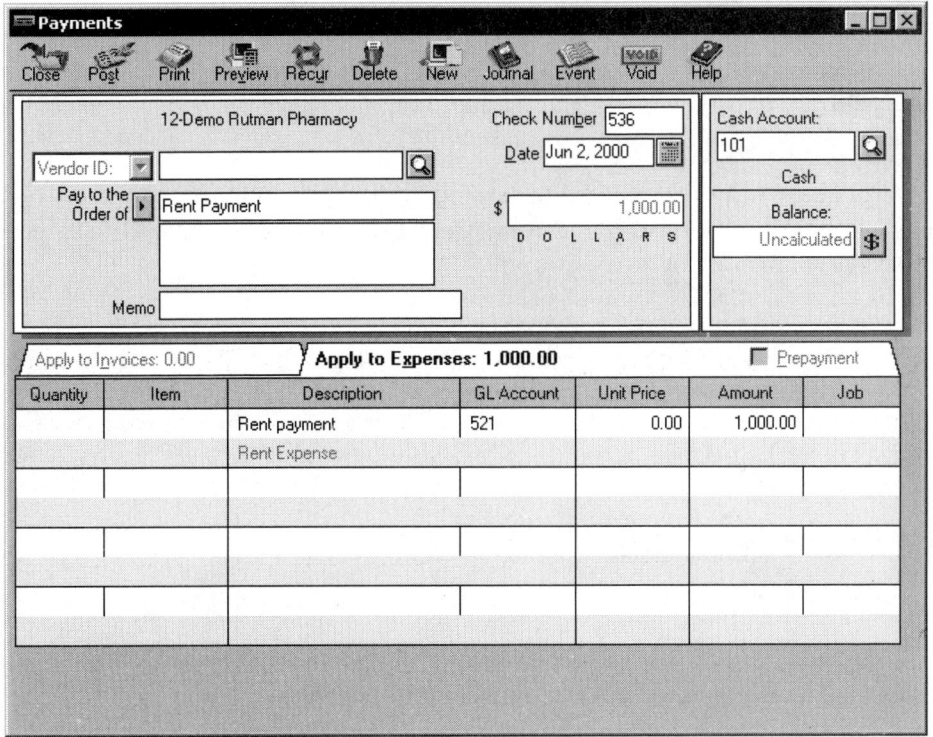

FIGURE 2.25 Payments Window (Direct Payment)

STEP 5: Display a General Ledger Trial Balance Report.

STEP 6: From the Reports menu, select the Accounts Payable option and display a schedule of accounts payable, purchases journal, check register, and cash disbursements journal with titles reports.

STEP 7: If errors are detected on the reports, return to the appropriate data-entry window (Purchases/Receive Inventory or Payments) and use the Edit Icon Bar button to select the transaction in error and make corrections.

See the solution section of this workbook for the solution to the demonstration problem.

PROBLEM 12-3A

Freddy Flint owns a small retail business called Flint's Fantasy. The cash account has a balance of $20,000 on July 1. The following transactions occurred during July.

July 1 Issued check no. 414 in payment of July rent, $1,500.
  1 Purchased merchandise on account from Tang's Toys, invoice no. 311, $2,700, terms 2/10, n/30.
  3 Purchased merchandise on account from Sillas & Company, invoice no. 812, $3,100, terms 1/10, n/30.
  5 Returned merchandise purchased from Tang's Toys, receiving a credit memo on the amount owed, $500.
  8 Purchased merchandise on account from Daisy's Dolls, invoice no. 139, $1,900, terms 2/10, n/30.
  11 Issued check no. 415 to Tang's Toys for merchandise purchased on account, less return of July 5 and less 2% discount.

13 Issued a check no. 416 to Sillas & Company for merchandise purchased on account, less 1% discount.

15 Returned merchandise purchased from Daisy's Dolls, receiving a credit memo on the amount owed, $400.

18 Issued check no. 417 to Daisy's Dolls for merchandise purchased on account, less return of July 15 and less 2% discount.

25 Purchased merchandise on account from Allied Business, invoice no. 489, $2,450, terms n/30.

26 Purchased merchandise on account from Tang's Toys, invoice no. 375, $1,980, terms 2/10, n/30.

29 Purchased merchandise on account from Sillas & Company, invoice no. 883, $3,460, terms 1/10, n/30.

31 Freddy Flint withdrew cash for personal use, $2,000. Issued check no. 418.

31 Issued check no. 419 to Glisan Distributors for a cash purchase of merchandise, $975.

In the Problem 12-3A you will use the Peachtree Accounting software to process purchases and cash payments, and to display a trial balance, schedule of accounts payable, purchases journal, check register, and cash disbursements journal. Follow the steps listed to complete the problem.

STEP 1: Open the data file for Problem 12-3A.

STEP 2: Restore the Opening Balance data.

STEP 3: From the Tasks menu, select the Purchases/Receive Inventory option and enter the purchases on account and returns or allowance transactions.

STEP 4: From the Tasks menu, select the Payments option and enter the cash payment transactions.

Note: Vendor credits for returns and allowances must be applied to the appropriate payment. For example, on the 11th, the amount of the check is $2,154.00. The $2,154.00 is arrived at by applying invoice number 311 for $2,700.00 less the credit of $500.00 less the discount. The discount is $54.00 on the original invoice amount of $2,700.00 minus the discount credit of $10.00 yielding a net discount of $44.00. ($2,700.00 − 500.00 − 44.00 = $2,154,00).

STEP 5: From the Reports menu, select the General Ledger option and display a General Ledger Trial Balance Report.

STEP 6: From the Reports menu, select the Accounts Payable option and display a schedule of accounts payable, purchases journal, check register, cash disbursements journal with titles, reports, and vendor ledgers.

PROBLEM 12-3B

Debbie Mueller owns a small retail business called Debbie's Doll House. The cash account has a balance of $20,000 on July 1. The following transactions occurred during July.

July 1 Issued check no. 314 for July rent, $1,400.

1 Purchased merchandise on account from Topper's Toys, invoice no. 211, $2,500, terms 2/10, n/30.

3 Purchased merchandise on account from Jones & Company, invoice no. 812, $2,800, terms 1/10, n/30.

5 Returned merchandise purchased from Topper's Toys receiving a credit memo on the amount owed, $400.

8 Purchased merchandise on account from Downtown Merchants, invoice no. 159, $1,600, terms 2/10, n/30.

11 Issued check no. 315 to Topper's Toys for merchandise purchased on account, less return of July 5 and less 2% discount.

13 Issued check no. 316 to Jones & Company for merchandise purchased on account, less 1% discount.

15 Returned merchandise purchased from Downtown Merchants receiving a credit memo on the amount owed, $600.

18 Issued check no. 317 to Downtown Merchants for merchandise purchased on account, less return of July 15 and less 2% discount.

25 Purchased merchandise on account from Columbia Products, invoice no. 468, $3,200, terms n/30.

26 Purchased merchandise on account from Topper's Toys, invoice no. 395, $1,430, terms 2/10, n/30.

29 Purchased merchandise on account from Jones & Company, invoice no. 853, $2,970, terms 1/10, n/30.

31 Mueller withdrew cash for personal use, $2,500. Issued check no. 318.

31 Issued check no. 319 to Burnside Warehouse for a cash purchase of merchandise, $1,050.

In Problem 12-3B, you will use the Peachtree Accounting software to process purchases and cash payments, and to display a trial balance, schedule of accounts payable, purchases journal, check register, and cash disbursements. Follow the steps listed to complete the problem.

STEP 1: Open the data file for Problem 12-3B.

STEP 2: Restore the Opening Balance data.

STEP 3: From the Tasks menu, select the Purchases/Receive Inventory option and enter the purchases on account and returns or allowance transactions.

STEP 4: From the Tasks menu, select the Payments option and enter the cash payment transactions.

STEP 5: From the Reports menu, select the General Ledger option and display a General Ledger Trial Balance Report.

STEP 6: From the Reports menu, select the Accounts Payable option and display a schedule of accounts payable, purchases journal, check register, cash disbursements journal reports, and vendor ledgers.

CHAPTER 12 MASTERY PROBLEM

Michelle French owns and operates Books and More, a retail book store. Selected account balances on June 1 are as follows:

General Ledger

Cash	$32,200.00
Accounts Payable	2,000.00
Michelle French, Drawing	18,000.00
Purchases	67,021.66
Purchases Returns and Allowances	2,315.23
Purchases Discounts	905.00
Freight-In	522.60
Rent Expense	3,125.00
Utilities Expense	1,522.87

Accounts Payable Ledger

North-Eastern Publishing Co.	$2,000.00

The following purchases and cash payment transactions took place during the month of June:

June 1   Purchased books on account from Irving Publishing Co., $2,100. Invoice no. 101, terms 2/10, n/30, FOB destination.

2   Issued check no. 300 to North-Eastern Publishing Co. for goods purchased on May 23, terms 2/10, n/30, $1,960 (the $2,000 invoice amount less the 2% discount).

3   Purchased books on account from Broadway Publishing, Inc., $2,880. Invoice no. 711, subject to 20% trade discount, and invoice terms of 3/10, n/30, FOB shipping point.

3   Issued check no. 301 to Mayday Shipping for delivery from Broadway Publishing, Inc., $250.

4   Issued check no. 302 for June rent, $625.

8   Purchased books on account from North-Eastern Publishing Co., $5,825. Invoice no. 268, terms 2/eom, n/60, FOB destination.

10   Received a credit memo from Irving Publishing Co., $550. Books had been returned because the covers were on upside down.

13   Issued check no. 304 to Broadway Publishing, Inc., for the purchase made on June 3. (Check no. 303 was voided because an error was made in preparing it.)

28   Made the following purchases:

Invoice No.	Company	Amount	Terms
579	Broadway Publishing, Inc.	$2,350	2/10, n/30 FOB destination
406	North-Eastern Publishing Co.	4,200	2/eom, n/60 FOB destination
964	Riley Publishing Co.	3,450	3/10, n/30 FOB destination

30   Issued check no. 305 to Taylor County Utility Co., for June utilities, $325.

30   French withdrew cash for personal use, $4,500. Issued check no. 306.

30   Issued check no. 307 to Irving Publishing Co. for purchase made on June 1 less returns made on June 10.

30   Issued check no. 308 to North-Eastern Publishing Co. for purchase made on June 8.

30   Issued check no. 309 for books purchased at an auction, $1,328.

In the Chapter 12 Mastery Problem, you will use the Peachtree Accounting software to process purchases and cash payments, and to display a trial balance, cost of goods sold statement, schedule of accounts payable, purchases journal, check register, and cash disbursements. Follow the steps listed to complete the problem.

STEP 1: Open the data file for the Chapter 12 Mastery Problem.

STEP 2: Restore the Opening Balance data.

STEP 3 From the Tasks menu, select the Purchases/Receive Inventory option and enter the purchases on account and returns or allowance transactions.

STEP 4: From the Tasks menu, select the Payments option and enter the cash payment transactions.

Note: In the cash payment on the 2nd to North-Eastern Publishing Co., you must enter $40.00 discount manually. The computer will not automatically calculate it. For the cash payment on the 30th (check no. 309), make the check payable to Auction.

STEP 5: From the Reports menu, select the Financial Statements option and display a Cost of Goods Sold Statement.

STEP 6: From the Reports menu, select the General Ledger option and display a General Ledger Trial Balance Report.

STEP 7: From the Reports menu, select the Accounts Payable option and display a schedule of accounts payable, purchases journal, check register, and cash disbursements journal reports.

CHAPTER 13 DEMONSTRATION PROBLEM (13-DEMO)

During the month of May, 2000, David's Specialty Shop engaged in the following transactions:

May 1 Sold merchandise on account to Molly Mac, $2,000 plus tax of $100. Sale no. 533.
2 Issued check no. 750 to Kari Co. in partial payment of May 1 balance, $800 less 2% discount.
3 Purchased merchandise on account from Scanlan Wholesalers $2,000. Invoice no. 621, dated May 3, terms 2/10, n/30.
4 Purchased merchandise on account from Simpson Enterprises $1,500. Invoice no. 767, dated May 4, 2/15, n/30.
4 Issued check no. 751 in payment of telephone expense for the month of December, $200.
8 Sold merchandise for cash, $3,600, plus tax of $180.
9 Received payment from Cody Slaton in full settlement of Invoice no 480, $2,500.
10 Issued check no. 752 to Scanlan Wholesalers in payment of May 1 balance of $1200.
12 Sold merchandise on account to Cody Slaton, $3,000 plus tax of $150. Sale no. 534.
12 Received payment from Kori Reynolds on account, $2,100.
13 Issued check no. 753 to Simpson Enterprises in payment of May 4 purchase. Invoice no. 767, less 2% discount.
13 Cody Slayton returned merchandise for credit, $1,000 plus sales tax, $50.00. Invoice no. 480.
17 Returned merchandise to Johnson Essentials for credit towards Invoice no. 580, $500.
22 Received payment from Natalie Gabbert on account, $1,555.
27 Sold merchandise on account to Natalie Gabbert, $2,000 plus tax of $100. Sale no. 535.
29 Issued check no. 754 in payment of wages (Wages Expense) for the four-week period ending May 30, $1,100.

STEP 1: Open the data file for the Chapter 13 Demonstration Problem.

STEP 2: Restore the Opening Balance data.

STEP 3 From the Tasks menu, select the Purchases/Receive Inventory option and enter the purchases on account and returns or allowance transactions.

STEP 4: From the Tasks Menu, select the Sales/Invoicing option and enter the sales on account transactions into the Sales/Invoicing window.

▶ Enter "Merchandise" in the Description field.
▶ Verify that "CT" is selected for the Sales Tax Code in the lower left portion of the window.

STEP 5: Enter the credit memo transactions into the Sales/Invoicing window.

▶ Enter CM followed by the credit memo number into the Invoice No. field (e.g., CM33).
▶ Enter "Credit Memo" in the Description field.
▶ Enter the account number for Sales Returns and Allowance in the GL Account field.
▶ Enter the credit memo amount as a negative number.

STEP 6: From the Tasks menu, select the Payments option and enter the cash payment transactions.

STEP 7: From the Tasks menu, select the Receipts option and enter the cash receipts on account transactions.

▶ Enter Deposit ticket ID of "05/09/00."
▶ Enter the invoice number provided as the reference.
▶ Enter "On account" in the Description Field.

▶ Be sure to apply in applicable credit memos.

STEP 8: Enter the cash sales into the Receipts window.

▶ Enter Deposit ticket ID of "05/31/00".
▶ Enter "Cash sales" in the Name field; enter "Cash sales" in the Description field.
▶ Enter the credit to sales in the Amount field.
▶ Select "CT" in the Sales Tax Code field near the bottom of the screen.

STEP 9: From the Reports menu, select the General Ledger option and display a General Ledger Trial Balance Report.

STEP 10: From the Reports menu, select the Accounts Payable option and display the following reports:

Vendors Ledgers Report
Purchases Journal
Check Register
Cash Disbursements Journal with Titles.

STEP 11: From the Reports menu select the accounts receivable option and display the following reports:

Sales Journal with Titles
Cash Receipts Journal with Titles
Invoice Register
Customers Ledgers Report

PROBLEM 13-2A

Zebra Imaginarium, a retail business, had the following cash receipts during December 2000. The sales tax is 6%.

Dec. 1 Received payment on account from Michael Anderson, $1,360.
    2   Received payment on account from Ansel Manufacturing, $382.
    7   Cash sales for the week, $3,160 plus tax. Bank credit card sales for the week, $1,000 plus tax. Bank credit card fee is 3%.
    8   Received payment on account from J. Gorbea, $880.
    11 Michael Anderson returned merchandise for a credit, $60 plus tax.; Invoice no. 892.
    14 Cash sales for the week, $2,800 plus tax. Bank credit card sales for the week, $800 plus tax. Bank credit card fee is 3%.
    20 Received payment on account from Tom Wilson, $1,110.
    21 Ansel Manufacturing returned merchandise for a credit,. $22 plus tax; Invoice no. 902
    21 Cash sales for the week, $3,200 plus tax.
    24 Received payment on account from Rachel Carson, $2,000.

STEP 1: Open the data file for the Problem 13-2A.

STEP 2: Restore the Opening Balance data.

STEP 3: From the Tasks menu, select the Receipts option and enter the cash receipts on account transactions.

▶ Enter Deposit ticket ID of "12/31/00."
▶ Enter the invoice number as the reference.

- Enter "On account" in the Description Field.
- Be sure to apply any applicable credit memos.

STEP 4: Enter the cash sales into the Receipts window.

- Enter Deposit ticket ID of "12/31/00".
- Enter "Cash sales" in the Name field; enter "Cash sales" in the Reference field..
- On the first line of the Apply to Revenues section, enter the cash sales; enter "Cash sales" in the Description.
- On the second line, enter the credit card sales; enter "Credit card sales" in the Description.
- On the third line, enter the bank fees as a negative number; enter "Bank fees" in the Description; enter the account number for Bank Credit Card Expense; enter a sales tax code of 2 (no sales tax).
- Select "Kansas" in the Sales Tax Code field near the bottom of the screen.

STEP 5: Enter the credit memo transactions into the Sales/Invoicing window.

- Enter CM followed by the credit memo number into the Invoice No. field (e.g., CM33).
- Enter "Credit Memo" in the Description field.
- Enter the account number for Sales Returns and Allowance in the GL Account field.
- Enter the credit memo amount as a negative number.
- Select a Sales Tax Code for Kansas.

STEP 6: Display the accounts receivable reports.

- From the Reports menu, select the Accounts Receivable option.
- Display the Sales Journal with Titles.
- Display the Cash Receipts Journal with Titles.
- Display the Customer Ledgers Report.
- Display a Trial Balance Report.

STEP 7: If errors are detected on the reports, return to the appropriate data entry window (Sales/Invoicing or Receipts) and use the Edit Icon Bar button to select the transaction in error and make corrections.

PROBLEM 13-2B

Color Florists, a retail business, had the following cash receipts during January 2000. The sales tax is 5%.

Jan.		
	1	Received payment on account from Ray Boyd, $880.
	3	Received payment on account from Clint Hassell, $271.
	5	Cash sales for the week, $2,800 plus tax. Bank credit card sales for the week, $1,200 plus tax. Bank credit card fee is 3%.
	8	Received payment on account from Jan Sowada, $912.
	11	Ray Boyd returned merchandise for a credit, $40 plus tax.; Invoice no. 892.
	12	Cash sales for the week, $3,100 plus tax. Bank credit card sales for the week, $1,900 plus tax. Bank credit card fee is 3%.
	15	Received payment on account from Robert Zehnle, $1,100.
	18	Robert Zehnle returned merchandise for a credit,. $31 plus tax; Invoice no. 902
	19	Cash sales for the week, $2,230 plus tax.
	25	Received payment on account from Dazai Manufacturing, $318.

STEP 1: Open the data file for the Problem 13-2B.

STEP 2: Restore the Opening Balance data.

STEP 3: From the Tasks menu, select the Receipts option and enter the cash receipts on account transactions.

- Enter Deposit ticket ID of "01/31/00."
- Enter the invoice number as the reference.
- Enter "On account" in the Description Field.
- Be sure to apply any applicable credit memos.

STEP 4: Enter the cash sales into the Receipts window.

- Enter Deposit ticket ID of "01/31/00".
- Enter "Cash sales" in the Name field; enter "Cash sales" in the Reference field..
- On the first line of the Apply to Revenues section, enter the cash sales; enter "Cash sales" in the Description.
- On the second line, enter the credit card sales; enter "Credit card sales" in the Description.
- On the third line, enter the bank fees as a negative number; enter "Bank fees" in the Description; enter the account number for Bank Credit Card Expense; enter a sales tax code of 2 (no sales tax).
- Select "Oregon" in the Sales Tax Code field near the bottom of the screen.

STEP 5: Enter the credit memo transactions into the Sales/Invoicing window.

- Enter CM followed by the credit memo number into the Invoice No. field (e.g., CM33).
- Enter "Credit Memo" in the Description field.
- Enter the account number for Sales Returns and Allowance in the GL Account field.
- Enter the credit memo amount as a negative number.
- Select a Sales Tax Code for Oregon.

STEP 6: Display the accounts receivable reports.

- From the Reports menu, select the Accounts Receivable option.
- Display the Sales Journal with Titles.
- Display the Cash Receipts Journal with Titles.
- Display the Customer Ledgers Report.
- Display a Trial Balance Report.

STEP 7: If errors are detected on the reports, return to the appropriate data entry window (Sales/Invoicing or Receipts) and use the Edit Icon Bar button to select the transaction in error and make corrections.

CHAPTER 13 MASTERY PROBLEM

During the month of Oct, 2000, The Pink Petal flower shop engaged in the following transactions:

Oct 1 Sold merchandise on account to Elizabeth Shoemaker, $1,000 plus sales tax. Sale no. 222.
    2 Issued check no. 190 to Jill Hand in payment of October 1 balance of $500, less 2% discount.

2	Purchased merchandise on account from Flower Wholesalers $4,000. Invoice no. 500, dated October 2, terms 2/10, n/30.
4	Purchased merchandise on account from Seidl Enterprises $700. Invoice no. 527, dated October 4, terms 2/15, n/30.
5	Issued check no. 191 in payment of telephone expense for the month of September, $150.
7	Sold merchandise for cash, $3500, plus tax of $175.
9	Received payment from Leigh Summers in full settlement of account, $2,000.
11	Issued check no. 192 to Flower Wholesalers in payment of October 1 balance of $1,500.
12	Sold merchandise on account to Leigh Summers, $2,000 plus sales tax. Sale no. 223.
12	Received payment from Meg Johnson on account, $3,100.
13	Issued check no. 193 to Seidl Enterprises in payment of October 4 purchase.
14	Meg Johnson returned merchandise for a credit, $300 plus sales tax; Invoice no. 212.
17	Returned merchandise to Vases Etc. for credit, $900; Invoice no. 580.
24	Received payment from David's Decorating on account, $2,135.
27	Sold merchandise on account to David's Decorating, $3,000 plus sales tax. Sale no. 224.
29	Issured check no. 194 in payment of wages (Wages Expense) for the four-week period ending October 30, $900.

STEP 1:   Open the data file for the Chapter 13 Demonstration Problem.

STEP 2:   Restore the Opening Balance data.

STEP 3   From the Tasks menu, select the Purchases/Receive Inventory option and enter the purchases on account and returns or allowance transactions.

STEP 4:   From the Tasks Menu, select the Sales/Invoicing option and enter the sales on account transactions into the Sales/Invoicing window.

▶ Enter "Merchandise" in the Description field.
▶ Verify that "CT" is selected for the Sales Tax Code in the lower left portion of the window.

STEP 5:   Enter the credit memo transactions into the Sales/Invoicing window.

▶ Enter CM followed by the credit memo number into the Invoice No. field (e.g., CM33).
▶ Enter "Credit Memo" in the Description field.
▶ Enter the account number for Sales Returns and Allowance in the GL Account field.
▶ Enter the credit memo amount as a negative number.

STEP 6:   From the Tasks menu, select the Payments option and enter the cash payment transactions.

STEP 7:   From the Tasks menu, select the Receipts option and enter the cash receipts on account transactions.

▶ Enter Deposit ticket ID of "05/09/00."
▶ Enter the invoice number provided as the reference.
▶ Enter "On account" in the Description Field.
▶ Be sure to apply in applicable credit memos.

STEP 8:   Enter the cash sales into the Receipts window.

▶ Enter "Cash sales" in the Name field; enter "Cash sales" in the Description field.
▶ Enter the credit to sales in the Amount field.
▶ Select "CT" in the Sales Tax Code field near the bottom of the screen.

STEP 9: From the Reports menu, select the General Ledger option and display a General Ledger Trial Balance Report.

STEP 10: From the Reports menu, select the Accounts Payable option and display the following reports:

Vendors Ledgers Report
Purchases Journal
Check Register
Cash Disbursements Journal with Titles.

STEP 11: From the Reports menu select the accounts receivable option and display the following reports:

Sales Journal with Titles
Cash Receipts Journal with Titles
Invoice Register
Customers Ledgers Report

CHAPTER 14 DEMONSTRATION PROBLEM (14-DEMO)

Harpo, Inc., is a retail novelty store. The following transactions relate to operations for the month of March.

March 2 Issued voucher no. 313 to Tremont Rental for March rent, $500.
2 Issued check no. 450 to Tremont Rental, $500. Voucher no. 313.
3 Purchased merchandise from Gail's Gags, $550, terms 2/15, n/60. Voucher no. 314.
4 Purchased merchandise from Silly Sam's, $200, terms 2/10, n/60. Voucher no. 315.
10 Issued check no. 451 to Jerry's Jokes, $500 less $10 discount. Voucher no. 310.
12 Received a credit memo from Silly Sam's for returned merchandise that was purchased on March 4, $100.
14 Issued check no. 452 to Resource Supplies, $250. Voucher no. 311.
16 Purchased merchandise from Giggles, $700, terms 2/10, n/30. Voucher no. 316.
18 Issued check no. 453 to Gail's Gags for purchase made on March 3 less 2% discount. Voucher no. 314.
19 Issued check no. 454 to Donnelly's, $750. Voucher no. 312.
21 Purchased merchandise from Creations, $870, terms 3/15, n/50. Voucher no. 317.
25 Purchased supplies from Hal's Supply, $120, terms 3/10, n/30. Voucher no. 318.
31 Issued check no. 455 to Silly Sam's for purchase made on March 4 less returns made on March 12. Voucher no. 315.
31 Issued voucher no. 319 to Payroll in payment of March wages, $1,250.
31 Issued check no. 456 to Payroll, $1,250. Voucher no. 319.

The Chapter 14 Demonstration Problem involves processing accounts payable transactions using a voucher system. All vouchers as well as returns and allowances will be entered into the Purchases/Receive Inventory window. Payment of vouchers will be processed through the Payments window. Once all the transactions have been entered, the various accounts payable reports will be generated. Follow the step-by-step instructions provided to solve the problem.

STEP 1: Open the data file for the Chapter 14 Demonstration Problem.

STEP 2: Restore the Opening Balance data.

STEP 3: From the Tasks menu, select the Purchases/Receive Inventory option and enter the vouchers and returns and allowance transactions.

Entering Voucher Transactions:

▶ Enter or select the vendor number.
▶ Enter the Voucher Number in the Invoice Number field.
▶ Enter the Date of the transaction.
▶ Verify that the terms of the sale are correctly indicated. If not, click on the right arrow button at the end of the Terms field and a Term Information window will appear allowing you to enter the pertinent discount data.
▶ On the Apply to Purchases tab, enter a description of the transaction in the Description field. For example, enter "March rent" for the rent payment on March 2nd.
▶ Enter or select the account number of the account to be debited in the GL Account field.
▶ Enter the amount of the voucher in the Amount field.
▶ Click on Post to record the transaction.

An example of the recording of a new voucher is illustrated in the Purchases/Receive Inventory window shown in Figure 2.26.

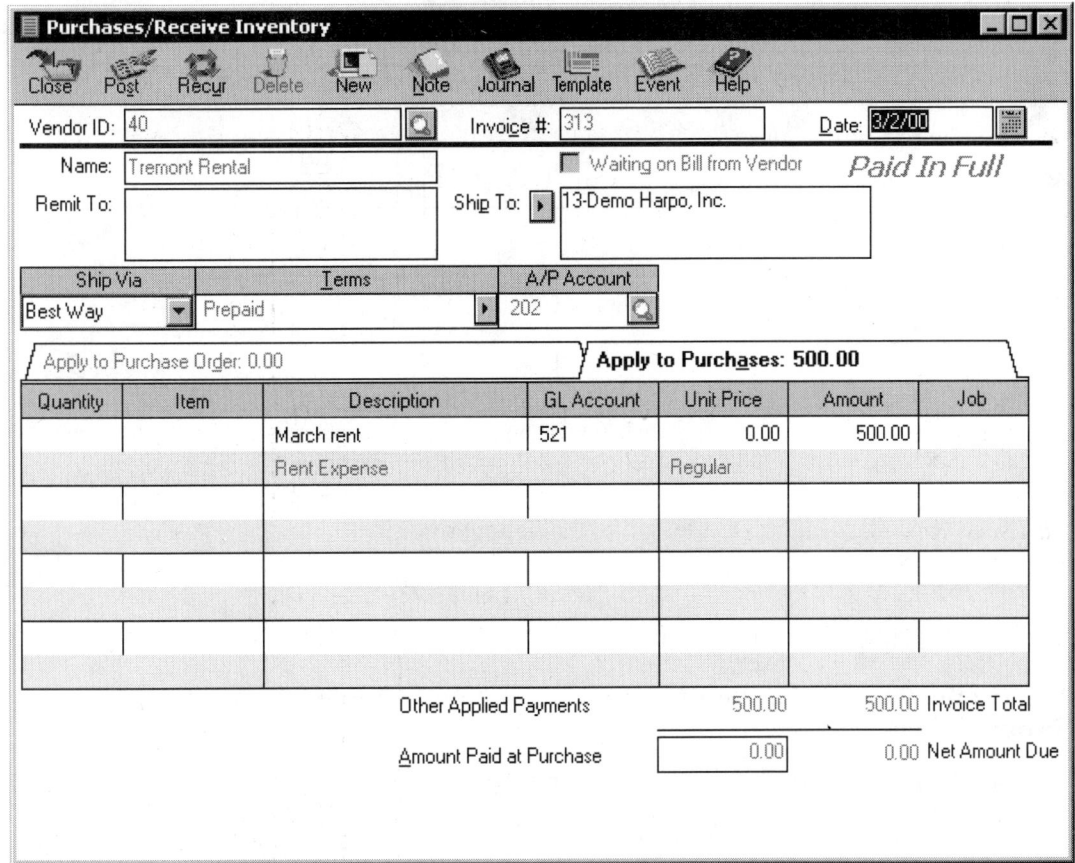

FIGURE 2.26 Purchases/Receive Inventory (New Voucher)

Entering Purchases Returns and Allowance Transactions:

▶ Enter or select the Vendor ID number.
▶ Enter an Invoice Number consisting of CM plus the original voucher number.
▶ Verify that the terms of the sale are correct; if not, click on the right arrow button in the Terms field and enter correct terms.

- ▶ Enter "Credit memo" as the Description.
- ▶ Enter the Purchases Returns and Allowances Account Number in the GL Account field.
- ▶ Enter the amount of the credit memo received as a negative number.
- ▶ Click on Post to record the transaction.

The recording of a Purchase Return transaction is illustrated in the Purchases/Receive Inventory window shown in Figure 2.27.

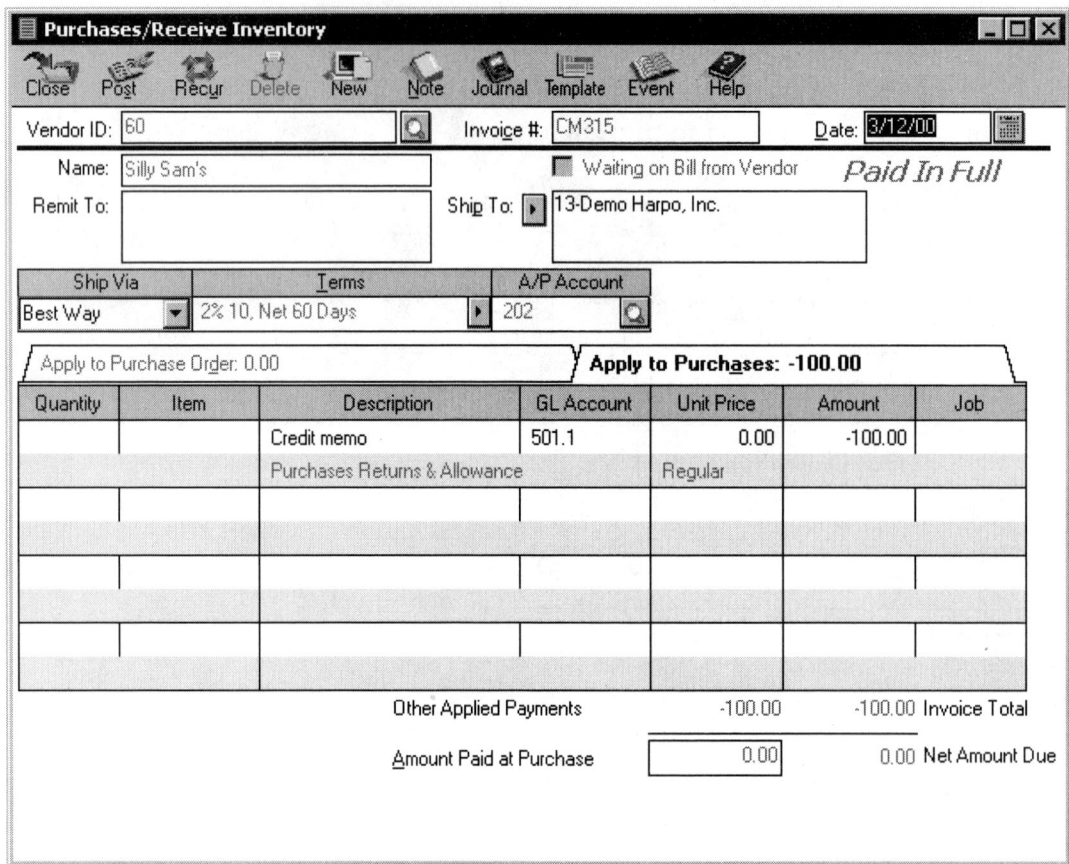

FIGURE 2.27 Purchases/Receive Inventory (Purchases Return)

STEP 4: From the Tasks menu, select the Payments option and enter the voucher payment transactions.

In the voucher system, all cash disbursements are vouchered and entered into the accounts payable system and later paid through the Payments window. There are no direct payments. Because all cash disbursements go through accounts payable, all voucher payments are, in effect, payments on account.

When entering voucher payments, you must select the vouchers you wish to pay and apply the appropriate credit memos to the voucher(s).

Voucher Payment (Apply to Invoices Tab):

- ▶ Enter or select the Vendor ID number.
- ▶ Enter the Check Number.
- ▶ Enter the Date of the check.

- Under the Apply to Invoices tab, click on the Pay box for the voucher or vouchers to be paid. Click on the Pay box for any credit memos that are to be applied to this payment.
- Click on Post to record the payment.

An example of a payment of a voucher transaction is illustrated in Figure 2.28.

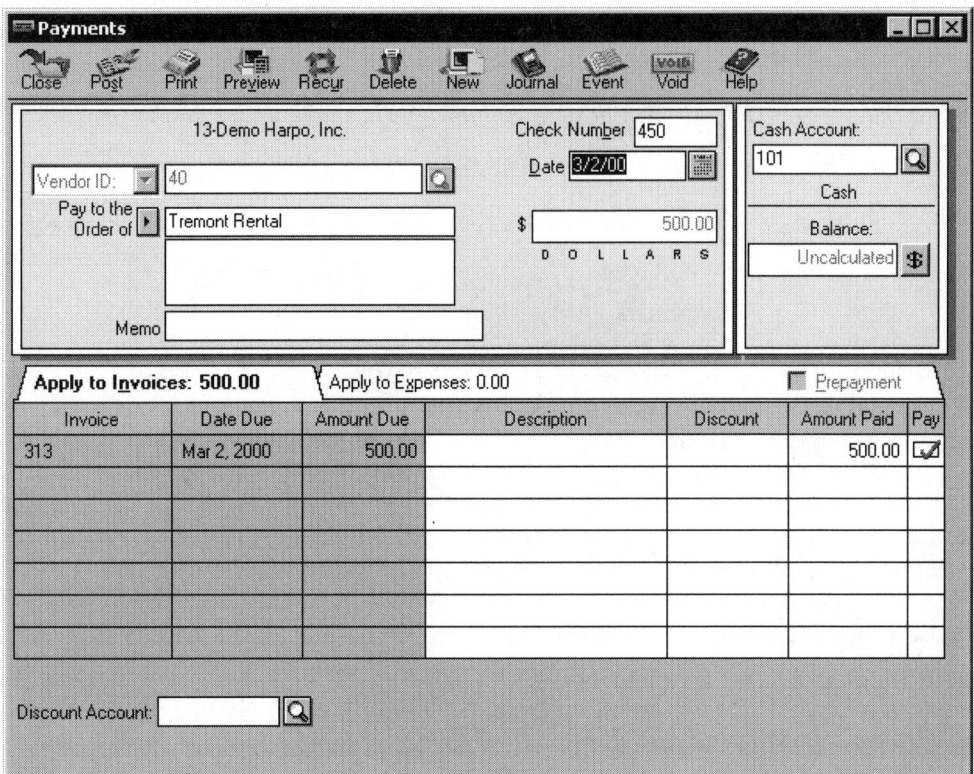

FIGURE 2.28 Payments Window (Payment of Voucher)

STEP 5:   Display a General Ledger Trial Balance Report.

STEP 6:   From the Reports menu, select the Accounts Payable option and display a schedule of vouchers payable, purchases journal, check register, and cash disbursements journal with titles reports.

STEP 7:   If errors are detected on the reports, return to the appropriate data entry window (Purchases/Receive Inventory or Payments) and use the Edit Icon Bar button to select the transaction in error and make corrections.

See the solution section of this workbook for the solution to the demonstration problem.

PROBLEM 14-3A

Betty Classic owns the Classic Candle Shop. The following transactions occurred during April 2000. The Classic Candle Shop uses a voucher register, a check register, and a general ledger. Unpaid vouchers are filed and listed at the end of the month. General ledger account balances on April 1 were: Cash, $5,189; and Supplies, $408.

Date	Voucher No.	Issued To	Amount	Purpose	Terms
4/1	1101	Landmark Realty	$ 500	April rent	
4/3	1102	Wax House	280	Merchandise	2/10, n/30
4/5	1103	Designs West	490	Merchandise	2/10, n/30
4/9	1104	Crane Stationers	180	Office supplies	
4/11	1105	Magic Solutions	600	Merchandise	2/10, n/30
4/15	1106	Payroll	1,500	Bimonthly payroll	
4/23	1107	Wax House	510	Merchandise	1/10, n/30
4/25	1108	Baskets & More	440	Merchandise	2/10, n/30
4/28	1109	Magic Solutions	450	Merchandise	2/10, n/30
4/30	1110	Payroll	1,500	Bimonthly payroll	

Checks issued:

Date	Check No.	Payee	Voucher No.	Amount
4/1	928	Landmark Realty	1101	$ 500
4/9	929	Crane Stationers	1104	180
4/11	930	Wax House	1102	280
4/15	931	Payroll	1106	1,500
4/19	932	Designs West	1103	490
4/30	933	Payroll	1110	1,500

In Problem 14-3A, all vouchers as well as returns and allowances will be entered into the Purchases/Receive Inventory window. Payment of vouchers will be processed through the Payments window. Once all the transactions have been entered, the various accounts payable reports will be generated. Follow the step-by-step instructions provided to solve the problem.

STEP 1: Open the data file for Problem 14-3A.

STEP 2: Restore the Opening Balance data.

STEP 3: From the Tasks menu, select the Purchases/Receive Inventory option and enter the vouchers and returns and allowance transactions. Verify that the default terms on the Purchases window are correct. If not, enter the correct terms for that transaction.

STEP 4: From the Tasks menu, select the Payments option and enter the voucher payment transactions.

STEP 5: Display a General Ledger Trial Balance Report.

STEP 6: From the Reports menu, select the Accounts Payable option and display a schedule of vouchers payable, purchases journal, check register, and cash disbursements journal with titles reports.

STEP 7: If errors are detected on the reports, return to the appropriate data entry window (Purchases/Receive Inventory or Payments) and use the Edit Icon Bar button to select the transaction in error and make corrections.

PROBLEM 14-3B

Jane Hledik is owner of Hledik Lawn Supply. The following transactions occurred during April 2000. Hledik Lawn Supply uses a voucher register, a check register, and a general ledger. Unpaid vouchers are filed and listed at the end of the month. General ledger account balances on April 1 were: Cash, $5,189; and Supplies, $408.

Vouchers issued:

Date	Voucher No.	Issued To	Amount	Purpose	Terms
4/2	662	Brenner's	$600	April rent	
4/4	663	Lawn Care Wholesale	300	Merchandise	2/10, n/30
4/7	664	Southern Supply	128	Office supplies	
4/10	665	Clay's Chemicals	420	Merchandise	1/20, n/30
4/13	666	Mendel & Son	530	Merchandise	2/10, n/30
4/15	667	Payroll	950	Bimonthly payroll	
4/19	668	Lawn Care Wholesale	570	Merchandise	1/10, n/30
4/27	669	Southern Supply	99	Office supplies	
4/29	670	Lakeside Fertilizer	280	Merchandise	2/10, n/30
4/30	671	Payroll	950	Bimonthly payroll	

Checks issued:

Date	Check No.	Payee	Voucher No.	Amount
4/2	748	Brenner's	662	$600
4/7	749	Southern Supply	664	128
4/11	750	Lawn Care Wholesale	663	300
4/15	751	Payroll	667	950
4/20	752	Mendel & Son	666	530
4/30	753	Payroll	671	950

In Problem 14-3B, all vouchers as well as returns and allowances will be entered into the Purchases/Receive Inventory window. Payment of vouchers will be processed through the Payments window. Once all the transactions have been entered, the various accounts payable reports will be generated. Follow the step-by-step instructions provided to solve the problem.

STEP 1: Open the data file for Problem 14-3B.

STEP 2: Restore the Opening Balance data.

STEP 3: From the Tasks menu, select the Purchases/Receive Inventory option and enter the vouchers and returns and allowance transactions. Verify that the default terms in the Purchases window are correct. If not, enter the correct terms for that transaction.

STEP 4: From the Tasks menu, select the Payments option and enter the voucher payment transactions.

STEP 5: Display a General Ledger Trial Balance Report.

STEP 6: From the Reports menu, select the Accounts Payable option and display a schedule of vouchers payable, purchases journal, check register, and cash disbursements journal with titles reports.

STEP 7: If errors are detected on the reports, return to the appropriate data entry window (Purchases/Receive Inventory or Payments) and use the Edit Icon Bar button to select the transaction in error and make corrections.

CHAPTER 14 MASTERY PROBLEM

Sunshine Flower Shop began operations in the month of July. The following transactions occurred during the first month of the business.

July 1   Purchased merchandise from Thorny Wholesale, $600. Voucher no. 1.
2   Issued check no. 1 to Strongs Rental for July rent, $1,000. Voucher no. 2
3   Purchased merchandise from Flowerbed, Inc., $470, terms 2/15, n/60, FOB shipping point. Voucher no. 3.
7   Issued check no. 2 to Thorny Wholesale in partial payment for goods purchased on July 1, $300. Voucher no. 1. Issued new voucher nos. 4 and 5.
9   Issued check no. 3 to Charlie's Trucking for shipping charges, $20. Voucher no. 6.
15   Issued check no. 4 to Payroll for wages, $600. Voucher no. 7.
16   Purchased merchandise from Petals Co., $377, terms 2/15, n/30. Voucher no. 8.
17   Purchased merchandise from Weeds Plus, $436, terms 3/15, n/60. Voucher no. 9.
18   Issued check no. 5 to Flowerbed, Inc., for goods purchased on July 3 less discount. Voucher no. 3.
23   Purchased supplies from Staples Supply, $150. Voucher no. 10.
25   Received a credit memo from Weeds Plus for returned merchandise that was purchased on July 17, $80.
31   Issued check no. 6 to Petals Co. for goods purchased on July 16 less discount. Voucher no. 8.
31   Issued check no. 7 to Payroll for wages, $600. Voucher no. 11.

The general ledger accounts are listed below. The $6,000 with which the Flower Shop began business is entered in the cash account. Only this account has a beginning balance.

Account	Number
Cash	101
Supplies	141
Vouchers Payable	202
Purchases	501
Purchases Returns and Allowances	501.1
Purchases Discounts	501.2
Freight-In	502
Wages Expense	511
Rent Expense	521

In the Chapter 14 Mastery Problem, all vouchers as well as returns and allowances will be entered into the Purchases/Receive Inventory window. Payment of vouchers will be processed through the Payments window. Once all the transactions have been entered, the various accounts payable reports will be generated. Follow the step-by-step instructions provided to solve the problem.

STEP 1: Open the data file for the Chapter 14 Mastery Problem.

STEP 2: Restore the Opening Balance data.

STEP 3: From the Tasks menu, select the Purchases/Receive Inventory option and enter the vouchers and returns and allowance transactions.

Note: Because a voucher system is being used, all cash disbursements must be first recorded in the Purchase/Receive Inventory window before payment is made.

STEP 4: From the Tasks menu, select the Payments option and enter the voucher payment transactions.

Note: The transaction on the 7th of July involves a partial payment to Thorny Wholesale. In the manual solution, the original voucher 1 is canceled and two new vouchers are issued to make the partial payments. With the Peachtree Accounting software, you simply specify the partial payment of $300.00. The software will handle the remaining payment. There is no need to issue the 2 additional vouchers.

STEP 5: Display a General Ledger Trial Balance Report.

STEP 6: From the Reports menu, select the Accounts Payable option and display a schedule of vouchers payable, purchases journal, check register, and cash disbursements journal with titles reports.

STEP 7: If errors are detected on the reports, return to the appropriate data entry window (Purchases/Receive Inventory or Payments) and use the Edit Icon Bar button to select the transaction in error and make corrections.

PROBLEM 15-1A

The trial balance for the Seaside Kite Shop, a business owned by Joyce Kennington, is shown in Figure 2.29 on the following page. Year-end adjustment information is as follows:

(a, b) Merchandise inventory costing $30,000 is on hand as of December 31, 2000.

(c) Supplies remaining at the end of the year, $2,700.

(d) Unexpired insurance on December 31, $2,900.

(e) Depreciation expense on the building for 2000, $5,000.

(f) Depreciation expense on the store equipment for 2000, $3,200.

(g) Unearned rent revenue as of December 31, $2,200.

(h) Wages earned but not paid as of December 31, $900.

In Problem 15-1A, you will enter the adjusting entries and display the financial statements for a merchandising business. When the Peachtree Accounting software prepares the income statement, it assumes that you are using a perpetual inventory and a cost of goods sold account approach. The income statement in the problems utilize a physical inventory approach whereby the cost of goods sold is calculated based on beginning inventory, cost accounts, and ending inventory. This can easily be circumvented by simply adding a cost account titled "Inventory Adjustment" and adjusting the merchandise inventory account to this account rather than the income summary account. This will allow the computer to total up a cost of goods sold figure on the income statement as shown in Figure 2.30. The inventory adjustment account gets closed to equity at the end of the period in the same way that Income Summary would in a manual system.

Cost of Goods Sold

Purchase	27,000.00
Purchases Returns and Allowances	<1,400.00>
Purchases Discounts	<1,800.00>
Freight-In	2,100.00
Inventory Adjustment	<5,000.00>
Total Cost of Goods Sold	20,900.00

FIGURE 2.30 Cost of Goods Sold Section of Income Statement

Seaside Kite Shop
Trial Balance
December 31, 20 - -

ACCOUNT TITLE	DEBIT BALANCE	CREDIT BALANCE
Cash	20 0 0 0 00	
Accounts Receivable	14 0 0 0 00	
Merchandise Inventory	25 0 0 0 00	
Supplies	8 0 0 0 00	
Prepaid Insurance	5 4 0 0 00	
Land	30 0 0 0 00	
Building	50 0 0 0 00	
Accumulated Depreciation—Building		20 0 0 0 00
Store Equipment	35 0 0 0 00	
Accumulated Depreciation—Store Equipment		14 0 0 0 00
Accounts Payable		9 6 0 0 00
Wages Payable		
Sales Tax Payable		5 9 0 0 00
Unearned Rent Revenue		8 9 0 0 00
Mortgage Payable		45 0 0 0 00
Joyce Kennington, Capital		65 4 1 0 00
Joyce Kennington, Drawing	26 0 0 0 00	
Income Summary		
Sales		118 0 0 0 00
Sales Returns and Allowances	1 7 0 0 00	
Rent Revenue		
Purchases	27 0 0 0 00	
Purchases Returns and Allowances		1 4 0 0 00
Purchases Discounts		1 8 0 0 00
Freight-In	2 1 0 0 00	
Wages Expense	32 0 0 0 00	
Advertising Expense	3 6 0 0 00	
Supplies Expense		
Telephone Expense	1 3 5 0 00	
Utilities Expense	8 0 0 0 00	
Insurance Expense		
Depreciation Expense—Building		
Depreciation Expense—Store Equipment		
Miscellaneous Expense	8 6 0 00	
	290 0 1 0 00	290 0 1 0 00

FIGURE 2.29 Seaside Kite Shop Trial Balance

STEP 1:   Open the data file for Problem 15-1A.

STEP 2:   Restore the Opening Balance data.

STEP 3:   Enter the adjusting entries for this problem. Use the letters (a), (b), etc., as the reference for the adjusting general journal entries.

STEP 4:   Display the General Journal Entries with Titles Report.

STEP 5:   Display a Trial Balance Report.

STEP 6:   Display the financial statements: Basic Income Statement, Owner's Equity Statement, and Balance Sheet.

PROBLEM 15-2A

The trial balance for Cascade Bicycle Shop, a business owned by David Lamond, is shown in Figure 2.31 on the following page. Year-end adjustment information is provided:

(a, b)   Merchandise inventory costing $22,000 is on hand as of December 31, 2000.

(c)   Supplies remaining at the end of the year, $2,400.

(d)   Unexpired insurance on December 31, $1,750.

(e)   Depreciation expense on the building for 2000, $4,000.

(f)   Depreciation expense on the store equipment for 2000, $3,600.

(g)   Unearned storage revenue as of December 31, $1,950.

(h)   Wages earned but not paid as of December 31, $750.

In Problem 15-2A, you will enter the adjusting entries and display the financial statements for a merchandising business. Follow the steps listed below to complete the problem.

STEP 1:   Open the data file for Problem 15-2A.

STEP 2:   Restore the Opening Balance data.

STEP 3:   Enter the adjusting entries for this problem. Use the worksheet letter (a), (b), etc., as the general journal reference for the adjusting entries.

STEP 4:   Display the General Journal Entries with Titles Report.

STEP 5:   Display a Trial Balance Report.

STEP 6:   Display the financial statements: Basic Income Statement, Owner's Equity Statement, and Balance Sheet.

Cascade Bicycle Shop
Trial Balance
December 31, 20- -

ACCOUNT TITLE	DEBIT BALANCE	CREDIT BALANCE
Cash	23 000 00	
Accounts Receivable	15 000 00	
Merchandise Inventory	31 000 00	
Supplies	7 200 00	
Prepaid Insurance	4 600 00	
Land	28 000 00	
Building	53 000 00	
Accumulated Depreciation—Building		17 000 00
Store Equipment	27 000 00	
Accumulated Depreciation—Store Equipment		9 000 00
Accounts Payable		3 800 00
Wages Payable		
Sales Tax Payable		3 050 00
Unearned Storage Revenue		5 600 00
Mortgage Payable		42 000 00
David Lamond, Capital		165 760 00
David Lamond, Drawing	33 000 00	
Income Summary		
Sales		51 000 00
Sales Returns and Allowances	2 400 00	
Storage Revenue		
Purchases	21 000 00	
Purchases Returns and Allowances		1 300 00
Purchases Discounts		1 900 00
Freight-In	1 800 00	
Wages Expense	35 000 00	
Advertising Expense	5 700 00	
Supplies Expense		
Telephone Expense	2 200 00	
Utilities Expense	9 600 00	
Insurance Expense		
Depreciation Expense—Building		
Depreciation Expense—Store Equipment		
Miscellaneous Expense	910 00	
	300 410 00	300 410 00

FIGURE 2.31 Cascade Bicycle Shop Trial Balance

PROBLEM 15-1B

A trial balance for the Basket Corner, a business owned by Linda Palermo, is shown in Figure 2.32 on the following page. Year-end adjustment information is provided:

(a, b) Merchandise inventory costing $24,000 is on hand as of December 31, 2000.

(c) Supplies remaining at the end of the year, $2,100.

(d) Unexpired insurance on December 31, $2,600.

(e) Depreciation expense on the building for 2000, $5,300.

(f) Depreciation expense on the store equipment for 2000, $3,800.

(g) Unearned decorating revenue as of December 31, $1,650.

(h) Wages earned but not paid as of December 31, $750.

In Problem 15-1B, you will enter the adjusting entries and display the financial statements for a merchandising business. Follow the steps listed below to complete the problem.

STEP 1: Open the data file for Problem 15-1B.

STEP 2: Restore the Opening Balance data.

STEP 3: Enter the adjusting entries for this problem. Use the worksheet letters (a), (b), etc., as the general journal reference for the adjusting entries.

STEP 4: Display the General Journal Entries with Titles Report.

STEP 5: Display a Trial Balance Report.

STEP 6: Display the financial statements: Basic Income Statement, Owner's Equity Statement, and Balance Sheet.

Basket Corner
Trial Balance
December 31, 20 - -

ACCOUNT TITLE	DEBIT BALANCE	CREDIT BALANCE
Cash	25 0 0 0 00	
Accounts Receivable	8 1 0 0 00	
Merchandise Inventory	32 0 0 0 00	
Supplies	7 1 0 0 00	
Prepaid Insurance	3 6 0 0 00	
Land	40 0 0 0 00	
Building	45 0 0 0 00	
Accumulated Depreciation—Building		16 0 0 0 00
Store Equipment	27 0 0 0 00	
Accumulated Depreciation—Store Equipment		5 5 0 0 00
Accounts Payable		3 6 0 0 00
Wages Payable		
Sales Tax Payable		6 2 0 0 00
Unearned Decorating Revenue		6 3 0 0 00
Mortgage Payable		36 0 0 0 00
Linda Palermo, Capital		112 0 5 0 00
Linda Palermo, Drawing	31 0 0 0 00	
Income Summary		
Sales		125 0 0 0 00
Sales Returns and Allowances	2 6 0 0 00	
Decorating Revenue		
Purchases	38 0 0 0 00	
Purchases Returns and Allowances		2 2 0 0 00
Purchases Discounts		1 7 0 0 00
Freight-In	1 9 0 0 00	
Wages Expense	38 0 0 0 00	
Advertising Expense	4 2 0 0 00	
Supplies Expense		
Telephone Expense	1 8 7 0 00	
Utilities Expense	8 4 0 0 00	
Insurance Expense		
Depreciation Expense—Building		
Depreciation Expense—Store Equipment		
Miscellaneous Expense	7 8 0 00	
	314 5 5 0 00	314 5 5 0 00

FIGURE 2.32 Basket Corner Trial Balance

PROBLEM 15-2B

The trial balance for Oregon Bike Company, a business owned by Craig Moody, is shown in Figure 2.33 on the following page. Year-end adjustment information is provided:

(a, b) Merchandise inventory costing $26,000 is on hand as of December 31, 2000.

(c) Supplies remaining at the end of the year, $2,500.

(d) Unexpired insurance on December 31, $1,820.

(e) Depreciation expense on the building for 2000, $6,400.

(f) Depreciation expense on the store equipment for 2000, $2,800.

(g) Unearned rent revenue as of December 31, $2,350.

(h) Wages earned but not paid as of December 31, $1,100.

In Problem 15-2B, you will enter the adjusting entries and display the financial statements for a merchandising business. Follow the steps listed below to complete the problem.

STEP 1: Open the data file for Problem 15-2B.

STEP 2: Restore the Opening Balance data.

STEP 3: Enter the adjusting entries for this problem. Use the worksheet letters (a), (b), etc., as the general journal reference for the adjusting entries.

STEP 4: Display the General Journal Entries with Titles Report.

STEP 5: Display a Trial Balance Report.

STEP 6: Display the financial statements: Basic Income Statement, Owner's Equity Statement, and Balance Sheet.

Oregon Bike Company
Trial Balance
December 31, 20- -

ACCOUNT TITLE	DEBIT BALANCE	CREDIT BALANCE
Cash	27 000 00	
Accounts Receivable	12 000 00	
Merchandise Inventory	39 000 00	
Supplies	6 200 00	
Prepaid Insurance	5 800 00	
Land	32 000 00	
Building	58 000 00	
Accumulated Depreciation—Building		27 000 00
Store Equipment	31 000 00	
Accumulated Depreciation—Store Equipment		14 000 00
Accounts Payable		4 900 00
Wages Payable		
Sales Tax Payable		2 900 00
Unearned Rent Revenue		6 100 00
Mortgage Payable		49 000 00
Craig Moody, Capital		169 500 00
Craig Moody, Drawing	36 000 00	
Income Summary		
Sales		58 000 00
Sales Returns and Allowances	3 300 00	
Rent Revenue		
Purchases	19 000 00	
Purchases Returns and Allowances		900 00
Purchases Discounts		1 450 00
Freight-In	800 00	
Wages Expense	47 000 00	
Advertising Expense	6 200 00	
Supplies Expense		
Telephone Expense	1 860 00	
Utilities Expense	8 100 00	
Insurance Expense		
Depreciation Expense —Building		
Depreciation Expense —Store Equipment		
Miscellaneous Expense	490 00	
	333 750 00	333 750 00

FIGURE 2.33 Oregon Bike Company Trial Balance

CHAPTER 15 MASTERY PROBLEM

John Neff owns and operates the Waikiki Surf Shop. A year-end trial balance is shown in Figure 2.34 on the following page. Year-end adjustment data for the Waikiki Surf Shop is as follows:

(a, b)   A physical count shows merchandise inventory costing $45,000 on hand as of December 31, 2000.

(c)   Supplies remaining at the end of the year, $600.

(d)   Unexpired insurance on December 31, $900.

(e)   Depreciation expense on the building for 2000, $6,000.

(f)   Depreciation expense on the store equipment for 2000, $4,500.

(g)   Wages earned but not paid as of December 31, $675.

(h)   Unearned boat rental revenue as of December 31, $3,000.

In the Chapter 15 Mastery Problem, you will enter the adjusting entries and display the financial statements for a merchandising business. Follow the steps listed below to complete the problem.

STEP 1:   Open the data file for the Chapter 15 Mastery Problem.

STEP 2:   Restore the Opening Balance data.

STEP 3:   Enter the adjusting entries. Use the letters (a), (b), etc., as the general journal reference for the adjusting entries.

STEP 4:   Display the General Journal Entries with Titles Report.

STEP 5:   Display a Trial Balance Report.

STEP 6:   Display the financial statements: Basic Income Statement, Owner's Equity Statement, and Balance Sheet.

CHAPTER 16 DEMONSTRATION PROBLEM (16-DEMO)

Tom McKinney owns and operates McK's Home Electronics. He has a store where he sells and repairs televisions and stereo equipment. A completed worksheet for 2000 is provided on page 127. McKinney made a $20,000 additional investment during 2000. The current portion of Mortgage Payable is $1,000. Credit sales for 2000 were $200,000, and the balance of Accounts Receivable on January 1 was $26,000.

In the Chapter 16 Demonstration Problem, you will enter the adjusting entries and display the financial statements for a merchandising business. After the financial statements have been prepared, you will close out the accounting period, and enter the reversing entries.

STEP 1:   Open the data file for the Chapter 16 Demonstration Problem.

STEP 2:   Restore the Opening Balance data.

STEP 3:   Enter the adjusting entries from the worksheet illustrated in the problem. Use the worksheet letters (a), (b), etc., as the reference for the adjusting general journal entries.

Waikiki Surf Shop
Trial Balance
December 31, 20- -

ACCOUNT TITLE	DEBIT BALANCE	CREDIT BALANCE
Cash	30 0 0 0 00	
Accounts Receivable	22 5 0 0 00	
Merchandise Inventory	57 0 0 0 00	
Supplies	2 7 0 0 00	
Prepaid Insurance	3 6 0 0 00	
Land	15 0 0 0 00	
Building	135 0 0 0 00	
Accumulated Depreciation—Building		24 0 0 0 00
Store Equipment	75 0 0 0 00	
Accumulated Depreciation—Store Equipment		22 5 0 0 00
Notes Payable		7 5 0 0 00
Accounts Payable		15 0 0 0 00
Wages Payable		
Unearned Boat Rental Revenue		33 0 0 0 00
John Neff, Capital		233 7 0 0 00
John Neff, Drawing	30 0 0 0 00	
Income Summary		
Sales		300 7 5 0 00
Sales Returns and Allowances	1 8 0 0 00	
Boat Rental Revenue		
Purchases	157 5 0 0 00	
Purchases Returns and Allowances		1 2 0 0 00
Purchases Discounts		1 5 0 0 00
Freight-In	4 5 0 00	
Wages Expense	63 0 0 0 00	
Advertising Expense	11 2 5 0 00	
Supplies Expense		
Telephone Expense	5 2 5 0 00	
Utilities Expense	18 0 0 0 00	
Insurance Expense		
Depreciation Expense—Building		
Depreciation Expense—Store Equipment		
Miscellaneous Expense	10 8 7 5 00	
Interest Expense	2 2 5 00	
	639 1 5 0 00	639 1 5 0 00

FIGURE 2.34 Waikiki Surf Shop Trial Balance

McK's Home Electronics
Work Sheet
For Year Ended December 31, 20-1

#	ACCOUNT TITLE	TRIAL BALANCE DEBIT	TRIAL BALANCE CREDIT	ADJUSTMENTS DEBIT	ADJUSTMENTS CREDIT	ADJUSTED TRIAL BALANCE DEBIT	ADJUSTED TRIAL BALANCE CREDIT	INCOME STATEMENT DEBIT	INCOME STATEMENT CREDIT	BALANCE SHEET DEBIT	BALANCE SHEET CREDIT
1	Cash	10 000 00				10 000 00				10 000 00	
2	Accounts Receivable	22 500 00				22 500 00				22 500 00	
3	Merchandise Inventory	39 000 00		(b) 45 000 00	(a) 39 000 00	45 000 00				45 000 00	
4	Supplies	2 700 00			(c) 2 100 00	600 00				600 00	
5	Prepaid Insurance	3 600 00			(d) 2 700 00	900 00				900 00	
6	Land	15 000 00				15 000 00				15 000 00	
7	Building	135 000 00				135 000 00				135 000 00	
8	Accum. Depr.—Building		24 000 00		(e) 6 000 00		30 000 00				30 000 00
9	Store Equipment	75 000 00				75 000 00				75 000 00	
10	Accum. Depr.—Store Equipment		22 500 00		(f) 4 500 00		27 000 00				27 000 00
11	Notes Payable		7 500 00				7 500 00				7 500 00
12	Accounts Payable		15 000 00				15 000 00				15 000 00
13	Wages Payable				(g) 675 00		675 00				675 00
14	Sales Tax Payable		2 250 00				2 250 00				2 250 00
15	Unearned Repair Fees		18 000 00	(h) 15 000 00			3 000 00				3 000 00
16	Mortgage Payable		45 000 00				45 000 00				45 000 00
17	Tom McKinney, Capital		151 600 00				151 600 00				151 600 00
18	Tom McKinney, Drawing	30 000 00				30 000 00				30 000 00	
19	Income Summary			(a) 39 000 00	(b) 45 000 00	39 000 00	45 000 00	39 000 00	45 000 00		
20	Sales		300 750 00				300 750 00		300 750 00		
21	Sales Returns and Allowances	1 800 00				1 800 00		1 800 00			
22	Repair Fees				(h) 15 000 00		15 000 00		15 000 00		
23	Interest Revenue		1 350 00				1 350 00		1 350 00		
24	Purchases	157 500 00				157 500 00		157 500 00			
25	Purchases Returns and Allowances		1 200 00				1 200 00		1 200 00		
26	Purchases Discounts		1 500 00				1 500 00		1 500 00		
27	Freight-In	450 00				450 00		450 00			
28	Wages Expense	63 000 00		(g) 675 00		63 675 00		63 675 00			
29	Advertising Expense	3 750 00				3 750 00		3 750 00			
30	Supplies Expense			(c) 2 100 00		2 100 00		2 100 00			
31	Telephone Expense	5 250 00				5 250 00		5 250 00			
32	Utilities Expense	18 000 00				18 000 00		18 000 00			
33	Insurance Expense			(d) 2 700 00		2 700 00		2 700 00			
34	Depr. Expense—Building			(e) 6 000 00		6 000 00		6 000 00			
35	Depr. Expense—Store Equipment			(f) 4 500 00		4 500 00		4 500 00			
36	Miscellaneous Expense	3 375 00				3 375 00		3 375 00			
37	Interest Expense	4 725 00				4 725 00		4 725 00			
38		590 650 00	590 650 00	114 975 00	114 975 00	646 825 00	646 825 00	312 825 00	364 800 00	334 000 00	282 025 00
39	Net Income							51 975 00			51 975 00
40								364 800 00	364 800 00	334 000 00	334 000 00

STEP 4: Display the General Journal Entries with Titles Report.

STEP 5: Display a Trial Balance Report.

STEP 6: Display the financial statements: Basic Income Statement, Owner's Equity Statement, and Balance Sheet.

STEP 7: Close out the accounting period by changing the accounting period to be "January 1, 2001, to January 31, 2001." To change the accounting period, select the System option from the Tasks menu and then choose the Change Accounting Period submenu option.

STEP 8: Display a Post-Closing Trial Balance Report.

STEP 9: Enter the reversing entries.

STEP 10: Display the General Journal Entries with Titles Report to display the reversing entries.

STEP 11: Manually compute the following:

a. current ratio,
b. quick ratio,
c. working capital,
d. return on owner's equity,
e. accounts receivable turnover and the average number of days required to collect receivables, and
f. inventory turnover and the average number of days required to sell inventory.

Compare your reports to the solutions shown in the Demonstration Problem Solutions in Section 4 of this workbook.

PROBLEM 16-1A

Ellis Fabric Store trial balance as of December 31, 2000 is shown in Figure 2.35 on the following page.

At the end of the year, the following adjustments need to be made:

(a, b) Merchandise Inventory as of December 31, $28,900.

(c) Unused supplies on hand, $1,350.

(d) Insurance expired, $300.

(e) Depreciation expense for the year, $500.

(f) Wages earned but not paid (Wages Payable), $480.

In Problem 16-1A, you will enter the adjusting entries and display the financial statements for a merchandising business. After the financial statements have been prepared, you will close out the accounting period and enter the reversing entries.

STEP 1: Open the data file for Problem 16-1A.

STEP 2: Restore the Opening Balance data.

Ellis Fabric Store
Trial Balance
For Year Ended December 31, 20 - -

ACCOUNT TITLE	ACCOUNT NO.	DEBIT BALANCE	CREDIT BALANCE
Cash		28 000 00	
Accounts Receivable		14 200 00	
Merchandise Inventory		33 000 00	
Supplies		1 600 00	
Prepaid Insurance		900 00	
Equipment		6 600 00	
Accumulated Depreciation—Equipment			1 000 00
Accounts Payable			16 620 00
Wages Payable			
Sales Tax Payable			850 00
W. P. Ellis, Capital			71 200 00
W. P. Ellis, Drawing		21 610 00	
Income Summary			
Sales			78 500 00
Sales Returns and Allowances		1 850 00	
Interest Revenue			1 200 00
Purchases		41 500 00	
Purchases Returns and Allowances			1 800 00
Purchases Discounts			830 00
Freight-In		660 00	
Wages Expense		14 880 00	
Advertising Expense		810 00	
Supplies Expense			
Telephone Expense		1 210 00	
Utilities Expense		3 240 00	
Insurance Expense			
Depreciation Expense—Equipment			
Miscellaneous Expense		920 00	
Interest Expense		1 020 00	
		172 000 00	172 000 00

FIGURE 2.35 Ellis Fabric Store Trial Balance

STEP 3: Enter the adjusting entries for this problem. Use the worksheet letters (a), (b), etc., as the reference for the adjusting general journal entries.

STEP 4: Display the General Journal Entries with Titles Report.

STEP 5: Display a Trial Balance Report.

STEP 6: Display the financial statements: Basic Income Statement, Owner's Equity Statement, and Balance Sheet.

STEP 7: Close out the accounting period by changing the accounting period to be "January 1, 2001, to January 31, 2001."

STEP 8: Display a Post-Closing Trial Balance Report.

STEP 9: Enter the reversing entries.

STEP 10: Display the General Journal Entries with Titles Report to display the reversing entries.

PROBLEM 16-1B

The trial balance for Darby Kite Store as of December 31, 2000 is shown in Figure 2.36 on the following page. At the end of the year, the following adjustments need to be made:

(a, b) Merchandise inventory as of December 31, $23,600.

(c) Unused supplies on hand, $1,050.

(d) Insurance expired, $250.

(e) Depreciation expense for the year, $400.

(f) Wages earned but not paid (Wages Payable), $360.

In Problem 16-1B, you will enter the adjusting entries and display the financial statements for a merchandising business. After the financial statements have been prepared, you will close out the accounting period, and enter the reversing entries.

STEP 1: Open the data file for the Problem 16-1B.

STEP 2: Restore the Opening Balance data.

STEP 3: Enter the adjusting entries for this problem. Use the worksheet letters (a), (b), etc., as the reference for the adjusting general journal entries.

STEP 4: Display the General Journal Entries with Titles Report.

STEP 5: Display a Trial Balance Report.

STEP 6: Display the financial statements: Basic Income Statement, Owner's Equity Statement, and Balance Sheet.

STEP 7: Close out the accounting period by changing the accounting period to be "January 1, 2001, to January 31, 2001."

Darby Kite Store
Trial Balance
For Year Ended December 31, 20- -

ACCOUNT TITLE	ACCOUNT NO.	DEBIT BALANCE	CREDIT BALANCE
Cash		11 700 00	
Accounts Receivable		11 200 00	
Merchandise Inventory		25 000 00	
Supplies		1 200 00	
Prepaid Insurance		800 00	
Equipment		5 400 00	
Accumulated Depreciation—Equipment			800 00
Accounts Payable			7 600 00
Wages Payable			
Sales Tax Payable			250 00
M. D. Akins, Capital			50 000 00
M. D. Akins, Drawing		10 500 00	
Income Summary			
Sales			57 990 00
Sales Returns and Allowances		1 450 00	
Purchases		34 500 00	
Purchases Returns and Allowances			1 100 00
Purchases Discounts			630 00
Freight-In		360 00	
Wages Expense		10 880 00	
Advertising Expense		740 00	
Supplies Expense			
Telephone Expense		1 100 00	
Utilities Expense		2 300 00	
Insurance Expense			
Depreciation Expense—Equipment			
Miscellaneous Expense		320 00	
Interest Expense		920 00	
		118 370 00	118 370 00

FIGURE 2.36 Darby Kite Store Trial Balance

STEP 8: Display a Post-Closing Trial Balance Report.

STEP 9: Enter the reversing entries.

STEP 10: Display the General Journal Entries with Titles Report to display the reversing entries.

CHAPTER 16 MASTERY PROBLEM

In the Chapter 16 Mastery Problem, you will enter the adjusting entries and display the financial statements for a merchandising business. After the financial statements have been prepared, you will close out the accounting period and enter the reversing entries.

STEP 1: Open the data file for the Chapter 16 Mastery Problem.

STEP 2: Restore the Opening Balance data.

STEP 3: Enter the adjusting entries from the worksheet illustrated in the problem. Use the worksheet letters (a), (b), etc., as the reference for the adjusting general journal entries.

STEP 4: Display the General Journal Entries with Titles Report.

STEP 5: Display a Trial Balance Report.

STEP 6: Display the financial statements: Basic Income Statement, Owner's Equity Statement, and Balance Sheet.

STEP 7: Close out the accounting period by changing the accounting period to be "January 1, 2001, to January 31, 2001."

STEP 8: Display a Post-Closing Trial Balance Report.

STEP 9: Enter the reversing entries.

STEP 10: Display the General Journal Entries with Titles Report to display the reversing entries.

Dominique's Doll House
Work Sheet
For Year Ended December 31, 20-3

#	ACCOUNT TITLE	TRIAL BALANCE DEBIT	TRIAL BALANCE CREDIT	ADJUSTMENTS DEBIT	ADJUSTMENTS CREDIT	ADJUSTED TRIAL BALANCE DEBIT	ADJUSTED TRIAL BALANCE CREDIT	INCOME STATEMENT DEBIT	INCOME STATEMENT CREDIT	BALANCE SHEET DEBIT	BALANCE SHEET CREDIT
1	Cash	5 2 0 0 00				5 2 0 0 00				5 2 0 0 00	
2	Accounts Receivable	3 2 0 0 00				3 2 0 0 00				3 2 0 0 00	
3	Merchandise Inventory	22 3 0 0 00		(b) 24 6 0 0 00	(a) 22 3 0 0 00	24 6 0 0 00				24 6 0 0 00	
4	Office Supplies	8 0 0 00			(c) 6 0 0 00	2 0 0 00				2 0 0 00	
5	Prepaid Insurance	1 2 0 0 00			(d) 4 0 0 00	8 0 0 00				8 0 0 00	
6	Store Equipment	85 0 0 0 00				85 0 0 0 00				85 0 0 0 00	
7	Accum. Depr.—Store Equipment		15 0 0 0 00		(e) 5 0 0 0 00		20 0 0 0 00				20 0 0 0 00
8	Notes Payable		6 0 0 0 00				6 0 0 0 00				6 0 0 0 00
9	Accounts Payable		5 5 0 0 00				5 5 0 0 00				5 5 0 0 00
10	Wages Payable				(g) 2 0 0 00		2 0 0 00				2 0 0 00
11	Sales Tax Payable		8 5 0 00				8 5 0 00				8 5 0 00
12	Unearned Rent Revenue		1 0 0 0 00	(f) 7 0 0 00			3 0 0 00				3 0 0 00
13	Long-Term Note Payable		10 0 0 0 00				10 0 0 0 00				10 0 0 0 00
14	Dominique Fouque, Capital		75 8 0 0 00				75 8 0 0 00				75 8 0 0 00
15	Dominique Fouque, Drawing	21 0 0 0 00				21 0 0 0 00				21 0 0 0 00	
16	Income Summary			(a) 22 3 0 0 00	(b) 24 6 0 0 00	22 3 0 0 00	24 6 0 0 00	22 3 0 0 00	24 6 0 0 00		
17	Sales		130 5 0 0 00				130 5 0 0 00		130 5 0 0 00		
18	Sales Returns and Allowances	9 0 0 00				9 0 0 00		9 0 0 00			
19	Rent Revenue		25 0 0 0 00		(f) 7 0 0 00		25 7 0 0 00		25 7 0 0 00		
20	Purchases	72 0 0 0 00				72 0 0 0 00		72 0 0 0 00			
21	Purchases Discounts		7 5 0 00				7 5 0 00		7 5 0 00		
22	Freight-In	1 2 0 0 00				1 2 0 0 00		1 2 0 0 00			
23	Wages Expense	42 0 0 0 00		(g) 2 0 0 00		42 2 0 0 00		42 2 0 0 00			
24	Rent Expense	6 0 0 0 00				6 0 0 0 00		6 0 0 0 00			
25	Office Supplies Expense			(c) 6 0 0 00		6 0 0 00		6 0 0 00			
26	Telephone Expense	1 5 0 0 00				1 5 0 0 00		1 5 0 0 00			
27	Utilities Expense	7 6 0 0 00				7 6 0 0 00		7 6 0 0 00			
28	Insurance Expense			(d) 4 0 0 00		4 0 0 00		4 0 0 00			
29	Depr. Expense—Store Equipment			(e) 5 0 0 0 00		5 0 0 0 00		5 0 0 0 00			
30	Interest Expense	5 0 0 00				5 0 0 00		5 0 0 00			
31		270 4 0 0 00	270 4 0 0 00	53 8 0 0 00	53 8 0 0 00	300 2 0 0 00	300 2 0 0 00	160 2 0 0 00	181 5 5 0 00	140 0 0 0 00	118 6 5 0 00
32	Net Income							21 3 5 0 00			21 3 5 0 00
33								181 5 5 0 00	181 5 5 0 00	140 0 0 0 00	140 0 0 0 00

SECTION 3

Setting Up a New Company

This section describes the process of setting up a new company. The process is very different depending on whether or not you have access to a CD-ROM drive.

COMPLETING NEW COMPANY SETUP

Follow the step-by-step instructions below to complete a new company setup:

▶ From the File menu, choose the New Company option.
▶ The New Company Setup Introduction screen shown in Figure 3.1 will appear.

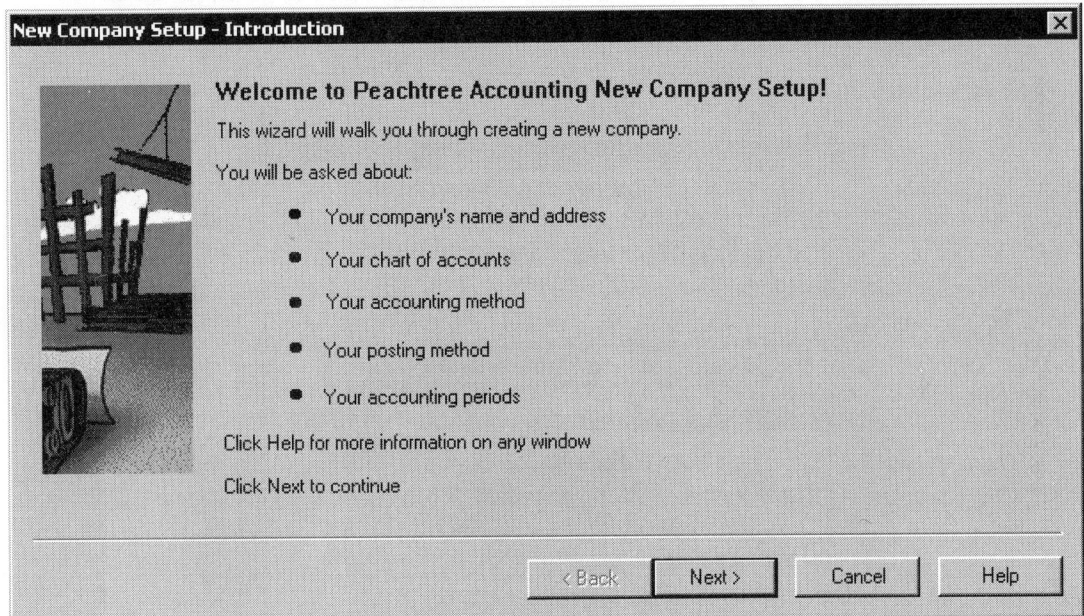

FIGURE 3.1 New Company Setup Introduction

▶ Click the Next button and follow the Wizard prompts to establish the new company.
▶ When the New Company setup Wizard finishes, the screen shown in Figure 3.2 on the following page will appear. It is recommended that you choose the "Yes, I would like to follow the Setup Checklist" option then click the Finish button.

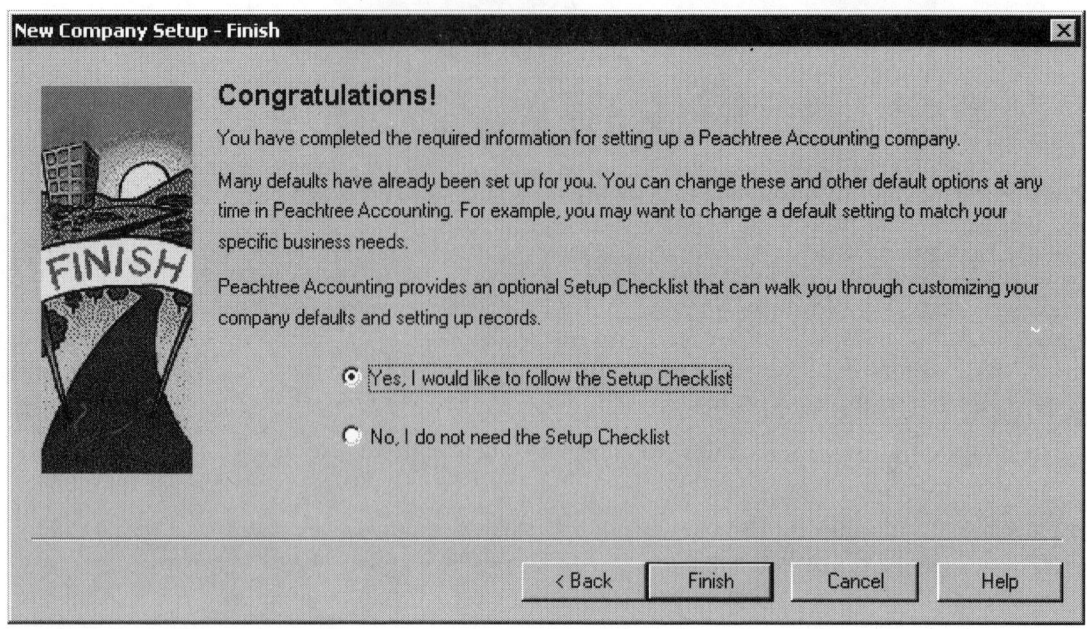

FIGURE 3.2 New Company Setup – Finish Window

▶ The Setup Checklist shown in Figure 3.3 will appear.

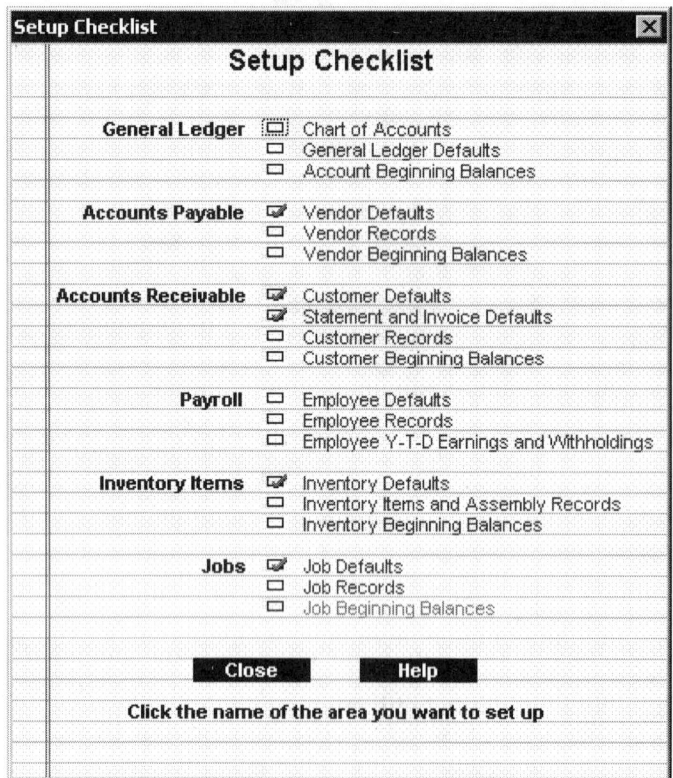

FIGURE 3.3 Setup Checklist

This list guides you through the process of setting up company data. It also helps you track your progress as you complete the setup process.

▶ Click the area (on the Checklist) you want to set up. Peachtree displays the appropriate window, where you can enter your settings or data.

SETUP CHECKLIST

To complete setup, click on each applicable option in the Setup Checklist and enter the appropriate data. Each of the Setup Checklist options is described in the following sections. As each data entry window appears, click on the Help button (or press F1) for a complete description of how to enter the data for that particular window. You do not have to complete the entire setup process in one session. You can return to the setup checklist at any time by choosing the Setup Checklist option from the Maintain menu. Each time you enter a function from the setup checklist, you will be asked whether you want to mark the task as complete when you exit the task. If you select the Yes button, a check mark is placed next to the task. You can still access options that are check marked. The check mark just tracks your progress towards completing setup.

GENERAL LEDGER CHECKLIST

▶ Enter general ledger chart of accounts. This window is used to set up an Account ID, Description and Account Type (Cash, Accounts Payable, Retained Earnings, etc.). You can also enter budget amounts for each accounting period, and copy the budget amounts into the next year. Click on the Help button for a detailed explanation of the various data fields.

▶ Enter general ledger account beginning balances. This screen allows you to select an account and enter the starting balance for that account.

ACCOUNTS PAYABLE CHECKLIST

▶ Enter vendor default settings. In this window, you set up default information for payment terms, account aging, and custom field labels. In most cases, the account aging and custom fields may be omitted. Again, remember to click on the Help button for detailed information about entering the data.

▶ Enter vendor records. In this window, enter the basic information about vendors, including address, the contact person, the terms of sale, and the tax authority for sales tax.

▶ Enter vendor beginning balances. In this window, enter the beginning balances for the vendors.

ACCOUNTS RECEIVABLE CHECKLIST

▶ Enter customer default settings. This data entry window allows you to set up default settings for terms of sale by customer, finance charges, account aging, custom fields, and payment types.

▶ Enter statement/invoice default settings. Enter the statement and invoice print options and dunning messages.

▶ Enter customer records. In this data entry window, you enter customer name and address information, including ship-to address (if different from regular address) and a Type code to use in categorizing customers. You can specify a general ledger account to use for sales to the customer, and a sales tax code, as well as terms of sale for each customer.

- Enter customer beginning balances. In this window, enter open invoices by customer. Optionally, you can simply enter the current balance with an invoice number of "Balance."
- Enter employee default settings. This window allows you to establish the unemployment percentage for your company, the state and locality you are in, and whether you deduct for 401K, Meals, or Tips. You can also set up default information for general employee information, pay levels, employee fields, employer fields, and custom field types. You can also enter the default cash account for payroll, define additional payroll fields, and assign fields for the W-2 forms.

PAYROLL CHECKLIST

- Enter employee records. In this screen, enter basic employee information including address, phone number, social security number, filing statuses, and pay information. Remember that you can press F1 or click on the Help button at any time to receive detailed information about a particular data entry window.
- Enter employee year-to-date earnings and withholdings. Enter year-to-date earnings and withholding amounts for up to 52 payroll periods.

INVENTORY CHECKLIST

- Enter inventory default settings. Enter the defaults for custom field types, item tax type, and ship methods.
- Enter inventory items and assemblies. In this window, enter your inventory account numbers—sales, merchandise inventory, and purchases. You may also enter the preferred vendor for each item and create a bill of materials for inventory items tracked as assembled items.
- Enter the inventory.
- Enter inventory beginning quantities. Enter the beginning quantities, unit costs, and total cost for each of the inventory items.

JOBS CHECKLIST

- Enter jobs default settings. This window allows you to set up labels for the customer fields to be used when entering jobs for the job costing system.
- Enter jobs. In this window, you can set up jobs and enter the customer, start date, and ending date.
- Enter job beginning balances. Enter the beginning balances for jobs. Enter the amount as a negative if it represents revenue.

SECTION 4

Demonstration Problem Solutions

Chapter 2 Demonstration Problem Solution

Page: 1

02-Demo Home and Away Inspections
Chart of Accounts
As of Dec 31, 2000

Filter Criteria includes: Report order is by ID. Report is printed with Accounts having Zero Amounts and in Detail Format.

Account ID	Account Description	Active?	Account Type
101	Cash	Yes	Cash
102	Accounts Receivable	Yes	Accounts Receivable
103	Supplies	Yes	Other Current Assets
104	Prepaid Insurance	Yes	Other Current Assets
105	Tools	Yes	Fixed Assets
106	Truck	Yes	Fixed Assets
201	Accounts Payable	Yes	Accounts Payable
300	Beginning Balance Equity	Yes	Equity-doesn't close
301	Damon Young, Capital	Yes	Equity-Retained Earnings
303	Damon Young, Drawing	Yes	Equity-gets closed
401	Inspection Fees	Yes	Income
501	Wages Expense	Yes	Expenses
503	Rent Expense	Yes	Expenses
505	Telephone Expense	Yes	Expenses
507	Utilities Expense	Yes	Expenses

02-Demo Home and Away Inspections
Balance Sheet
December 31, 2000

ASSETS

Cash	$ 7,665.00	
Accounts Receivable	1,300.00	
Supplies	300.00	
Prepaid Insurance	600.00	
Tools	3,000.00	
Truck	8,000.00	
Total Assets		$ 20,865.00

LIABILITIES AND CAPITAL

Liabilities		
Accounts Payable	$ 2,200.00	
Total Liabilities		2,200.00
Capital		
Damon Young, Capital	15,000.00	
Damon Young, Drawing	<500.00>	
Net Income	4,165.00	
Total Capital		18,665.00
Total Liabilities & Capital		$ 20,865.00

Page: 1

02-Demo Home and Away Inspections
Income Statement
For the Twelve Months Ending December 31, 2000

	Year to Date
Revenues	
Inspection Fees	$ 5,000.00
Total Revenues	5,000.00
Expenses	
Wages Expense	450.00
Rent Expense	300.00
Telephone Expense	35.00
Utilities Expense	50.00
Total Expenses	835.00
Net Income	$ 4,165.00

02-Demo Home and Away Inspections
Statement of Owner's Equity
December 31, 2000

Capital, Beginning of Period		15,000.00
Net Income for the Period	4,165.00	
Less Withdrawals for Period	500.00	
Increase in Capital		3,665.00
Capital, End of Period		$ 18,665.00

Chapter 3 Demonstration Problem Solution

03-Demo We-Buy, You-Pay Shopping Serv.
Balance Sheet
December 31, 2000

ASSETS

Assets			
Cash	$	20,010.00	
Accounts Receivable		8,400.00	
Office Equipment		10,000.00	
Computer Equipment		4,800.00	
Total Assets			$ 43,210.00

LIABILITIES AND CAPITAL

Liabilities			
Accounts Payable	$	6,000.00	
Notes Payable		4,000.00	
Total Liabilities			10,000.00
Capital			
Celia Pints, Capital		30,000.00	
Celia Pints, Drawing		<2,000.00>	
Net Income		5,210.00	
Total Capital			33,210.00
Total Liabilities & Capital		$	43,210.00

03-Demo We-Buy, You-Pay Shopping Serv.
Income Statement
For the Twelve Months Ending December 31, 2000

	Year to Date
Revenues	
Shopping Fees	$ 18,400.00
Total Revenues	18,400.00
Expenses	
Rent Expense	500.00
Telephone Expense	90.00
Commissions Expense	10,500.00
Utilities Expense	600.00
Travel Expense	1,500.00
Total Expenses	13,190.00
Net Income	$ 5,210.00

03-Demo We-Buy, You-Pay Shopping Serv.
Statement of Owner's Equity
December 31, 2000

Capital, Beginning of Period		30,000.00
Net Income for the Period	5,210.00	
Less Withdrawals for Period	2,000.00	
Increase in Capital		3,210.00
Capital, End of Period		$ 33,210.00

Chapter 4 Demonstration Problem Solution

Page: 1

04-Demo George Fielding Fin. Conslt.
General Journal
For the Period From Dec 1, 2000 to Dec 31, 2000

Date	Account ID	Reference	Account Description	Debit Amt	Credit Amt
12/1/00	101		Cash	20,000.00	
	311		George Fielding, Capital		20,000.00
12/3/00	521		Rent Expense	1,000.00	
	101		Cash		1,000.00
12/4/00	101		Cash	2,500.00	
	401		Professional Fees		2,500.00
12/6/00	533		Utilities Expense	75.00	
	101		Cash		75.00
12/7/00	101		Cash	2,000.00	
	401		Professional Fees		2,000.00
12/12/00	538		Automobile Expense	60.00	
	101		Cash		60.00
12/14/00	511		Wages Expense	600.00	
	101		Cash		600.00
12/17/00	142		Office Supplies	280.00	
	202		Accounts Payable		280.00
12/20/00	525		Telephone Expense	100.00	
	101		Cash		100.00
12/21/00	312		George Fielding, Drawing	1,100.00	
	101		Cash		1,100.00
12/24/00	534		Charitable Contribution Exp.	100.00	
	101		Cash		100.00
12/27/00	101		Cash	2,000.00	
	401		Professional Fees		2,000.00
12/28/00	511		Wages Expense	600.00	
	101		Cash		600.00
12/29/00	202		Accounts Payable	100.00	
	101		Cash		100.00
		Total		30,515.00	30,515.00

04-Demo George Fielding Fin. Conslt.

General Ledger Trial Balance
As of Dec 31, 2000

Filter Criteria includes: Report order is by ID. Report is printed in Detail Format.

Account ID	Account Description	Debit Amt	Credit Amt
101	Cash	22,765.00	
142	Office Supplies	280.00	
202	Accounts Payable		180.00
311	George Fielding, Capital		20,000.00
312	George Fielding, Drawing	1,100.00	
401	Professional Fees		6,500.00
511	Wages Expense	1,200.00	
521	Rent Expense	1,000.00	
525	Telephone Expense	100.00	
533	Utilities Expense	75.00	
534	Charitable Contribution Exp.	100.00	
538	Automobile Expense	60.00	
	Total:	26,680.00	26,680.00

04-Demo George Fielding Fin. Conslt.

General Ledger

For the Period From Dec 1, 2000 to Dec 31, 2000

Filter Criteria includes: Report order is by ID. Report is printed with Truncated Transaction Descriptions and in Detail Format.

Account ID Account Description	Date	Reference	Jrnl	Trans Description	Debit Amt	Credit Amt	Balance
101 Cash	12/1/00			Beginning Balance			
	12/1/00		GENJ		20,000.00		
	12/3/00		GENJ			1,000.00	
	12/4/00		GENJ		2,500.00		
	12/6/00		GENJ			75.00	
	12/7/00		GENJ		2,000.00		
	12/12/00		GENJ			60.00	
	12/14/00		GENJ			600.00	
	12/20/00		GENJ			100.00	
	12/21/00		GENJ			1,100.00	
	12/24/00		GENJ			100.00	
	12/27/00		GENJ		2,000.00		
	12/28/00		GENJ			600.00	
	12/29/00		GENJ			100.00	
				Current Period Change	26,500.00	3,735.00	22,765.00
	12/31/00			Ending Balance			22,765.00
142 Office Supplies	12/1/00			Beginning Balance			
	12/17/00		GENJ		280.00		
				Current Period Change	280.00		280.00
	12/31/00			Ending Balance			280.00
202 Accounts Payable	12/1/00			Beginning Balance			
	12/17/00		GENJ			280.00	
	12/29/00		GENJ		100.00		
				Current Period Change	100.00	280.00	-180.00
	12/31/00			Ending Balance			-180.00
311 George Fielding, Capital	12/1/00			Beginning Balance			
	12/1/00		GENJ			20,000.00	
				Current Period Change		20,000.00	-20,000.00
	12/31/00			Ending Balance			-20,000.00
312 George Fielding, Drawing	12/1/00			Beginning Balance			
	12/21/00		GENJ		1,100.00		
				Current Period Change	1,100.00		1,100.00
	12/31/00			Ending Balance			1,100.00
401 Professional Fees	12/1/00			Beginning Balance			
	12/4/00		GENJ			2,500.00	
	12/7/00		GENJ			2,000.00	
	12/27/00		GENJ			2,000.00	
				Current Period Change		6,500.00	-6,500.00
	12/31/00			Ending Balance			-6,500.00
511 Wages Expense	12/1/00			Beginning Balance			
	12/14/00		GENJ		600.00		
	12/28/00		GENJ		600.00		
				Current Period Change	1,200.00		1,200.00
	12/31/00			Ending Balance			1,200.00

04-Demo George Fielding Fin. Conslt.

General Ledger

For the Period From Dec 1, 2000 to Dec 31, 2000

Filter Criteria includes: Report order is by ID. Report is printed with Truncated Transaction Descriptions and in Detail Format.

Account ID Account Description	Date	Reference	Jrnl	Trans Description	Debit Amt	Credit Amt	Balance
521 Rent Expense	12/1/00 12/3/00		GENJ	Beginning Balance	1,000.00		
	12/31/00			Current Period Change Ending Balance	1,000.00		1,000.00 1,000.00
525 Telephone Expense	12/1/00 12/20/00		GENJ	Beginning Balance	100.00		
	12/31/00			Current Period Change Ending Balance	100.00		100.00 100.00
533 Utilities Expense	12/1/00 12/6/00		GENJ	Beginning Balance	75.00		
	12/31/00			Current Period Change Ending Balance	75.00		75.00 75.00
534 Charitable Contribution Ex	12/1/00 12/24/00		GENJ	Beginning Balance	100.00		
	12/31/00			Current Period Change Ending Balance	100.00		100.00 100.00
538 Automobile Expense	12/1/00 12/12/00		GENJ	Beginning Balance	60.00		
	12/31/00			Current Period Change Ending Balance	60.00		60.00 60.00

Chapter 5 Demonstration Problem Solution

Page: 1

05-Demo Justin Park Legal Services
General Journal
For the Period From Dec 1, 2000 to Dec 31, 2000

Date	Account ID	Reference	Trans Description	Account Description	Debit Amt	Credit Amt
12/31/00	523	(a)	Adjusting Entry	Office Supplies Expense	500.00	
	142		Adjusting Entry	Office Supplies		500.00
12/31/00	541	(b)	Adjusting Entry	Depr. Expense—Office Equip.	3,000.00	
	181.1		Adjusting Entry	Accum. Depr.—Office Equipment		3,000.00
12/31/00	542	(c)	Adjusting Entry	Depr. Expense—Computer Equip.	1,000.00	
	187.1		Adjusting Entry	Accum. Depr.—Computer Equip.		1,000.00
12/31/00	535	(d)	Adjusting Entry	Insurance Expense	100.00	
	145		Adjusting Entry	Prepaid Insurance		100.00
12/31/00	511	(e)	Adjusting Entry	Wages Expense	300.00	
	219		Adjusting Entry	Wages Payable		300.00
		Total			**4,900.00**	**4,900.00**

Page: 1

05-Demo Justin Park Legal Services
Income Statement
For the Twelve Months Ending December 31, 2000

	Year to Date
Revenues	
Client Fees	$ 40,000.00
Total Revenues	40,000.00
Expenses	
Wages Expense	12,300.00
Rent Expense	5,000.00
Office Supplies Expense	500.00
Telephone Expense	1,000.00
Utilities Expense	3,900.00
Insurance Expense	100.00
Depr. Expense--Office Equip.	3,000.00
Depr. Expense--Computer Equip.	1,000.00
Total Expenses	26,800.00
Net Income	$ 13,200.00

05-Demo Justin Park Legal Services
Balance Sheet
December 31, 2000

ASSETS

Assets			
Cash	$	7,000.00	
Office Supplies		300.00	
Prepaid Insurance		1,100.00	
Office Equipment		15,000.00	
Accum. Depr.--Office Equipment		<3,000.00>	
Computer Equipment		6,000.00	
Accum. Depr.--Computer Equip.		<1,000.00>	
Total Assets		$	25,400.00

LIABILITIES AND CAPITAL

Liabilities			
Notes Payable	$	5,000.00	
Accounts Payable		500.00	
Wages Payable		300.00	
Total Liabilities			5,800.00
Capital			
Justin Park, Capital		11,400.00	
Justin Park, Drawing		<5,000.00>	
Net Income		13,200.00	
Total Capital			19,600.00
Total Liabilities & Capital		$	25,400.00

05-Demo Justin Park Legal Services
Statement of Owner's Equity
December 31, 2000

Capital, Beginning of Period		11,400.00
Net Income for the Period	13,200.00	
Less Withdrawals for Period	5,000.00	
Increase in Capital		8,200.00
Capital, End of Period	$	19,600.00

Chapter 6 Demonstration Problem Solution

06-Demo Hard Copy Printers
General Journal
For the Period From Dec 1, 2000 to Dec 31, 2000

Page: 1

Date	Account ID	Reference	Account Description	Debit Amt	Credit Amt
12/31/00	543	(a)	Paper Supplies Expense	3,550.00	
	151		Paper Supplies		3,550.00
12/31/00	547	(b)	Insurance Expense	505.00	
	155		Prepaid Insurance		505.00
12/31/00	541	(c)	Wages Expense	30.00	
	219		Wages Payable		30.00
12/31/00	546	(d)	Depr. Exp.--Printing Equipment	1,200.00	
	185.1		Accum. Depr.--Printing Equip.		1,200.00
		Total		**5,285.00**	**5,285.00**

06-Demo Hard Copy Printers
General Ledger Trial Balance
As of Dec 31, 2000

Page: 1

Filter Criteria includes: Report order is by ID. Report is printed in Detail Format.

Account ID	Account Description	Debit Amt	Credit Amt
111	Cash	1,180.00	
151	Paper Supplies	50.00	
155	Prepaid Insurance	495.00	
185	Printing Equipment	5,800.00	
185.1	Accum. Depr.--Printing Equip.		1,200.00
211	Accounts Payable		500.00
219	Wages Payable		30.00
311	Timothy Chang, Capital		10,000.00
312	Timothy Chang, Drawing	13,000.00	
411	Printing Fees		35,100.00
541	Wages Expense	12,000.00	
542	Rent Expense	7,500.00	
543	Paper Supplies Expense	3,550.00	
544	Telephone Expense	550.00	
545	Utilities Expense	1,000.00	
546	Depr. Exp.--Printing Equipment	1,200.00	
547	Insurance Expense	505.00	
	Total:	46,830.00	46,830.00

06-Demo Hard Copy Printers
Balance Sheet
December 31, 2000

ASSETS

Assets		
Cash	$ 1,180.00	
Paper Supplies	50.00	
Prepaid Insurance	495.00	
Printing Equipment	5,800.00	
Accum. Depr.--Printing Equip.	<1,200.00>	
Total Assets		$ 6,325.00

LIABILITIES AND CAPITAL

Liabilities		
Accounts Payable	$ 500.00	
Wages Payable	30.00	
Total Liabilities		530.00
Capital		
Timothy Chang, Capital	10,000.00	
Timothy Chang, Drawing	<13,000.00>	
Net Income	8,795.00	
Total Capital		5,795.00
Total Liabilities & Capital		$ 6,325.00

06-Demo Hard Copy Printers
Income Statement
For the Month Ended December 31, 2000

Revenues		
Printing Fees	$	35,100.00
Total Revenues		35,100.00
Expenses		
Wages Expense		12,000.00
Rent Expense		7,500.00
Paper Supplies Expense		3,550.00
Telephone Expense		550.00
Utilities Expense		1,000.00
Depr. Exp.--Printing Equipment		1,200.00
Insurance Expense		505.00
Total Expenses		26,305.00
Net Income	$	8,795.00

06-Demo Hard Copy Printers
Statement of Owner's Equity
December 31, 2000

Capital, Beginning of Period		10,000.00
Net Income for the Period	8,795.00	
Less Withdrawals for Period	13,000.00	
Increase in Capital		<4,205.00>
Capital, End of Period	$	5,795.00

06-Demo Hard Copy Printers
General Ledger Trial Balance
As of Jan 31, 2001

teria includes: Report order is by ID. Report is printed in Detail Format.

t ID	Account Description	Debit Amt	Credit Amt
	Cash	1,180.00	
	Paper Supplies	50.00	
	Prepaid Insurance	495.00	
	Printing Equipment	5,800.00	
	Accum. Depr.--Printing Equip.		1,200.00
	Accounts Payable		500.00
	Wages Payable		30.00
	Timothy Chang, Capital		5,795.00
	Total:	7,525.00	7,525.00

Chapter 7 Demonstration Problem Solution

Page: 1

07-Demo Kuhn's Wilderness Outfitters
Account Reconciliation
As of Mar 31, 2000
101 - Cash
Bank Statement Date: March 31, 2000

Filter Criteria includes: Report is printed in Detail Format.

Beginning GL Balance				4,870.57
Add: Cash Receipts				
Less: Cash Disbursements				<197.45>
Add <Less> Other				<158.10>
Ending GL Balance				4,515.02
Ending Bank Balance				5,419.00
Add back deposits in transit				
	Feb 12, 2000	3/12/00	926.10	
Total deposits in transit				926.10
<Less> outstanding checks				
	Feb 1, 2000	462	<524.26>	
	Feb 5, 2000	465	<213.41>	
	Feb 22, 2000	473	<543.58>	
	Feb 22, 2000	476	<351.38>	
	Mar 31, 2000	477	<197.45>	
Total outstanding checks				<1,830.08>
Add <Less> Other				
Total other				
Unreconciled difference				0.00
Ending GL Balance				4,515.02

Page: 1

07-Demo Kuhn's Wilderness Outfitters
Account Register
For the Period From Mar 1, 2000 to Mar 31, 2000
101 - Cash

Filter Criteria includes: Report order is by Date.

Date	Trans No	Type	Trans Desc	Deposit Amt	Withdrawal Amt	Balance
			Beginning Balance			4,870.57
3/31/00		Other	Bank service charge		4.10	4,866.47
3/31/00		Other	Error on check no. 456		54.00	4,812.47
3/31/00		Other	ATM withdrawal		100.00	4,712.47
3/31/00	477	Withdrawal	Petty Cash		197.45	4,515.02
			Total		355.55	

Chapter 8 Demonstration Problem Solution

Page: 1

08-Demo Canine Coiffures
Check Register
For the Period From Jan 15, 2000 to Jan 21, 2000

Filter Criteria includes: Report order is by Check Date. Report is printed in Detail Format.

Reference	Date	Employee	Amount
811	1/21/00	Katie DeNourie	409.26
812	1/21/00	Pete Garriott	360.70
813	1/21/00	Sheila Martinez	396.90
814	1/21/00	Nancy Parker	399.20
815	1/21/00	John Shapiro	341.83
		1/15/00 thru 1/21/00	1,907.89
		1/15/00 thru 1/21/00	1,907.89

08-Demo Canine Coiffures
Payroll Journal
For the Period From Jan 15, 2000 to Jan 21, 2000

Filter Criteria includes: Report order is by Check Date. Report is printed in Detail Format.

Date Employee	GL Acct ID	GL Acct Description	Reference	Debit Amt	Credit Amt
1/21/00	511	Wages and Salaries Expense	811	460.00	
Katie DeNourie	511	Wages and Salaries Expense		69.00	
	211	Employee Income Tax Payable			54.98
	212	Social Security Tax Payable			32.80
	213	Medicare Tax Payable			7.67
	215	City Earnings Tax Payable			5.29
	216	Health Ins. Premiums Payable			4.00
	217	Credit Union Payable			15.00
	212	Social Security Tax Payable			32.80
	213	Medicare Tax Payable			7.67
	219	Payroll Taxes Payable			21.69
	513	Payroll Taxes Expense		32.80	
	513	Payroll Taxes Expense		7.67	
	513	Payroll Taxes Expense		21.69	
	101	Cash			409.26
1/21/00	511	Wages and Salaries Expense	812	480.00	
Pete Garriott	211	Employee Income Tax Payable			45.03
	212	Social Security Tax Payable			29.76
	213	Medicare Tax Payable			6.96
	215	City Earnings Tax Payable			4.80
	216	Health Ins. Premiums Payable			14.00
	218	Savings Bond Deduction Payable			18.75
	212	Social Security Tax Payable			29.76
	213	Medicare Tax Payable			6.96
	219	Payroll Taxes Payable			19.68
	513	Payroll Taxes Expense		29.76	
	513	Payroll Taxes Expense		6.96	
	513	Payroll Taxes Expense		19.68	
	101	Cash			360.70
1/21/00	511	Wages and Salaries Expense	813	487.50	
Sheila Martinez	211	Employee Income Tax Payable			29.42
	212	Social Security Tax Payable			30.23
	213	Medicare Tax Payable			7.07
	215	City Earnings Tax Payable			4.88
	216	Health Ins. Premiums Payable			4.00
	217	Credit Union Payable			15.00
	212	Social Security Tax Payable			30.23
	213	Medicare Tax Payable			7.07
	219	Payroll Taxes Payable			19.99
	513	Payroll Taxes Expense		30.23	
	513	Payroll Taxes Expense		7.07	
	513	Payroll Taxes Expense		19.99	
	101	Cash			396.90
1/21/00	511	Wages and Salaries Expense	814	440.00	
Nancy Parker	511	Wages and Salaries Expense		33.00	
	211	Employee Income Tax Payable			18.88
	212	Social Security Tax Payable			29.33
	213	Medicare Tax Payable			6.86
	215	City Earnings Tax Payable			4.73
	216	Health Ins. Premiums Payable			14.00
	212	Social Security Tax Payable			29.33
	213	Medicare Tax Payable			6.86
	219	Payroll Taxes Payable			19.39
	513	Payroll Taxes Expense		29.33	
	513	Payroll Taxes Expense		6.86	
	513	Payroll Taxes Expense		19.39	
	101	Cash			399.20
1/21/00	511	Wages and Salaries Expense	815	460.00	
John Shapiro	211	Employee Income Tax Payable			44.63
	212	Social Security Tax Payable			28.52
	213	Medicare Tax Payable			6.67

08-Demo Canine Coiffures
Payroll Journal
For the Period From Jan 15, 2000 to Jan 21, 2000

Filter Criteria includes: Report order is by Check Date. Report is printed in Detail Format.

Date Employee	GL Acct ID	GL Acct Description	Reference	Debit Amt	Credit Amt
	215	City Earnings Tax Payable			4.60
	217	Credit Union Payable			15.00
	218	Savings Bond Deduction Payable			18.75
	212	Social Security Tax Payable			28.52
	213	Medicare Tax Payable			6.67
	219	Payroll Taxes Payable			18.86
	513	Payroll Taxes Expense		28.52	
	513	Payroll Taxes Expense		6.67	
	513	Payroll Taxes Expense		18.86	
	101	Cash			341.83
				2,714.98	2,714.98

08-Demo Canine Coiffures
Payroll Register
For the Period From Jan 15, 2000 to Jan 21, 2000

Filter Criteria includes: Report order is by Check Date. Report is printed in Detail Format.

Employee ID Employee SS No Reference Date	Pay Type	Pay Hrs	Pay Amt	Amount	Gross Local Soc_Sec_ER	Fed_Income Health Ins. Medicare_E	Soc_Sec Cred. Union FUTA_ER	Medicare Saving Bo SUI_ER
1 Katie DeNourie 436-44-2712 811 1/21/00	Regular Overtime	40.00 4.00	460.00 69.00	409.26	529.00 -5.29 -32.80	-54.98 -4.00 -7.67	-32.80 -15.00	-7.67 -21.69
2 Pete Garriott 568-88-8722 812 1/21/00	Regular	40.00	480.00	360.70	480.00 -4.80 -29.76	-45.03 -14.00 -6.96	-29.76	-6.96 -18.75 -19.68
3 Sheila Martinez 455-73-3478 813 1/21/00	Regular	39.00	487.50	396.90	487.50 -4.88 -30.23	-29.42 -4.00 -7.07	-30.23 -15.00	-7.07 -19.99
4 Nancy Parker 423-28-2769 814 1/21/00	Regular Overtime	40.00 2.00	440.00 33.00	399.20	473.00 -4.73 -29.33	-18.88 -14.00 -6.86	-29.33	-6.86 -19.39
5 John Shapiro 877-228214 815 1/21/00	Regular	40.00	460.00	341.83	460.00 -4.60 -28.52	-44.63 -6.67	-28.52 -15.00	-6.67 -18.75 -18.86
Summary Total 1/15/00 thru 1/21/00	Regular Overtime	199.00 6.00	2,327.50 102.00	1,907.89	2,429.50 -24.30 -150.64	-192.94 -36.00 -35.23	-150.64 -45.00	-35.23 -37.50 -99.61
Report Date Final Total 1/15/00 thru 1/21/00	Regular Overtime	199.00 6.00	2,327.50 102.00	1,907.89	2,429.50 -24.30 -150.64	-192.94 -36.00 -35.23	-150.64 -45.00	-35.23 -37.50 -99.61

Chapter 9 Demonstration Problem Solution

09-Demo Hart Company
General Journal
For the Period From Dec 1, 2000 to Dec 31, 2000

Filter Criteria includes: Report order is by Date. Report is printed with Accounts having Zero Amounts and with Truncated Transaction Descriptions and in Detail Format.

Date	Account ID	Reference	Trans Description	Account Description	Debit Amt	Credit Amt
12/31/00	511		Record December 31 payroll	Wages and Salaries Expense	3,800.00	
	211		Record December 31 payroll	Employee Income Tax Payable		380.00
	212		Record December 31 payroll	Social Security Tax		235.60
	213		Record December 31 payroll	Medicare Tax Payable		55.10
	216		Record December 31 payroll	Health Insurance Premium Pay.		50.00
	217		Record December 31 payroll	United Way Contribution Pay.		100.00
	101		Record December 31 payroll	Cash		2,979.30
	513		Employer payroll taxes	Payroll Taxes Expense	315.50	
	212		Employer payroll taxes	Social Security Tax		235.60
	213		Employer payroll taxes	Medicare Tax Payable		55.10
	219		Employer payroll taxes	FUTA Tax Payable		3.20
	220		Employer payroll taxes	SUTA Tax Payable		21.60
	510		Adjustment for insurance pre	Workers' Comp. Ins. Expense	18.00	
	221		Adjustment for insurance pre	Workers' Comp. Ins. Payable		18.00
			Total		4,133.50	4,133.50

09-Demo Hart Company
General Journal
For the Period From Jan 1, 2001 to Jan 31, 2001

Filter Criteria includes: Report order is by Date. Report is printed with Accounts having Zero Amounts and with Truncated Transaction Descriptions and in Detail Format.

Date	Account ID	Reference	Trans Description	Account Description	Debit Amt	Credit Amt
1/15/01	211		Paid employees withholding li	Employee Income Tax Payable	1,520.00	
	212		Paid employees withholding li	Social Security Tax	1,847.00	
	213		Paid employees withholding li	Medicare Tax Payable	433.00	
	101		Paid employees withholding li	Cash		3,800.00
1/31/01	219		Paid FUTA taxes	FUTA Tax Payable	27.20	
	101		Paid FUTA taxes	Cash		27.20
	220		Paid SUTA tax	SUTA Tax Payable	183.60	
	101		Paid SUTA tax	Cash		183.60
			Total		4,010.80	4,010.80

09-Demo Hart Company
General Ledger Trial Balance
As of Jan 31, 2001

Filter Criteria includes: Report order is by ID. Report is printed in Detail Format.

Account ID	Account Description	Debit Amt	Credit Amt
101	Cash	64,156.52	
103	Accounts Receivable	21,250.00	
142	Office Supplies	1,200.00	
143	Prepaid Insurance	560.00	
180	Equipment	178,575.00	
180.1	Accum. Depr.--Equipment		40,286.00
201	Accounts Payable		8,165.00
216	Health Insurance Premium Pay.		50.00
217	United Way Contribution Pay.		100.00
221	Workers' Comp. Ins. Payable		18.00
311	Beatrice Hart, Capital		217,122.52
	Total:	265,741.52	265,741.52

Chapter 10 Demonstration Problem Solution

10-Demo Vietor Financial Planning
General Journal
For the Period From Dec 1, 2000 to Dec 31, 2000

Filter Criteria includes: Report order is by Date. Report is printed with Accounts having Zero Amounts and with Truncated Transaction Descriptions and in Detail Format.

Date	Account ID	Reference	Trans Description	Account Description	Debit Amt	Credit Amt
12/1/00	101		Original investment by	Cash	20,000.00	
	311		Original investment by	Maria Vietor, Capital		20,000.00
12/3/00	521		Paid rent	Rent Expense	1,000.00	
	101		Paid rent	Cash		1,000.00
12/4/00	101		Fee for services	Cash	2,500.00	
	401		Fee for services	Professional Fees		2,500.00
12/6/00	533		Paid utilities	Utilities Expense	75.00	
	101		Paid utilities	Cash		75.00
12/7/00	101		Fee for services	Cash	2,000.00	
	401		Fee for services	Professional Fees		2,000.00
12/12/00	526		Gas & oil	Automobile Expense	60.00	
	101		Gas & oil	Cash		60.00
12/14/00	511		Secretarial services	Wages Expense	600.00	
	101		Secretarial services	Cash		600.00
12/17/00	142		Cleat Office Supply	Office Supplies	280.00	
	202		Cleat Office Supply	Accounts Payable		280.00
12/20/00	525		Long distance service	Telephone Expense	100.00	
	101		Long distance service	Cash		100.00
12/21/00	312		Owner withdrawal	Maria Vietor, Drawing	1,100.00	
	101		Owner withdrawal	Cash		1,100.00
12/24/00	534		National Multiple Scler	Charitable Contributions Exp.	100.00	
	101		National Multiple Scler	Cash		100.00
12/27/00	101		Fee for services	Cash	2,000.00	
	401		Fee for services	Professional Fees		2,000.00
12/28/00	511		Secretarial services	Wages Expense	600.00	
	101		Secretarial services	Cash		600.00
12/29/00	202		Cleat Office Supply	Accounts Payable	100.00	
	101		Cleat Office Supply	Cash		100.00
			Total		**30,515.00**	**30,515.00**

10-Demo Vietor Financial Planning
General Ledger Trial Balance
As of Dec 31, 2000

Filter Criteria includes: Report order is by ID. Report is printed in Detail Format.

Account ID	Account Description	Debit Amt	Credit Amt
101	Cash	22,765.00	
142	Office Supplies	280.00	
202	Accounts Payable		180.00
311	Maria Vietor, Capital		20,000.00
312	Maria Vietor, Drawing	1,100.00	
401	Professional Fees		6,500.00
511	Wages Expense	1,200.00	
521	Rent Expense	1,000.00	
525	Telephone Expense	100.00	
526	Automobile Expense	60.00	
533	Utilities Expense	75.00	
534	Charitable Contributions Exp.	100.00	
	Total:	26,680.00	26,680.00

Chapter 11 Demonstration Problem Solution

11-Demo Hunt's Audio-Video Store
Sales Journal
For the Period From Apr 1, 2000 to Apr 30, 2000
Filter Criteria includes: Report order is by Invoice Date. Report is printed in Detail Format.

Date	Account ID	Invoice No	Line Description	Account Description	Debit Amnt	Credit Amnt
4/1/00	231	46	MO: Missouri 7% sales tax	Sales Tax Payable		12.57
	401		Merchandise	Sales		179.50
	122		Kellie Cokley	Accounts Receivable	192.07	
4/3/00	231	41	MO: Missouri 7% sales tax	Sales Tax Payable		11.17
	401		Merchandise	Sales		159.50
	122		Susan Haberman	Accounts Receivable	170.67	
4/4/00	231	42	MO: Missouri 7% sales tax	Sales Tax Payable		21.00
	401		Merchandise	Sales		299.95
	122		Goro Kimura	Accounts Receivable	320.95	
4/7/00	231	CM1	MO: Missouri 7% sales tax	Sales Tax Payable	2.80	
	401.1		Credit Memo	Sales Returns & Allowance	39.95	
	122		Kenneth Watt	Accounts Receivable		42.75
4/11/00	231	43	MO: Missouri 7% sales tax	Sales Tax Payable		35.00
	401		Merchandise	Sales		499.95
	122		Victor Cardona	Accounts Receivable	534.95	
4/17/00	231	44	MO: Missouri 7% sales tax	Sales Tax Payable		26.60
	401		Merchandise	Sales		379.95
	122		Susan Haberman	Accounts Receivable	406.55	
4/19/00	231	45	MO: Missouri 7% sales tax	Sales Tax Payable		4.20
	401		Merchandise	Sales		59.95
	122		Tera Scherrer	Accounts Receivable	64.15	
4/21/00	231	CM2	MO: Missouri 7% sales tax	Sales Tax Payable	3.50	
	401.1		Credit Memo	Sales Returns & Allowance	49.95	
	122		Goro Kimura	Accounts Receivable		53.45
4/28/00	231	47	MO: Missouri 7% sales tax	Sales Tax Payable		3.50
	401		Merchandise	Sales		49.95
	122		Kenneth Watt	Accounts Receivable	53.45	
		Total			1,838.99	1,838.99

11-Demo Hunt's Audio-Video Store
Cash Receipts Journal
For the Period From Apr 1, 2000 to Apr 30, 2000

Date	Account ID	Transaction Ref	Line Description	Account Description	Debit Amnt	Credit Amnt
4/6/00	122	1	Invoice: Balance	Accounts Receivable		69.50
	101		Tera Scherrer	Cash	69.50	
4/10/00	122	2	Invoice: Balance	Accounts Receivable		99.95
	101		Kellie Cokley	Cash	99.95	
4/14/00	122	3	Invoice: Balance	Accounts Receivable		199.75
	122		Invoice: CM1	Accounts Receivable	42.75	
	101		Kenneth Watt	Cash	157.00	
4/24/00	122	4	Invoice: Balance	Accounts Receivable		299.95
	101		Victor Cardona	Cash	299.95	
4/26/00	122	5	Invoice: Balance	Accounts Receivable		79.98
	122		Invoice: 41	Accounts Receivable		170.67
	101		Susan Haberman	Cash	250.65	
4/30/00	231	6	MO: Missouri 7% sales tax	Sales Tax Payable		85.40
	401		Credit card receipts	Sales		1,220.00
	231		Credit card expense	Sales Tax Payable	65.27	
	101		Credit card receipts	Cash	1,240.13	
4/30/00	231	7	MO: Missouri 7% sales tax	Sales Tax Payable		140.00
	401		Cash sales	Sales		2,000.00
	101		Cash sales	Cash	2,140.00	
					4,365.20	4,365.20

11-Demo Hunt's Audio-Video Store
Invoice Register
For the Period From Apr 1, 2000 to Apr 30, 2000

Filter Criteria includes: Report order is by Invoice Number.

Invoice No	Date	Quote No	Name	Amount
41	4/3/00		Susan Haberman	170.67
42	4/4/00		Goro Kimura	320.95
43	4/11/00		Victor Cardona	534.95
44	4/17/00		Susan Haberman	406.55
45	4/19/00		Tera Scherrer	64.15
46	4/1/00		Kellie Cokley	192.07
47	4/28/00		Kenneth Watt	53.45
CM1	4/7/00		Kenneth Watt	-42.75
CM2	4/21/00		Goro Kimura	-53.45
Total				1,646.59

11-Demo Hunt's Audio-Video Store
Customer Ledgers
For the Period From Apr 1, 2000 to Apr 30, 2000

Filter Criteria includes: Report order is by ID. Report is printed in Detail Format.

Customer ID Customer	Date	Trans No	Typ	Debit Amt	Credit Amt	Balance
10 Victor Cardona	4/1/00 4/11/00 4/24/00	Balance Fwd 43 4	 SJ CRJ	 534.95 	 299.95	299.95 834.90 534.95
20 Kellie Cokley	4/1/00 4/1/00 4/10/00	Balance Fwd 46 2	 SJ CRJ	 192.07 	 99.95	99.95 292.02 192.07
30 Susan Haberman	4/1/00 4/3/00 4/17/00 4/26/00	Balance Fwd 41 44 5	 SJ SJ CRJ	 170.67 406.55 	 250.65	79.98 250.65 657.20 406.55
40 Goro Kimura	4/1/00 4/4/00 4/21/00	Balance Fwd 42 CM2	 SJ SJ	 320.95 	 53.45	379.50 700.45 647.00
50 Tera Scherrer	4/1/00 4/6/00 4/19/00	Balance Fwd 1 45	 CRJ SJ	 64.15	 69.50 	149.50 80.00 144.15
60 Kenneth Watt	4/1/00 4/7/00 4/14/00 4/28/00	Balance Fwd CM1 3 47	 SJ CRJ SJ	 53.45	 42.75 157.00 	199.75 157.00 0.00 53.45

Chapter 12 Demonstration Problem Solution

12-Demo Rutman Pharmacy
General Ledger Trial Balance
As of Jun 30, 2000

Filter Criteria includes: Report order is by ID. Report is printed in Detail Format.

Account ID	Account Description	Debit Amt	Credit Amt
101	Cash	5,481.74	
202	Accounts Payable		952.12
311	Jodi Rutman, Capital		26,264.48
501	Purchases	16,378.27	
501.1	Purchases Returns & Allowance		412.53
501.2	Purchases Discounts		230.88
521	Rent Expense	6,000.00	
	Total:	27,860.01	27,860.01

12-Demo Rutman Pharmacy
Schedule of Accounts Payable
As of Jun 30, 2000

Vendor	Invoice No	Amount Due
Flites Pharmaceuticals	675	638.47
Flites Pharmaceuticals		**638.47**
University Drug Co.	914A	367.35
	CM914A	-53.70
University Drug Co.		**313.65**
		952.12

12-Demo Rutman Pharmacy
Check Register
For the Period From Jun 1, 2000 to Jun 30, 2000

Filter Criteria includes: Report order is by Date.

Check #	Date	Payee	Cash Account	Amount
536	6/2/00	Rent Payment	101	1,000.00
537	6/9/00	Sullivan Company	101	229.52
538	6/16/00	Amfac Drug Supply	101	511.04
539	6/23/00	Mutual Drug Company	101	469.81
540	6/29/00	Merchandise	101	270.20
541	6/30/00	Vashon Medical Supply	101	1,217.69
Total				3,698.26

12-Demo Rutman Pharmacy
Cash Disbursements Journal
For the Period From Jun 1, 2000 to Jun 30, 2000

Filter Criteria includes: Report order is by Date. Report is printed in Detail Format.

Date	Check #	Account ID	Line Description	Account Description	Debit Amount	Credit Amount
6/2/00	536	521	Rent payment	Rent Expense	1,000.00	
		101	Rent Payment	Cash		1,000.00
6/9/00	537	501.2	Discounts Taken	Purchases Discounts		4.68
		202	Invoice: 71	Accounts Payable	234.20	
		101	Sullivan Company	Cash		229.52
6/16/00	538	501.2	Discounts Taken	Purchases Discounts		5.16
		202	Invoice: 196	Accounts Payable	562.40	
		202	Invoice: CM106	Accounts Payable		46.20
		101	Amfac Drug Supply	Cash		511.04
6/23/00	539	501.2	Discounts Taken	Purchases Discounts		9.59
		202	Invoice: 745	Accounts Payable	479.40	
		101	Mutual Drug Company	Cash		469.81
6/29/00	540	501	Cash Purchase Merchandise	Purchases	270.20	
		101	Merchandise	Cash		270.20
6/30/00	541	202	Invoice: Balance	Accounts Payable	1,217.69	
		101	Vashon Medical Supply	Cash		1,217.69
	Total				3,763.89	3,763.89

12-Demo Rutman Pharmacy
Purchase Journal
For the Period From Jun 1, 2000 to Jun 30, 2000

Filter Criteria includes: Report order is by Date. Report is printed in Detail Format.

Date	Account ID / Account Description	Invoice #	Line Description	Debit Amount	Credit Amount
6/1/00	501 Purchases	71	Merchandise	234.20	
	202 Accounts Payable		Sullivan Company		234.20
6/5/00	501 Purchases	196	Merchandise	562.40	
	202 Accounts Payable		Amfac Drug Supply		562.40
6/7/00	501 Purchases	914A	Merchandise	367.35	
	202 Accounts Payable		University Drug Co.		367.35
6/12/00	501.1 Purchases Returns & Allowanc	CM106	Credit Memo		46.20
	202 Accounts Payable		Amfac Drug Supply	46.20	
6/14/00	501 Purchases	745	Merchandise	479.40	
	202 Accounts Payable		Mutual Drug Company		479.40
6/15/00	501.1 Purchases Returns & Allowanc	CM914A	Credit Memo		53.70
	202 Accounts Payable		University Drug Co.	53.70	
6/27/00	501 Purchases	675	Merchandise	638.47	
	202 Accounts Payable		Flites Pharmaceuticals		638.47
				2,381.72	2,381.72

Chapter 13 Demonstration Problem Solution

13- Demo David's Specialty Shop
Vendor Ledgers
For the Period From May 1, 2000 to May 31, 2000

Filter Criteria includes: Report order is by ID.

Vendor ID / Vendor	Date	Trans No	Type	Paid	Debit Amt	Credit Amt	Balance
10 Johnson Essentials	5/1/00	Balance Fwd					2,350.00
	5/17/00	CM580	PJ		500.00		1,850.00
20 Kari Co.	5/1/00	Balance Fwd					1,000.00
	5/2/00	750	CDJ		16.00	16.00	1,000.00
	5/2/00	750	CDJ		800.00		200.00
30 Scanlan Wholesalers	5/1/00	Balance Fwd					1,200.00
	5/3/00	621	PJ			2,000.00	3,200.00
	5/10/00	752	CDJ		1,200.00		2,000.00
40 Simpson Enterprises	5/4/00	767	PJ	*		1,500.00	1,500.00
	5/13/00	753	CDJ		30.00	30.00	1,500.00
	5/13/00	753	CDJ		1,500.00		0.00

13- Demo David's Specialty Shop
Purchase Journal
For the Period From May 1, 2000 to May 31, 2000

Filter Criteria includes: Report order is by Date. Report is printed in Detail Format.

Date	Account ID / Account Description	Invoice #	Line Description	Debit Amount	Credit Amount
5/3/00	501 Purchases	621	Merchandise	2,000.00	
	202 Accounts Payable		Scanlan Wholesalers		2,000.00
5/4/00	501 Purchases	767	Merchandise	1,500.00	
	202 Accounts Payable		Simpson Enterprises		1,500.00
5/17/00	501.1 Purchases Returns & Allowanc	CM580	Credit memo		500.00
	202 Accounts Payable		Johnson Essentials	500.00	
				4,000.00	4,000.00

13- Demo David's Specialty Shop
Check Register
For the Period From May 1, 2000 to May 31, 2000

Filter Criteria includes: Report order is by Date.

Check #	Date	Payee	Cash Account	Amount
750	5/2/00	Kari Co.	101	784.00
751	5/4/00	Telephone Expense	101	200.00
752	5/10/00	Scanlan Wholesalers	101	1,200.00
753	5/13/00	Simpson Enterprises	101	1,470.00
754	5/29/00	Wages Expense	101	1,100.00
Total				4,754.00

13- Demo David's Specialty Shop
Cash Disbursements Journal
For the Period From May 1, 2000 to May 31, 2000

Filter Criteria includes: Report order is by Date. Report is printed in Detail Format.

Date	Check #	Account ID	Account Description	Line Description	Debit Amount	Credit Amou
5/2/00	750	501.2	Purchases Discounts	Discounts Taken		16.00
		202	Accounts Payable	Invoice: 600	800.00	
		101	Cash	Kari Co.		784.00
5/4/00	751	545	Telephone Expense	Telephone Expense	200.00	
		101	Cash	Telephone Expense		200.00
5/10/00	752	202	Accounts Payable	Invoice: 605	1,200.00	
		101	Cash	Scanlan Wholesalers		1,200.00
5/13/00	753	501.2	Purchases Discounts	Discounts Taken		30.00
		202	Accounts Payable	Invoice: 767	1,500.00	
		101	Cash	Simpson Enterprises		1,470.00
5/29/00	754	542	Wages Expense	Wages Expense	1,100.00	
		101	Cash	Wages Expense		1,100.00
	Total				4,800.00	4,800.00

13- Demo David's Specialty Shop
Sales Journal
For the Period From May 1, 2000 to May 31, 2000

Filter Criteria includes: Report order is by Invoice Date. Report is printed in Detail Format.

Date	Account ID	Invoice No	Account Description	Line Description	Debit Amnt	Credit Amnt
5/1/00	204	533	Sales Tax Payable	State: State Sales Tax		100.00
	401		Sales	Merchandise		2,000.00
	131		Accounts Receivable	Molly Mac	2,100.00	
5/12/00	204	534	Sales Tax Payable	State: State Sales Tax		150.00
	401		Sales	Merchandise		3,000.00
	131		Accounts Receivable	Cody Slaton	3,150.00	
5/13/00	204	CM480	Sales Tax Payable	State: State Sales Tax	50.00	
	401.1		Sales Returns & Allowanc	Credit memo	1,000.00	
	131		Accounts Receivable	Cody Slaton		1,050.00
5/27/00	204	535	Sales Tax Payable	State: State Sales Tax		100.00
	401		Sales	Merchandise		2,000.00
	131		Accounts Receivable	Natalie Gabbert	2,100.00	
			Total		8,400.00	8,400.00

13- Demo David's Specialty Shop
Cash Receipts Journal
For the Period From May 1, 2000 to May 31, 2000

Filter Criteria includes: Report order is by Check Date. Report is printed in Detail Format.

Date	Account ID	Transaction Ref	Account Description	Line Description	Debit Amnt	Credit Amnt
5/8/00	204	Cash sales	Sales Tax Payable	State: State Sales Tax		180.00
	401		Sales	Cash sales		3,600.00
	101		Cash	Cash sales	3,780.00	
5/9/00	122	480	Supplies	Invoice: 480		2,500.00
	101		Cash	Cody Slaton	2,500.00	
5/12/0	122	479	Supplies	Invoice: 479		2,100.00
	101		Cash	Kori Reynolds	2,100.00	
5/22/0	122	466	Supplies	Invoice: 466		1,555.00
	101		Cash	Natalie Gabbert	1,555.00	
					9,935.00	9,935.00

13- Demo David's Specialty Shop
Invoice Register
For the Period From May 1, 2000 to May 31, 2000

Filter Criteria includes: Report order is by Invoice Number.

Invoice No	Date	Quote No	Name	Amount
533	5/1/00		Molly Mac	2,100.00
534	5/12/00		Cody Slaton	3,150.00
535	5/27/00		Natalie Gabbert	2,100.00
CM480	5/13/00		Cody Slaton	-1,050.00
Total				6,300.00

13- Demo David's Specialty Shop
Customer Ledgers
For the Period From May 1, 2000 to May 31, 2000

Filter Criteria includes: Report order is by ID. Report is printed in Detail Format.

Customer ID / Customer	Date	Trans No	Typ	Debit Amt	Credit Amt	Balance
10	5/1/00	Balance Fwd				1,821.00
Natalie Gabbert	5/22/00	466	CRJ		1,555.00	266.00
	5/27/00	535	SJ	2,100.00		2,366.00
20	5/1/00	Balance Fwd				279.00
Molly Mac	5/1/00	533	SJ	2,100.00		2,379.00
30	5/1/00	Balance Fwd				2,300.00
Kori Reynolds	5/12/00	479	CRJ		2,100.00	200.00
40	5/1/00	Balance Fwd				2,500.00
Cody Slaton	5/9/00	480	CRJ		2,500.00	0.00
	5/12/00	534	SJ	3,150.00		3,150.00
	5/13/00	CM480	SJ		1,050.00	2,100.00

Chapter 14 Demonstration Problem Solution

14-Demo Harpo, Inc.
General Ledger Trial Balance
As of Mar 31, 2000

Filter Criteria includes: Report order is by ID. Report is printed in Detail Format.

Account ID	Account Description	Debit Amt	Credit Amt
101	Cash	2,121.00	
141	Supplies	520.00	
202	Vouchers Payable		1,690.00
301	Capital Stock		12,500.00
501	Purchases	6,570.00	
501.1	Purchases Returns & Allowance		200.00
501.2	Purchases Discounts		71.00
511	Wages Expense	3,750.00	
521	Rent Expense	1,500.00	
	Total:	14,461.00	14,461.00

14-Demo Harpo, Inc.
Schedule of Vouchers Payable
As of Mar 31, 2000

Vendor ID / Vendor	Invoice No	Amount Due
70 Giggles	316	700.00
70 Giggles		**700.00**
80 Creations	317	870.00
80 Creations		**870.00**
90 Hal's Supply	318	120.00
90 Hal's Supply		**120.00**
Report Total		**1,690.00**

14-Demo Harpo, Inc.

Purchase Journal

For the Period From Mar 1, 2000 to Mar 31, 2000

Filter Criteria includes: Report order is by Date. Report is printed in Detail Format.

Date	Account ID / Account Description	Invoice #	Line Description	Debit Amount	Credit Amount
3/2/00	521 Rent Expense	313	March rent	500.00	
	202 Vouchers Payable		Tremont Rental		500.00
3/3/00	501 Purchases	314	Merchandise	550.00	
	202 Vouchers Payable		Gail's Gags		550.00
3/4/00	501 Purchases	315	Merchandise	200.00	
	202 Vouchers Payable		Silly Sam's		200.00
3/12/00	501.1 Purchases Returns & Allowanc	CM315	Credit memo		100.00
	202 Vouchers Payable		Silly Sam's	100.00	
3/16/00	501 Purchases	316	Merchandise	700.00	
	202 Vouchers Payable		Giggles		700.00
3/21/00	501 Purchases	317	Merchandise	870.00	
	202 Vouchers Payable		Creations		870.00
3/25/00	141 Supplies	318	Merchandise	120.00	
	202 Vouchers Payable		Hal's Supply		120.00
3/31/00	511 Wages Expense	319	Payroll	1,250.00	
	202 Vouchers Payable		Payroll		1,250.00
				4,290.00	4,290.00

14-Demo Harpo, Inc.
Check Register
For the Period From Mar 1, 2000 to Mar 31, 2000

Filter Criteria includes: Report order is by Date.

Check #	Date	Payee	Cash Account	Amount
450	3/2/00	Tremont Rental	101	500.00
451	3/10/00	Jerry's Jokes	101	490.00
452	3/14/00	Resource Supplies	101	250.00
453	3/18/00	Gail's Gags	101	539.00
454	3/19/00	Donnelly's	101	750.00
455	3/31/00	Silly Sam's	101	100.00
456	3/31/00	Payroll	101	1,250.00
Total				3,879.00

14-Demo Harpo, Inc.
Cash Disbursements Journal
For the Period From Mar 1, 2000 to Mar 31, 2000

Filter Criteria includes: Report order is by Date. Report is printed in Detail Format.

Date	Check #	Account ID	Line Description	Debit Amount	Credit Amou
3/2/00	450	202	Invoice: 313	500.00	
		101	Tremont Rental		500.00
3/10/00	451	501.2	Discounts Taken		10.00
		202	Invoice: 310	500.00	
		101	Jerry's Jokes		490.00
3/14/00	452	202	Invoice: 311	250.00	
		101	Resource Supplies		250.00
3/18/00	453	501.2	Discounts Taken		11.00
		202	Invoice: 314	550.00	
		101	Gail's Gags		539.00
3/19/00	454	202	Invoice: 312	750.00	
		101	Donnelly's		750.00
3/31/00	455	202	Invoice: 315	200.00	
		202	Invoice: CM315		100.00
		101	Silly Sam's		100.00
3/31/00	456	202	Invoice: 319	1,250.00	
		101	Payroll		1,250.00
	Total			4,000.00	4,000.00

Chapter 16 Demonstration Problem Solution

16-Demo McK's Home Electronics
General Journal
For the Period From Dec 1, 2000 to Dec 31, 2000

Date	Account ID	Reference	Trans Description	Account Description	Debit Amt	Credit Amt
12/31/00	503	(a)	Adjusting Entry	Inventory Adjustment	39,000.00	
	131		Adjusting Entry	Merchandise Inventory		39,000.00
12/31/00	131	(b)	Adjusting Entry	Merchandise Inventory	45,000.00	
	503		Adjusting Entry	Inventory Adjustment		45,000.00
12/31/00	521	(c)	Adjusting Entry	Supplies Expense	2,100.00	
	141		Adjusting Entry	Supplies		2,100.00
12/31/00	527	(d)	Adjusting Entry	Insurance Expense	2,700.00	
	145		Adjusting Entry	Prepaid Insurance		2,700.00
12/31/00	529	(e)	Adjusting Entry	Depr. Expense—Building	6,000.00	
	190.1		Adjusting Entry	Accum. Depr.—Building		6,000.00
12/31/00	531	(f)	Adjusting Entry	Depr. Expense—Store Equipment	4,500.00	
	195.1		Adjusting Entry	Accum. Depr.—Store Equipment		4,500.00
12/31/00	511	(g)	Adjusting Entry	Wages Expense	675.00	
	214		Adjusting Entry	Wages Payable		675.00
12/31/00	221	(h)	Adjusting Entry	Unearned Repair Fees	15,000.00	
	601		Adjusting Entry	Repair Fees		15,000.00
		Total			114,975.00	114,975.00

16-Demo McK's Home Electronics
Balance Sheet
December 31, 2000

ASSETS

Current Assets		
Cash	$ 10,000.00	
Accounts Receivable	22,500.00	
Merchandise Inventory	45,000.00	
Supplies	600.00	
Prepaid Insurance	900.00	
Total Current Assets		79,000.00
Property and Equipment		
Building	135,000.00	
Accum. Depr.--Building	<30,000.00>	
Store Equipment	75,000.00	
Accum. Depr.--Store Equipment	<27,000.00>	
Total Property and Equipment		153,000.00
Other Assets		
Land	15,000.00	
Total Other Assets		15,000.00
Total Assets	$	247,000.00

LIABILITIES AND CAPITAL

Current Liabilities		
Notes Payable	$ 7,500.00	
Accounts Payable	15,000.00	
Wages Payable	675.00	
Sales Tax Payabe	2,250.00	
Total Current Liabilities		25,425.00
Long-Term Liabilities		
Mortgage Payable	45,000.00	
Total Long-Term Liabilities		45,000.00
Total Liabilities		70,425.00
Capital		
Tom McKinney, Capital	151,600.00	
Tom McKinney, Drawing	<30,000.00>	
Net Income	54,975.00	
Total Capital		176,575.00
Total Liabilities & Capital	$	247,000.00

Unaudited - For Management Purposes Only

16-Demo McK's Home Electronics
Statement of Owner's Equity
December 31, 2000

Capital, Beginning of Period		151,600.00
Net Income for the Period	54,975.00	
Less Withdrawals for Period	30,000.00	
Increase/Decrease in Capital		24,975.00
Capital, End of Period	$	176,575.00

16-Demo McK's Home Electronics
Income Statement
For the Period Ending December 31, 2000

Revenues		
Sales	$	300,750.00
Sales Returns & Allowance		<1,800.00>
Total Revenues		298,950.00
Cost of Goods Sold		
Purchases		157,500.00
Purchases Returns & Allowance		<1,200.00>
Purchases Discounts		<1,500.00>
Freight-In		450.00
Inventory Adjustment		<6,000.00>
Total Cost of Goods Sold		149,250.00
Gross Profit		149,700.00
Expenses		
Wages Expense		63,675.00
Advertising Expense		3,750.00
Supplies Expense		2,100.00
Telephone Expense		5,250.00
Utilities Expense		18,000.00
Insurance Expense		2,700.00
Depr. Expense--Building		6,000.00
Depr. Expense--Store Equipment		4,500.00
Miscellaneous Expense		3,375.00
Total Expenses		109,350.00
Income from Operations		40,350.00
Other Revenue		
Repair Fees		15,000.00
Interest Revenue		1,350.00
Other Expenses		
Interest Expense		4,725.00
Net Income	$	51,975.00

For Management Purposes Only

16-Demo McK's Home Electronics
General Ledger Trial Balance
As of Dec 31, 2000

Filter Criteria includes: Report order is by ID. Report is printed in Detail Format.

Account ID	Account Description	Debit Amt	Credit Amt
101	Cash	10,000.00	
102	Accounts Receivable	22,500.00	
131	Merchandise Inventory	45,000.00	
141	Supplies	600.00	
145	Prepaid Insurance	900.00	
185	Land	15,000.00	
190	Building	135,000.00	
190.1	Accum. Depr.--Building		30,000.00
195	Store Equipment	75,000.00	
195.1	Accum. Depr.--Store Equipment		27,000.00
201	Notes Payable		7,500.00
202	Accounts Payable		15,000.00
214	Wages Payable		675.00
219	Sales Tax Payabe		2,250.00
221	Unearned Repair Fees		3,000.00
285	Mortgage Payable		45,000.00
311	Tom McKinney, Capital		151,600.00
312	Tom McKinney, Drawing	30,000.00	
401	Sales		300,750.00
401.1	Sales Returns & Allowance	1,800.00	
501	Purchases	157,500.00	
501.1	Purchases Returns & Allowance		1,200.00
501.2	Purchases Discounts		1,500.00
502	Freight-In	450.00	
503	Inventory Adjustment		6,000.00
511	Wages Expense	63,675.00	
518	Advertising Expense	3,750.00	
521	Supplies Expense	2,100.00	
523	Telephone Expense	5,250.00	
524	Utilities Expense	18,000.00	
527	Insurance Expense	2,700.00	
529	Depr. Expense--Building	6,000.00	
531	Depr. Expense--Store Equipment	4,500.00	
534	Miscellaneous Expense	3,375.00	
601	Repair Fees		15,000.00
602	Interest Revenue		1,350.00
701	Interest Expense	4,725.00	
	Total:	607,825.00	607,825.00

16-Demo McK's Home Electronics
General Ledger Trial Balance
As of Jan 31, 2001

Filter Criteria includes: Report order is by ID. Report is printed in Detail Format.

Account ID	Account Description	Debit Amt	Credit Amt
101	Cash	10,000.00	
102	Accounts Receivable	22,500.00	
131	Merchandise Inventory	45,000.00	
141	Supplies	600.00	
145	Prepaid Insurance	900.00	
185	Land	15,000.00	
190	Building	135,000.00	
190.1	Accum. Depr.--Building		30,000.00
195	Store Equipment	75,000.00	
195.1	Accum. Depr.--Store Equipment		27,000.00
201	Notes Payable		7,500.00
202	Accounts Payable		15,000.00
219	Sales Tax Payabe		2,250.00
285	Mortgage Payable		45,000.00
311	Tom McKinney, Capital		176,575.00
511	Wages Expense		675.00
	Total:	304,000.00	304,000.00

16-Demo McK's Home Electronics
General Journal
For the Period From Jan 1, 2001 to Jan 31, 2001

Date	Account ID	Reference	Trans Description	Account Description	Debit Amt	Credit Amt
1/1/01	214	(a)	Reversing Entry	Wages Payable	675.00	
	511		Reversing Entry	Wages Expense		675.00
			Total		675.00	675.00